Happily Ever After

KELLY L. HOWARTH, M.Ed., PPCC
LAURIE JOHNSON, B.F.A., PPCC

Copyright © 2024 Kelly L. Howarth and Laurie Johnson
All rights reserved.
Montreal, Quebec, Canada.
Printed in Canada.
InfiniteU Press

HAPPILY EVER AFTER—A REALITY CHECK

ISBN 978-1-7753154-9-0 (Print)
ISBN 978-1-7387137-1-4 (Digital)

Do not reprint, reproduce, or distribute this book without the co-authors' written consent. For any inquiries, contact Kelly L. Howarth at www.infiniteUcoaching.com and Laurie Johnson at www.thefineartofyou.com.

Cover concept by Laurie Johnson
Front and back cover images by Sadeugra (See Bibliography)
Cover design and layout by Eswari Kamireddy
Interior layout by Eswari Kamireddy
Author photo of Kelly L. Howarth by Luigi Perrotta
Author photo of Laurie Johnson by Laurie Johnson
Vector Art on Parting Words page by Sophie Gallo (See Bibliography)

Disclaimers:

- ❖ Kelly L. Howarth and Laurie Johnson are not liable for the accuracy or availability of external website URLs mentioned in this publication. They do not guarantee that any content on such websites remains accurate or appropriate.
- ❖ The person in the cover image is a model unrelated to the characters mentioned in this book (except Froggie).
- ❖ The co-authors bear no responsibility for frogs or fairy-tale endings.
- ❖ No frogs were harmed in writing this book.

You and Me. Me and you.
We go together like a sock and a shoe!

Dedication

We dedicate this book to our devoted partners, who celebrate our successes and stand by us during our challenges. Your unwavering love and support have been constant sources of inspiration, reminding us to never abandon our dreams. We are grateful for your presence in our worlds.

Contents

Preface — xv

Prelude - The Dating Game — xvii
   Know Your Worth — xviii
   You are not Auditioning — xix
   Unrequited Love — xix
   Online Dating — xxi
   Meeting Through Friends — xxv
   Rekindling the Fairy Tale — xxvi
   The First Date — xxvii

Introduction - Welcome to Getting Clear — 1
   How This Book Can Help — 2
   Working This Book — 8

Chapter 1 - Once Upon a Time — 11
   The Fairy Tale Begins — 11
   The House Key — 17
   Commitment — 19

Chapter 2 - Compatibility — 29
   Values — 30
   Traditions and Celebrations — 37
   Arranged Marriage — 39
   Child Marriage — 39
   Money Values — 41
   Political Values — 47
   Conflicting Values — 48
   Needs Versus Wants — 49

Interests	52
Goals	52
Other Aspects of Compatibility	57
Truly Knowing Each Other	63
Defining your Non-Negotiables	64

Chapter 3 - Self-Care — 69

Caring for Ourselves	70
Baggage	75
Boundaries	80
Expectations	84
Mirror, Mirror on the Wall	89

Chapter 4 - Red Flags and Deal Breakers — 93

Distinguishing Red Flags and Deal Breakers	94
Abuse and Coercive Control	95
Mental Illness	104
Addiction and Compulsion	109
Failure to Launch	113
Difficult In-laws	114
Chronic Under or Unemployment	118
When Your Relationship is a Secret	119
When Your Partner Leads a Double Life	120
When You Love a Prisoner	121
Scams and Shams	125
Falling with a Safety Net	126

Chapter 5 - Sex and Intimacy — 131

Types of Intimacy	132
Being Vulnerable	133
Sexual Myths and the Media	137
Sex Across the Lifespan	138

Sexual Orientation	140
Virginity	140
The Hookup Culture	141
Love Bombing	144
Your Healthy Sex Life	146
Sexy Seniors	151
Sexual Disorders	153
Sexual Deviance	154

Chapter 6 - Infidelity — 157

Excuses! Excuses!	157
Two Types of Infidelity	158
Myths About Cheating	160
The Other Woman/Man	163
Coming Clean	165
What Motivates us to Stay	166
The Hit to Your Self-Esteem	174
Earning Back Trust	175

Chapter 7 - Communication — 179

The Language of Love	180
Grievances	181
Four Communication Styles	183
Applying Active Listening	184
Conflict Management	185
Jealousy and Possessiveness	190
Solving Common Problems	193
Fighting Fair	194
Couple Therapy	196
Decisions, Decisions	196

Chapter 8 - Becoming Mr. & Mrs. (or any combo)   **199**
  Preparing for Marriage   199
  Lifestyle and Living Arrangements   200
  Living Together or Apart   205
  The Wedding   208
  Cohabiting Instead of Marrying   214
  Labels Matter   215

Chapter 9 - Work, Career, and Learning   **219**
  Work Versus Career   219
  Entrepreneurship   220
  Parental Leave   221
  Taking a Sabbatical   222
  Continuing Education   223
  Life Balance and Blend   224

Chapter 10 - Money and Spending   **229**
  Managing Money as a Couple   229

Chapter 11 - Sharing the Load   **237**
  Stereotypes   237
  Categories of Household Chores   238
  Negotiating Roles   246
  Splitting Chores   247
  Outsourcing   248

Chapter 12 - Expanding Your Family   **251**
  Pets: I don't wanna your iguana!   251
  Deciding to have Children   254
  Raising Children   265
  Empty Nest   276

Chapter 13 - Blended and Extended Families — 281
- Exes and Uh-Ohs — 281
- Alimony and Palimony — 284
- Co-parenting — 285
- Stepparenting — 286
- Extended Family — 290
- Multi-Generational Living — 291

Chapter 14 - Making Time Count — 295
- Me Time — 295
- Couple Time — 296
- Family Time — 299
- Extended Family and Friendships — 300
- Couple Friendships — 302
- Visitors — 303

Chapter 15 - Life Transitions — 305
- Transitions as Stressors — 306
- Loss — 332
- Death — 333
- Grieving — 335

Chapter 16 - Growing Together or Growing Apart — 339
- Deepening your Connection — 340
- Loss of Connection — 343
- Separation and Divorce — 347
- Getting an Annulment — 349
- Getting Back on the Horsey — 357

Chapter 17 - Love and Legal Matters — 363
- Marriage — 363
- Prenuptial Agreements — 364

Domestic Partnerships and Civil Unions	364
Cohabitation Agreement	364
Adoption and Surrogacy	364
Separation and Divorce	365
Child Custody and Support	366
Protection Orders and Restraining Orders	366
Putting Your Affairs in Order	367
Chapter 18 - Your Happily Ever After	**375**
An Alternative to Kissing Frogs	376
Parting Words	**380**
Bibliography	**383**

Preface

Kelly and Laurie remember their mothers reading fairy tales to them as little girls. The fantastical stories told of princes saving princesses and living happily ever after in a gorgeous castle. But does this happen in real life? Hardly! It is rare to fall in love, marry, and live the fairy tale that misled us as children. This is the issue: when we expect a fairy tale, we are often shocked and bewildered when reality hits. That is why we feel it's important to acknowledge the reality of *your* situation.

Laurie experienced many failed relationships often because of her poor choices and misguided belief that love was flowers and unicorns. She also watched as friends struggled with dating—having no realistic guideline to help with maneuvering through unhealthy perspectives.

Over two years ago, Kelly witnessed a close family member end an intimate relationship because of each partner's conflicting values. She understood that when partners have conflicting values, it's challenging to build a sound foundation of trust, understanding, and compromise. There was an ever-elusive ideal plaguing this couple (and likely many other couples), preventing them from moving forward together.

During an impromptu chat, Kelly and Laurie quipped about authoring a book to debunk the fairy tale notion of the perfect relationship by providing a reality check for couples. Thus, *Happily Ever After—A Reality Check* was born! Kelly and Laurie wanted to delve deeper into the concept of values and their influence on relationships and began exploring ways in which individuals can identify and align their values to foster healthier and more fulfilling connections.

Through their respective experiences, self-reflection, and research, Kelly and Laurie gained valuable insights into the vital roles open communication, empathy, and compromise play in navigating conflicting values within intimate relationships. We believe that by acknowledging and addressing diverse values, a couple can build a stronger and more rewarding partnership.

In her coaching practice, Kelly helps her clients find clarity in themselves and their relationships. Her specialty is supporting people through personal and work life transitions, including career change, and cultivating their sense of '*enoughness*' in all aspects of their lives.

And Laurie has found her long-term partner (Dare she say soul mate? Yes!) and is living a happy and healthy relationship. Laurie uses her unique expertise in coaching and therapeutic art exercises to help you shift perspectives, break through barriers, and create a life filled with purpose, passion, and possibility!

We both acknowledge and promote the beauty of diverse couples, including those of different ages, genders, sexual orientations, capacities, and other variables. We also acknowledge our westernised, white, middle-class privilege and how this book may portray traditional heterosexual relationships. Our aim is to foster a dialogue that questions the expectations and stereotypes perpetuated by the Happily Ever After fairy tale.

There is a positive quality to fairy tales that inspires us to work through the challenges of relationships. While we may crave the control and predictability of a happily ever after, fairy tales aren't passive occurrences that happen *to* us. Happiness does not depend on how the stars align to decide our fate. We possess the power to create the relationship we dream of. And this is the reality check.

Prelude

The Dating Game

Also Known as Twenty Questions

WTF has happened to dating? People used to court each other for months before committing. The first date was a prime opportunity to play twenty questions with your date to learn what made them tick. The twenty questions have sadly dwindled to: *Hey, wanna hook up?*

Society pushes us to be unwilling to delay gratification, whether eating, making money, buying items, or finding the right partner. The urge to own and experience everything quickly can lead to debt, ill health, or losing assets in a divorce. Once we get the things we want so badly, we sometimes discard them just as fast. Sometimes we are attracted to shiny new things, including dating partners.

Some people enjoy serial dating and opt for the familiarity of monogamy. Others struggle with knowing when to end an unhealthy relationship and stay despite feeling unsatisfied. But one reality we often share is the desire for connection in an intimate relationship. We continue to strive for that, kissing loads of frogs along the way.

In the film *Jerry Maguire* (Crowe, 1996, 2:08:23) Jerry (Tom Cruise) tells Dorothy (Renée Zellweger), "You complete me." Although we may melt at this ideal and expect love to feel like this, we must be complete in ourselves before entering a relationship. That we have worked on ourselves shows a higher level of self-awareness. This doesn't mean we cannot grow more with a partner or complement one another. We must acknowledge our baggage, pack our life's toolbox with tools like communication and listening, and apply them. No one is perfect; we must take responsibility for our issues and gain the tools to enter a relationship as whole as possible.

Know Your Worth

Before you even contemplate dating, you must do a deep inner dive to know and affirm your worth. This means you've done your inside work to develop healthy self-esteem and self-love that are not dependent on a romantic relationship. You engage in activities that bring you joy, practice self-care, and surround yourself with uplifting people. And this has nothing to do with any monetary value you bring to the table but your value as a person—what you will and will not tolerate, what you expect, what you want for yourself, how you care for yourself and your needs, and your self-confidence in your own deservingness.

There is no need to voice this because you know the qualities you bring to a relationship. You show your worth through your actions with everyone you meet. You trust your instincts, communicate your needs and boundaries clearly, and are assertive while being respectful. It is not about being demanding or expecting a perfect partner. You simply refuse to settle for anything less than what you deserve. Only then can you choose relationships that value and appreciate you for who you are.

You are not Auditioning

Be aware of the tendency to over-give and be exploited or treated as though you are their wife/husband. The date who keeps you waiting, asks you to chauffeur them around, do their laundry, make them meals, care for their children, or help clean their home is not looking to date you so much as they are looking to be taken care of.

We sometimes erroneously think that if we agree to every request or whim, our date will appreciate us more and want to be with us. It's the opposite! Skip ahead to Boundaries in Chapter Three to understand how critical early limit-setting is. We are not suggesting you avoid doing wonderful things for the other person. Tamper your giving with sound judgment. You don't have to audition for the role because dating is not a simulation nor playing house—it is a fun time designed to learn about each other. Court and let yourself be courted!

Unrequited Love

You have a terrible crush on someone who barely notices you, let alone returns your feelings of infatuation. Your mind does somersaults trying to figure out why this person does not acknowledge you or ask you out, and it feels heartbreaking. You are trying to live out the fairy tale romance you have built in your head, longing for a love that never happens.

Unrequited love results when one person develops powerful emotions towards someone who does not reciprocate those feelings with the same intensity or at all. And it can be deeply challenging and painful. Dealing with unrequited love requires self-reflection and emotional resilience because you risk falling into the trap of harbouring unrealistic notions of couple relationships that feed the fairy tale of Happily Ever After.

This unbalanced affection can create a sense of longing, disappointment, and heartache for the person who is not receiving the desired response from their love interest. When you experience this unreciprocated affection, you may constantly think about the object of your desire, daydreaming about a potential relationship and hoping your love interest returns your feelings. Despite your best efforts, the other person may not feel the same way or may not even be aware of the depth of your emotions.

Many of us experience unrequited love as high school and college students. Kelly knows of a woman who held a torch for a young man who never knew the extent of this woman's admiration because she could not bring herself to share her feelings about pursuing a romantic relationship. The woman watched as this guy embarked on other love relationships, eventually marrying. She never dated and married later in life, as it had taken her many years to come to terms with her loss and the pain of her unreciprocated feelings.

The reasons for unrequited love vary; it could be mismatched feelings, differences in personal preferences, lack of maturity, or simply because love is a complex and unpredictable emotion. Regardless of the cause, it can be difficult for the person experiencing unrequited love to move on and let go of their feelings. According to Dr. Dianne Grande (2020), this may be a fantasy bond resulting from early attachment trauma (childhood neglect and abuse) where you may need professional help to work through it to practice self-restraint—especially if this is a repetitive and addictive pattern.

While unrequited love can be a painful experience, remember that love is a two-way street. It is not a reflection of your worth or desirability if someone does not reciprocate your feelings. Acknowledge and accept that the other person's feelings are beyond your control.

Distance yourself from your object of affection, allowing time and space for healing and self-growth. Pivot your love obsession towards yourself. Seek support from friends, family, or a therapist to navigate the emotional challenges. Use it as a learning experience and believe that your Person Charming is somewhere out there; someone special who will appreciate and return the love you offer.

> **REFLECTION**
>
> Do you find yourself in non-reciprocal love relationships, and if so, think about these questions:
>
> 1. Is this a pattern for me?
> 2. How does this unrequited love serve me?
> 3. What can I do to shift my thoughts and behaviour away from this unavailable person?
> 4. Alternatively, what steps can I take to let the person know how I feel?

Online Dating

The rise in dating apps and online dating has changed the dating landscape. We don't always have the time or means to go to places where we can meet others, or we may suffer from social anxiety, and interacting with others from the comfort of home can cure loneliness. Our Person Charming might be one click away!

While meeting people online can be fun and safe, it can also be risky. Tune into any news channel for examples of how online dating can go wrong—from stories of individuals who have fallen victim to scams and catfishing to more serious crimes. These incidents remind us that while online interactions can be exciting and secure, we must exercise caution when forming relationships in the digital world.

Behind the screen, someone may have ulterior motives or hidden agendas. They may display a persona they want us to see, projecting an image that is not reflective of who they are. This can lead to deception and manipulation, as they capitalize on our shared interests and mutual goals to gain our trust. They may shower us with compliments and affection, making us feel valued and loved. These online connections can boost our self-esteem and create a strong bond with us, but those with nefarious intentions may use these tactics to exploit our vulnerabilities and manipulate us emotionally.

Prioritise your well-being and safety, pay attention to your intuition, and ask the right questions to filter out incompatible individuals. At the risk of sounding overly cautious, we challenge you to activate your critical thinking by asking specific questions and validating the answers you receive. Research your date's name online. Do a reverse telephone number lookup, and check for legal notifications, such as arrests or any other public notices (Your date may do the same research on you). The more intensive your search, the better! If you have any doubts or uncomfortable feelings, reach out to a trusted friend, family member, or professional for guidance and support. It's better to lose a bit of your pride versus thousands of dollars.

Before starting a committed relationship, it is crucial to clarify your values and goals, establish boundaries, and have confidence in your intuition (Read more in the next chapters). You get to decide whether to meet, and only when you have conducted thorough research about this new person and feel confident in your decision. You should never feel pressured or given ultimatums to meet or engage in any other activity.

Next, do video chats! It's important to see the individual you're going to meet before meeting in person. Video chats allow you to get a better sense of their personality, body language, and overall demeanour. It's a wonderful way to build a connection and ensure there's a level of comfort and compatibility. Plus, it's a convenient way to have face-to-face conversations with no physical proximity.

During online chats, remember to keep your personal information, like pictures of your kids or any other sensitive details, out of sight. No stranger should see anything of personal value to you before meeting in person. Refusing to video chat screams 'Scammer!' If someone is unwilling to live video chat with you after a week of messaging, it is a clear red flag, so end all communication despite whatever excuse the person gives. They may have a fake profile picture or be in another relationship. If you are not aware, there is a way to check online to verify from where images originate.

It's challenging to uncover if someone is already in a relationship and seeking online affairs outside their marriage, but there are ways. Anyone who sounds like they are whispering over the phone or can only speak at odd hours (and insist on calling you) is obviously in a relationship or hiding something. They could be married and not want their partner to know they are on a dating app.

Laurie connected with a man via an online dating app. After a couple of days of texting, she suggested they take the next step of having a phone chat. She noticed he was talking in hushed tones, which her intuition told her was strange. And minutes later, her gut feeling proved correct! There was a kerfuffle and another voice in the background as this guy's wife wrestled the phone out of his hand, yelling about catching her "serial cheating asshole husband red-handed!" Laurie remained on the phone with the woman for another thirty minutes, providing free relationship coaching. True story!

The timeline for meeting should be within a couple of weeks. While texting someone can be a fantastic way to connect on a mental level, long-term messaging can lead to building a fantasy image of the other person in your mind. So, if you are serious about taking your relationship further, we recommend an in-person date within two weeks. Here are some guidelines:

If you feel comfortable to meet, do so in a public place and during the day. Neutral spaces and daylight make our first-time meeting safer. Give friends or family members all the details of your meeting and the contact information of your date. If you choose to meet in a coffee shop, don't be shy to tell the barista (or anyone else close by) that you are on a blind date. While having an ally can help you feel safer, you have sole responsibility for your safety.

No spark? If you meet, chat for a while, and realise you never want to see this person again, be honest and empathic. Rejection sucks! Understand they may see a future with you. And it would feel disappointing for you to be rejected, too. It's critical to ensure the person you reject doesn't know where you live or have any of your personal details in case of potential stalking.

Your connection feels unbelievably perfect! The person is such an ideal catch that you wonder why no one has snatched them up yet. This individual may be the infamous soulmate that people speak of. Or they are a professional love chameleon (or iguana) expert in wooing and conquering before moving to their next prey. If it feels too good to be true, put on your critical thinking cap and investigate. Be discerning and follow your gut feelings. If their actions match their words, everyone gets along, and your loved ones approve, then decide what comes next for your relationship.

Prepare for worst-case scenarios. Ugh! No one wants to think of these, but we learn through newscasts about a family searching for their missing loved one who met up with a stranger. And this is happening somewhere every day! We offer dating tips and safety measures, but it's your responsibility to exercise caution and vigilance to avoid dating horrors.

Here are critical safety considerations for dating:

- ❖ If you plan to meet someone online, ensure another adult has details of that plan. Teenagers may roll their eyes at this, but most parents want to protect their children from predators. Considering they've been on the earth longer, humour them and let your parents help you date safely.
- ❖ Phone apps will show someone where you are. Download,

activate, and share! You can deactivate the feature once you are safely home.
- Never get into a car on your first (and even second) date. Arrange a neutral meeting place and go with your own transportation.
- Do not drink alcohol or use the bathroom until you have finished eating and drinking. Never leave your food or drink unattended.
- Trust any feelings that arise (your intuition). If you do not feel secure and are second-guessing yourself, opt to be overly cautious and find a safe way to end the date.
- If you're uncomfortable and do not feel confident about ending the date, pre-arrange for a friend to call you an hour into your meeting to check in and create a fake emergency. This is your moment to be nominated for an Oscar, so break a leg! *I'm sorry I must leave, but there's a family emergency.* Offer to pay, then take a taxi home.
- Always text your designated someone when you arrive home.
- Repeat this mantra: *It's better to be safe than sorry.*

Meeting Through Friends

Your best friend's boyfriend knows someone single and thinks you would be a perfect match! Could this be the ideal set-up? Yes. And no.

Yes, if they know the person very well, know their family, have grown up together and hang out regularly. They know all the tea about this person: their past relationships and why they failed, their values, unhealthy habits, good habits, and what they seek in a relationship. This could be a best friend, a family member, a neighbour (as in one of the author's cases), or a colleague.

No, because although your friend has known *you* for years, they may not know the other person as well. Although you may feel safe, it's important to remember that your blind date is a stranger. Recognise that your blind date is someone you don't know and prioritise your safety by asking the right questions to both your friend and your date. It could turn out that your friend thinks you'd be a brilliant match with 'some person' they met last week at a keg party. In that case, get a new friend!

Thirty-nine percent of sexual assaults happen at the hands of someone known to the victim, according to RAINN (Rape, Abuse & Incest National Network). This alarming statistic makes it crucial to trust the power of our intuition. That little voice inside often warns us when something doesn't feel right—listen to it!

Questions to ask your friend (the same as if you were online dating) when they are setting you up on a date with someone they know:

- How long have you known this person, and in what capacity (close friend, acquaintance, colleague)?
- Why do you think we would be a good match?
- What is their full name (so you can perform an online search)?
- Why are they single (or what is wrong with them)?

Safety first. Always. We all want to feel loved. There is nothing wrong with that chemistry. But, when desire overcomes the cognisant part of our brain, we can convince ourselves that we can spin poop into gold. Desperately wanting something can cause us to make a wrong decision in a millisecond.

Rekindling the Fairy Tale

How often do people find each other again via social media with the goal of rekindling the flame of their adolescent love? Or someone is obsessed with an old flame and finds them online only to discover they are happily married to someone else!

The Internet makes it easy to find anyone from our past—despite that sometimes it is best to leave them there! Recreating the fantasy of what once was, hence, the fairy tale bears mentioning here because we may feel what we had was so special and that person is "The One that got away." We may have spent years thinking about "What if…?"

Who you once were is not who you are today. Life has happened in between. Take the time to get to know the person as they are now. It may be best to treat them as a stranger because technically they are!

Kelly experienced this feeling about someone she was engaged to in her early twenties. For years she dreamt of him and regretted their hasty split. She eventually learned these feelings stemmed from her unhappiness in herself, especially when she realised how she'd settled for less by living in an unhealthy relationship with the long-term partner she eventually chose.

Sometimes we meet an old flame after many years apart and resume as if we've never been apart. Because of the death of or desertion by spouses, now we are free to pursue and rekindle that long-ago-but-not-forgotten romance. It can be the making of a beautiful love story to tell grandchildren from our respective families!

The First Date

Usually superficial, the first date is often based on appearance and ease of conversation. Or sparks fly because you have this amazing chemistry! (Whoa, Horsey!) The second or third date is foundational and allows you to discover your partner on a deeper level. Their answers can help you gain critical information to evaluate your desire to pursue a relationship.

We are daring, even double daring, you to move out of your

comfort zone by asking specific questions. If you seek a long-term relationship, you can make the best decision by taking things slower and using every opportunity to learn about the other person. As you would interview someone for a position in your company, you can pose questions to your date. Except in this case, *you* are the position (Oops, Freudian slip)!

Here are questions to ask your date:

1. *How do you spend your free time?* This helps establish common ground, that the person has a life outside work and other obligations and gives insight into how they engage with the world.
2. *What kind of music/bands do you like?* This fun question establishes a cultural bent that the person likes entertainment and is not all work and no play.
3. *What do you do for work?* You want to know their job and financial status.
4. *Do you consider yourself a leader or a follower?* While this sounds like a job interview question, you want to know if your potential partner is an initiative-taker with ambition.
5. *What would you do if you had the money to do whatever you wanted?* This question uncovers financial well-being, values, mission, and what is meaningful to the person.

In today's fast-paced society, finding time to eat or take a break, let alone date someone, is challenging. Hence the get-to-the-point-questions above. You can be curious about someone without acting interrogating; pepper your conversation as the dialogue fits the context. Pay attention to body language, such as eye contact and nervousness, when your date responds. If your date avoids answering or hedges when you ask a question, it may show they have something to hide.

Two weeks into dating, Laurie devised and used these in-depth questions with her partner:

1. How would your last partner describe you?
2. How long have you been with your employer?
3. What part did you play in your last relationship break-up?
4. What did you learn about yourself from your previous relationship?
5. Would you accept it if everyone insisted the world is flat? Why?
6. How many relationships have you had in the past five years?
7. Would your mother say you are easily influenced?
8. What are your top three short and long-term goals?
9. What elements define an abusive relationship?
10. To what lengths would you go to preserve a relationship, and at what point would you decide to walk away?
11. What is the most important to you: money, love, happiness, independence, and integrity?
12. How would your best friends describe you?
13. How would your enemies describe you?
14. What are your best and worst qualities?
15. In a partner, what qualities do you look for and respect?
16. What kind of relationship do/did your parents have?
17. What type of parent are you? Authoritarian or friend?
18. How important are your friends to you?
19. What do you enjoy most when you meet someone new?

These are suggested questions you can ask. Create a list based on your values and goals. For more examples, visit the link to an expanded list of first-date questions in the Bibliography.

Dating conventions continue to develop, so knowing and honouring your values can keep you grounded (See Values in Chapter 2). *Happily Ever After—A Reality Check* aims to help you achieve clarity as you cut through all the noise to listen to yourself (and your potential partner). If dating is a game, determine your objectives and develop a strategy!

Introduction

Welcome to Getting Clear

And we lived happily ever after!

You are dating someone and it's serious; you feel ready to take the plunge to commit. This exciting step could involve moving in together or getting engaged. Understanding your motivation is crucial when making a major life choice. Knowing your 'why' will help you navigate the complexities of living with a chosen partner, spouse, husband, wife, or even a roommate. Sustainable relationships begin with a clear understanding about your reason for being together. Your 'why' will motivate you when the going gets tough and you want to get going!

If you enter a living arrangement or marriage without working on yourself, you may end up with the opposite of what you desire in a relationship. Critical thinking often goes out the window in love relationships. When everything is rosy at the beginning of a new relationship, it's easy to overlook the warning signs. You must do your homework. Otherwise, you may wonder why your couple is fraught with discord, anger, resentment, or even violence as time passes!

EXERCISE: Know your 'Why?'

Check all that apply:

☐ We are in love and have a mutual goal of building a life together.
☐ We've been dating for X amount of time, and we want to take our relationship to the next level.
☐ Time to fly the coop (leave my family's home/another home, the system).
☐ I want a parental figure for my children.
☐ I'm looking for stability or financial security.
☐ My biological clock is ticking.
☐ I don't want to be alone.
☐ All the above.
☐ None of the above.

How This Book Can Help

This book aims to help you clarify why you want to move forward with your current love interest. It delves into the depths of your emotions, thoughts, and motivations, helping you understand the underlying factors that drive your attraction. Whether it's their unique qualities, shared values, or the chemistry between you, this book encourages introspection and self-reflection to empower you to make informed decisions and build a solid foundation for a fulfilling and meaningful romantic connection.

As life coaches who help clients identify the gap between where they are and where they want to be, we authored this book in the same style to help you determine how your wishes compare with your reality. The Oxford Learner's Dictionaries (online) defines a reality check as:

"An occasion when you are reminded of how things are in the real world, rather than how you would like things to be." This book encourages you to conduct reality checks on a wide range of relationship topics.

Each chapter covers a subject with questions and exercises to help you reflect on your motivations, learning, and steps you can take toward change. When you meditate and reflect on the questions, it may amaze you how the answers percolate and bubble up. If a question eludes you, skip it. You can ponder it and return later.

As you complete the exercises, we will ask you to identify red flags, deal breakers, and decide *if* you choose to move forward and how. There are no correct answers; it's merely a way to put your thoughts into black-and-white and practise a deeper connection to your intuition.

Red Flags

Why did the suspicious math teacher always pay attention to red flags? Because she knew they were the square roots of trouble! We find red flags on a beach, alerting us to the dangers of the tides. We see them on construction sites and vehicles carrying awkward, heavy loads or hazardous materials. They tell us to proceed with caution, promoting our safety and preventing harm.

Red flags arise from our intuition or what we know as a gut feeling or 'Spidey sense' when our subconscious processes allow thoughts or feelings to surface. Sensing through intuition lets us use associative thinking to connect unrelated ideas and make conclusions based on our knowledge and experiences.

Our insights form our convictions and reinforce our feelings of certainty. The powerful emotion of discomfort and the little voice inside tells us something feels off. As we become intuitively or overtly aware, we notice the red flag or warning signal that means danger.

Sometimes, we see red flags in our relationships and wonder: *How can a fairy tale have red flags?* We may refuse to see them because we subconsciously desire a relationship so much that we want the connection to work. When our expectations clash with reality, we doubt ourselves and question our instincts.

Enter DENIAL. And denial is not a river in Egypt but a massive canal running through our backyard! Because we feel committed, we may minimize the severity of these danger signals. We may feel humiliated and angry because we have already invested much of ourselves in the relationship. Hence, we develop a defence mechanism that can shield us from the pain of facing an unpleasant reality until we are emotionally prepared. When we deny a red flag, we pretend it does not exist.

Trusting our instincts can be misleading, so it's crucial to use evidence and critical thinking when something feels off. While a red flag is not always a deal breaker, it is something to which we must pay attention.

An Opportunity for Growth

When you're in the initial stages of a relationship, the honeymoon phase can make you see your partner as perfect. But when a red flag appears, that illusion shatters. It may prematurely become a deal-breaker, and you end the relationship. It's important to pay attention to red flags and address them through communication without ignoring them. When red flags occur early on, this presents an opportunity to manage conflict and differences as a couple.

A caveat about red flags signalling abuse: Do not overlook or attempt to work through any red flags if your partner engages in intimate partner violence. Abuse only escalates. You must exit the dynamic safely (Read more about abuse in Chapter 4).

Deal Breakers

Deal breakers are non-negotiable issues in a relationship that can cause one or both people to withdraw if they can't tolerate or live with them. They differ from red flags because even though something presents as a red flag; it does not mean it's a deal breaker. A red flag can be a point of discussion whereby you double-check their importance and severity through honest, open communication. Deal breakers are those toxic behaviours that lead to wanting to end a relationship; there usually is no communication because you are not expecting change, nor are you willing to wait for it.

For example, if my boyfriend sometimes (*sometimes* being the operative word here) watches pornography, this may be a red flag. We discuss it, and since this is not an addiction or something he craves, he stops viewing it. He shows me he is sensitive to my feelings.

When is a red flag a deal breaker? When you notice the behaviour, you also see a pattern. For example, your boyfriend constantly looks at porn on his computer and tries to hide it by closing the screen whenever you approach. Suppose he overly defends or explains his habit. This may signal a pattern of compulsive behaviour and merits a direct conversation where I listen carefully to what my partner is not saying. I choose not to tolerate someone constantly consuming pornography. In my mind, this could be an active sex addiction which has the potential to escalate and rob the relationship of intimacy. Excessive porn use is a deal breaker, and I choose to end the relationship.

A deal breaker is present when:

- ❖ The issue becomes a point of contention in the relationship and causes arguments between you.
- ❖ Your focus on the problem distracts you from the relationship.
- ❖ Being around your partner doesn't make you feel good.

❖ You feel anxious when you think about your relationship or wonder what will happen when your partner shows up.

Your gut tells you something is wrong, and everything inside screams to get out of the relationship. Doubts creep in, and you question your self-worth as it continues to plummet. Each hit to your self-esteem chips away at your confidence, leaving you feeling smaller and less valuable.

Sometimes, we have blind spots or are in denial concerning our partner's behaviour. We may tell ourselves he or she will change when we move in or marry (See Rescuing and Fixing in Chapter 3). Not true! When you notice your discomfort, this is your internal radar alerting you to a potential problem and your intolerance to it. It's smarter to take more time dating before committing to see how your partner's actions and your couple dynamic affect your relationship.

Mind the Gap

In the United Kingdom, when we board trains, we are frequently reminded to "Mind the gap" to ensure our safety. This cautionary phrase warns about the space between the platform and the train, which could cause us to trip, stumble, or even fall. Similarly, in life, we often encounter a gap between the current state of things and our desired outcomes. It is this discrepancy that we must acknowledge and reconcile to progress and pursue our plans in an intimate relationship.

A Step Towards Change

We fear the unknown because change is hard for us emotionally, psychologically, and socially. The following list highlights those reasons:

- ❖ The unknown is scary - it triggers anxiety and fear, making us crave familiarity and security.
- ❖ Loss of control - we cannot control the situation or outcomes.
- ❖ Habitual behaviour and comfort zone - we are creatures of habit, comfortable in our way of being—even if it doesn't serve us well.
- ❖ Cognitive dissonance - we resist change to avoid the discomfort of conflicting thoughts or realities.
- ❖ Emotional attachment - we have difficulty releasing our attachment to people, places, and things.
- ❖ Perceived effort and overwhelm - it may feel like too much work to effect change.
- ❖ Social pressure - we want to keep the status quo to please others or toe the line because of others' judgements.
- ❖ Experiences - past negative events associated with change, especially failure, can lead to resistance.
- ❖ Identity and image - change can challenge our sense of identity based on our current roles, habits, and behaviours.
- ❖ Lack of resources - we need more time, money, or other resources.
- ❖ Lack of motivation - we do not feel the impetus to change.

While change can be challenging, it's not always negative. So, for habits to stick, we must take incremental action. Tiny steps are critical. The last line of each chapter asks you to consider one small action you can take. Remember: Little steps can lead to notable progress when we take enough of them. Embracing the unknown can lead to personal growth, improved skills, new opportunities, and enhanced resilience. And this is how we grow!

Working This Book

This book takes a coaching approach based on positive psychology; we are merely planting seeds for thought. It is a guide with suggestions to help you navigate your relationship with yourself and your partner. Trust your intuition, choose whichever chapter speaks to you the most, and jump in!

Performing Your Reality Check

Each chapter ends with an opportunity for you to do a reality check about your relationship as it relates to the information presented regarding:

How things are: Currently, the situation either works for me or is not ideal, meaning there are aspects out of line with my expectations or desires.

How I would like things to be: Ideally, I would like things to be different and aligned with my preferences and aspirations. Or my situation is ideal—wonderful!

Red Flag(s): I am noticing warning signs or indicators suggesting the current situation may not be favourable or healthy, and I must pay attention.

Deal Breaker(s): Specific factors or circumstances are unacceptable to me because they do not fit with my values and prompt me to reconsider the relationship entirely.

One action I can take: To address these concerns and work towards a more desired outcome, I can take specific steps or make a decision that will lead to positive change.

As you consider the diverse topics, you may wonder how relevant they are to you. (*Like retirement—really? Must I think about that now? I've got years to go!*) What may appear irrelevant now can figure into the grander picture as you consider building a life for yourself and with a partner. And that includes the not-so-pressing items because critical conversations and choices will come—sometimes faster than you think!

You'll notice we emphasize clear, honest, open communication as it relates to each topic. The constant reminder is to prevent relationship failure because this is the major reason couples drift apart and break up. Communication is a powerful tool to maintain a strong and healthy couple in every aspect of the relationship. We aim to equip couples with the skills to overcome challenges and resolve conflicts to foster a deeper connection.

Whether you're in a relationship or using a dating app, this information can also help you understand yourself better. We recommend keeping a separate journal to document your reflections and answers, and we encourage you to do these as a couple. If your partner is unwilling, move ahead and complete the exercises yourself.

It's time to do your homework—your reality check for building your *happily ever after*. Let's get started!

Chapter 1

Once Upon a Time

She kissed the frog, hoping he would become a prince. P.S. He is still a frog!

The Fairy Tale Begins

Who knows what attracts us to a particular person? There are so many variables that it would be impossible to name because attraction often overrides appearance. We swear we have a type. But then we meet that off-beat someone who makes us laugh or has other characteristics or values that melt our heart and BOOM—we feel attracted!

Our heart has a memory of its own and connects so deeply to someone that it catches us off guard. It could be how they laugh, their confident walk, their intelligence, their sense of adventure, or any other characteristic, and we feel drawn to them. Not all people we feel drawn to fit our ideal image of whom we see ourselves committing to. 'On paper,' there may be reasons we would not feel attracted to a particular person, but the heart does not have eyes or reasoning. Despite our intense connection with someone, we must explore the possibilities of what life with this person might be long term. Keep an open mind and take steps to address unexpected challenges in your relationship.

WYSIWYG (What you see is what you get) applies in all relationships. As a couple, if we are lucky, we will grow old and ugly together. Time and gravity are realities, so naturally, our appearance changes. The svelte young woman with enormous boobs may become curvier and sport sagging, pendulous breasts. A man with a full head of hair may become bald. These are all surface changes. Beauty is skin deep, so it's vital to love each other's core.

REFLECTION

- ☐ OMG, I kissed a frog, and he is still a frog! (If you think this, please head to the nearest wall, and bang your head on it multiple times.)
- ☐ I love frogs! (This is not a deal breaker.)
- ☐ What frog? (You may still be in the honeymoon phase.)

Every perfect love story charts this course: Boy meets girl, they fall in love, get married and live happily ever after—the making of a fantastic fairy tale! No one mentions the choppy waters, sea storms, and tsunamis! Managing this union can be challenging because of factors like personalities, ethnicity, religion, values, and life changes. Past traumas, societal pressures, and ideologies can complicate relationships and make them less than perfect.

How society defines relationships also influences perceptions of the ideal union. There are same-sex couples, 'throuples,' multicultural, multi-religion, and multi-binary, which comprise people forming relationships, every one of which has its challenges. Movies, television, magazines, and social media create and feed the expectation of the fairy tale. Open any bridal magazine, and we enter a world of flowing white tulle, flowers, romantic venues, and getaways—all the trappings of a fairy tale wedding.

In Western countries, children's beliefs are shaped by traditional fairy tales like *Cinderella*, popularised by Disney (Geronimi et al., 1950). Prince Charming sweeps the girl off her feet and takes her to his castle to live happily ever after. No one tells us we'll have to kiss loads of frogs before meeting 'Person Charming.' We grow up believing we will merit the prince (or princess) and a happy ending if we do things correctly. Like Cinderella, we may have learned to be people-pleasers. We believe that if we scrub enough floors, we'll earn the opportunity to attend the Ball, and the handsome prince will whisk us away to a castle.

The unconscious influence of outdated gender stereotypes may still affect our modern relationships. Perpetuated by fairy tales based on patriarchal constructs, these roles imply tasks are gender specific, instead of flexible or interchangeable. Today's reality is that parents must work long hours to meet rising living costs, requiring them to take on multiple roles, actively working toward equality and sharing household responsibilities. In relationships, both partners contribute to the financial stability of the family and share the emotional and domestic workload. It isn't easy balancing a fairy tale romance with everyday chores, bills, and children.

How We Came to Be a Couple

Each couple has a story that includes how they met, their first date, and their initial declarations of love. You may have met by chance or through mutual friends, took the online dating route, scrolling through myriad profiles to find 'The One.' Or you met through your workplace, school, or a shared hobby or social club. Ultimately, forming a couple involves mutual attraction and a desire to be in a relationship.

It requires getting to know each other, spending time together, and building a connection that may lead to a long-term commitment.

Considering your initial motivations when times are challenging can be helpful because it reminds you why you are together. Return to this often to recall your 'why' when things get tough.

> **EXERCISE A: The Story of Us**
>
> Tell the story of *us*. How did you meet? Make notes, draw a picture, write a poem, or compose several paragraphs describing your beginning. Does a song or piece of music resonate as in 'our song'? Perhaps it's a film you watched or a place you visited together.
>
> Telling your story is critical because when relationships get rocky (and they will!), it can help to remember why you became a couple.

> **REFLECTION**
>
> Does your partner agree to do the work of this book?
>
> ☐ Yes
> ☐ No
> ☐ I can't ask (*Why not?*)

The Honeymoon Period

The honeymoon period happens in every romantic relationship. It is nature's way of creating the bonding required for coupling. You are in love. Endorphins course through your system, turning your brain to mush. The idea of love is glamorous and highly seductive. Why is that? It's part fairy tale, part society's expectations—mixed with biology. Everything feels fantastic, and your 'prince' or 'princess' can do no wrong.

However, this period is fleeting and not ideal for moving in together or marrying. In this phase, your hormones align with your biology to trick you into making life-changing decisions you may regret later. The hits of serotonin can combine with a lack or void that causes people to feel a relationship will fulfill them. It's a euphoria fuelled by the desperate need to find a partner. When you have an emptiness to fill, it's perilous because you risk attracting someone who mirrors that positive image of yourself. You might rely on someone to feel special, as their positive actions and words boost your self-esteem.

Something about the honeymoon phase entices people to take the path of least resistance and avoid engaging in hard conversations. Things are going exceptionally well. Why rock the boat? In the honeymoon period, we may:

- Miss red flags.
- Tolerate the unacceptable—ignore our values and deal breakers (See Chapter 2 for more details).
- Tell ourselves the other person will change.
- Convince ourselves we will adapt to what we don't like.
- Fall deeper and inextricably in love with the idea of love rather than see the reality.
- Feel too invested to back out, telling ourselves we can make it work. *I couldn't change my dysfunctional family of origin, and here is my golden second chance* (Subconsciously, of course)!

> ### REFLECTION
>
> Ask yourself these questions:
>
> 1. Are you constantly trying to convince your partner to love you?
> 2. Do you hide parts of yourself/your habits from your partner?
> 3. Are your boundaries being respected?

Here's a challenge: during the honeymoon period, postpone sex. Wait! Before protesting, consider the reasoning. Engaging in physical intimacy, particularly sexual intercourse, impairs our judgement. A therapist told Kelly that men lose their rationality while waiting to have sex, while women lose it after having sex.

Women connect deeply by communicating and expressing their feelings. Men connect through activities and view intimacy as doing things together. It's no wonder that sex for men is doing something that potentially connects them. Hence, men view sex as intimacy. Ending a troubled relationship becomes difficult after we become emotionally attached through sex. A vast emotional responsibility arises from having sex; often, when hormones are raging, your brain takes a vacation.

Now, it's only fair to warn you that biology has a sneaky plan: to get us to procreate. So, by design, as humans, often we enter a state of denial, compounded by the honeymoon period. Therefore, avoiding sex while endorphins are raging is best. Cloud buster, right? We're raining on your sex parade! But consider that we cannot make rational, life-altering decisions when so many feel-good hormones are coursing through us.

Whether you believe in fairy tales or know they aren't true, you still struggle to deal with their effect. Good for you if you are living a fairy tale with your partner! (Are you still in the honeymoon phase?)

Consider the quote about doing the same thing and expecting different outcomes. Stop kissing frogs and expecting princes/princesses!

You know when this intense and all-consuming honeymoon period begins, but how do you know when this giddy, drunk-on-love-period is over? The second you feel annoyed by your partner's behaviour, you understand they're not perfect, and this marks the start of the end of the honeymoon phase.

The honeymoon phase can be a delicious period to get to know one another while learning how you can be as a couple. Stay vigilant (it will be over soon enough when you pick up that first dirty sock wedged under the night table). You have options regarding how you want to move forward together or apart. Allow yourselves to use this period to discover and test the reality of your future.

REFLECTION

1. How long did your relationship's honeymoon phase last (Or are you still in it)?
2. What significant decisions did you make during this period?
3. Before deciding about anything critical, can you wait for the honeymoon phase to end? If not, why?
4. Is there something you (half-heartedly) agreed to in the honeymoon phase that you now regret?
5. Did your honeymoon phase affect your physical intimacy with your partner? How?

The House Key

For some couples, exchanging house keys means you have committed to one another and are exclusive. Perhaps you want your partner to water your plants and feed your cats while you are travelling for work.

Consider the implications of giving your key during the honeymoon phase. A key to your home means that any person has full access to your belongings and sacred space, including your sensitive documents. If either of you have children, *their* lives will be directly affected. Just because you feel deeply connected to your partner doesn't mean your children will feel the same way and may need more time. While they may not pay rent or own the property, your children must consent.

How early in a relationship would you give your partner the password to your bank account, social security number, or other legal documents? Consider the following motivations for giving your house key based on your 'why':

- It's for convenience.
- Out of necessity, to look after your house while you are away (You can ask for your key back when you return).
- You're feeling pressured by the other person.
- You've been together for a long time and trust one another.

In his book *Act Like a Lady, Think Like a Man* (2014), Steve Harvey advises to never give your house key. His rationale: unless you share a lease or deed. You should only give your house key when you commit and there is implicit trust between you.

Sometimes, we fear the relationship will end if we don't act the way we think our partner wants us to. However, the opposite is true. A healthy relationship can withstand delay because it tests the strength of the couple and their ability to stay together for the long haul.

Waiting to offer our house key helps us establish and maintain healthy boundaries. Please do not rush into giving your key. The person you are dating must earn your trust before freely accessing your home. Over time, just as your partner gains the key to your heart, they get the key to your home. Besides, if you give your key too early, you may want it back, especially if the relationship sours or you develop safety concerns. It's challenging to retrieve your key and costly to change the locks. Once you fully commit to making a home together, either leased or purchased, you will share a key.

> **EXERCISE B: The Idea of Being in Love**
>
> Check out the video about Marlon Brando and Rita Moreno's relationship, *How Marlon Brando Love-Tortured Rita Moreno* (See the link in the Bibliography).
>
> 1. Are there any elements of your relationship that resonate?
> 2. Are you in love with the idea of love?
> 3. How does your relationship help you be your best self?

Commitment

Sometimes, we float into a living arrangement. Other times, we plan it. We may plan a legally binding commitment that involves a contract, such as a cohabitation or prenuptial agreement (See Chapter 17). And we marry, declaring our commitment before various parties (God, family, friends). Or we move in together with the goal to marry in the future (or not). It's widespread practice today to live together before marrying or opt out of entering the legal union of marriage. We are no less committed when we decide to cohabit.

We must be clear on our values and communicate honestly to make our intentions transparent while protecting ourselves. Worse is to harbour expectations based on a lack of or false information. We avoid discussing our living situation and make impulsive choices without thinking about the outcomes. We invest emotionally and financially, and when the relationship ends, it surprises us to learn we do not have the same rights as if we had legally married.

The Stages of Commitment

Committing to another person happens in stages and builds slowly along a continuum. We may discuss our status when we date: *What are we doing here? What is this? What do we call ourselves?* We hold conversations about being exclusive because we are spending more time together. We may notice that keeping two apartments is costly and decide to find one home to share because we're together all the time.

When we commit to another person, we pledge to preserve the integrity of our relationship by:

- ❖ Respecting and supporting each other's values
- ❖ Wanting for our partner what we want for ourselves
- ❖ Having each other's back
- ❖ Installing healthy interdependence

Open communication, trust, empathy, and cooperation are hallmarks of healthy interdependence. Foundational for all relationships, it is the mutually supportive and beneficial relationship between individuals. Each relies on the other while maintaining a sense of autonomy and independence. In a healthy relationship, individuals respect each other's needs and work towards common goals.

By working together, we can accomplish more than we could on our own because everyone has unique strengths and weaknesses. Healthy interdependence applies to all relationships, including romantic, family, friendships, and professional collaborations.

The benefits of healthy interdependence include:

- ❖ Increased emotional support
- ❖ Improved problem-solving abilities
- ❖ Greater resilience in the face of challenges

Balancing each other's needs and desires can lead to greater self-awareness and personal growth. While independent of thought, feelings, and personhood, you become emotionally interdependent with your partner. Shifting from 'me' to 'we' and prioritising communication, respect, and cooperation can create a valuable relationship dynamic.

Milestones

There are dating milestones, then there are relationship milestones. We deepen and renew our feelings with every stage we experience as a couple. Dating milestones depend on variables related to our personalities and relationship dynamics. While you get to decide when your own milestones will unfold, the following milestones appear in the order in which they usually happen:

- Going on your first date: This is the initial meeting where you get to know each other and decide if you want to continue dating.
- Touching, such as hugging, hand-holding, putting your arm around each other, which can be a prelude to a more intimate touch.
- Enjoying your first kiss: A kiss can be a significant moment in a relationship, signalling that you are becoming more intimate.
- Becoming exclusive: You might stop dating other people and commit to a monogamous relationship with your partner. You label the relationship, often referring to the other as girlfriend/boyfriend (girlfriend/girlfriend, boyfriend/boyfriend).
- Having sex for the first time: You become physically intimate with your partner.
- Meeting family and friends: Introducing your partner to your

family signifies you are serious and intend to integrate them into your life.
- ❖ Declaring your love: "I love you" is a big step in a relationship, displaying and wanting to express powerful feelings for your partner.
- ❖ Moving in together: Cohabiting is a significant commitment and a major step in a relationship.
- ❖ Getting engaged: An engagement is a formal commitment to get married and often involves a proposal and giving an engagement ring.
- ❖ Marrying: Marriage expresses the ultimate commitment in a romantic relationship and can be a milestone couples aspire to.
- ❖ Making financial and legal commitments: Completing legal documents and merging finances may involve opening a joint bank account, buying a home together, and creating a legal will.
- ❖ Having a child together: Deciding to expand your family to include a child is a major decision that affects your couple and creates your joint responsibility for someone dependent.

You may choose to cohabitate and not marry. Communicate regularly with your partner to ensure you're heading in the same direction regarding your relationship.

When you move in together with the expectation of getting married, and that never materializes, it can lead to feelings of being trapped and unable to move forward from that important milestone. You've invested, and you may feel as though you wasted your time. So, you stick with the relationship because it feels odd to pack up and leave. Kelly experienced this very thing: she felt frustrated waiting around for a marriage proposal only to discover her then common-law partner was not the marrying type.

> **REFLECTION**
>
> 1. What are the main milestones in your relationship?
> 2. What do they mean to you?
> 3. Are there any desired relationship milestones that you are not achieving, and what is stopping you?

Types of Commitment

Commitments often follow milestones, representing significant achievement or progress towards a goal. When we reach a milestone, this shows we are advancing in our relationship. This motivates us to make commitments to continue our progress.

We propose three types of commitment: emotional, physical/sexual, and legal.

Emotional commitment refers to the degree of emotional attachment and investment in a relationship. It involves feelings of love, care, and support for the other person and a desire to maintain a long-term relationship with them. Emotional commitment involves trust, loyalty, and overcoming relationship challenges. You show respect for your partner and form an allegiance, defining the relationship and nurturing each other. Of course, chemistry—that attraction you have for your partner—is your starting point. An emotional commitment in a monogamous relationship means being faithful to your partner.

Physical/sexual commitment refers to intimacy and sexual exclusivity between two people in a relationship. This type of commitment involves a mutual agreement to be sexually exclusive and to engage in physical acts of affection and intimacy. Physical (/sexual) commitment describes sexual faithfulness. We agree to be exclusive with our partner and engage physically and sexually with them. We are present to our partner and commit to accompanying and caring for them through the challenging and good times. You make a physical commitment by sharing space and financial responsibilities with your partner.

Legal commitment refers to the formal recognition of a relationship. This covers marriage, civil unions, or domestic partnerships and involves legal obligations and responsibilities. Legal commitment provides certain rights and protections to individuals in a relationship. This includes the ability to make medical decisions for your partner and the right to inherit property upon your partner's death. Legal commitment includes prenuptial and agreements and marriage certificates that have legal and financial obligations. A legal marriage involves shared monetary responsibility for debt, taxes, property, and children.

The other aspect of legally committing is signing a cohabitation agreement if you live as a common-law couple. Unmarried couples can legally establish joint parenthood for shared children. Moving in with your partner may leave you no legal rights, depending on your country and province. Use your local government website for research, and if you don't understand the legal terms, seek help from a legal clinic. Always prepare to pay for the legal services of a lawyer to officialise your documents. This is the best way to ensure you create an emotionally and financially transparent, fair, and wise future.

Relationships often involve a combination of emotional, physical/sexual, and legal commitment. However, it's also possible for a relationship to have one type of commitment without the others. For example, a couple might choose to live together rather than marry legally.

You can be married but not feel emotionally committed; sometimes, people get married for reasons other than love. In certain provinces, couples must file taxes together but are not eligible for spousal support in case of separation. Both spouses must look at their situation and finances and decide what is best for them if their relationship ends. It's not about expecting your relationship to end, and instead, being optimistic and ready for any outcome.

We may have witnessed our parents' bitter, unsalvageable marriages where one spouse controlled the other and all the money. We may have watched how the divorce was so hateful and expensive that it took years for one or both parents to rebuild their lives and finances. Like sponges, we absorbed lessons from their resentment and fall-out. Laurie witnessed her parent's unhappy marriage for decades. Because of this, she remembers telling her mother she never wanted to get married—and hasn't yet!

Every couple must openly discuss what works best for them. It comes back to your 'Why,' defined by your personal choices, family, and cultural expectations. You must determine and be transparent about the type(s) of commitment you desire in your relationship.

Celebrating Your Commitment

Happy Anniversary! You've made it to one year, two…five, ten! Time to celebrate! Except your partner forgets! You want to honour your special date with a romantic candlelight dinner, and your partner barely remembers to wish you a Happy Anniversary.

Celebrating your commitment is more than celebrating a date. It reminds you why you're together—and persevere despite the rough patches. It's vital to communicate your expectations about how you would like to honour your union. Your celebration may depend on a ritual with symbols (flowers, an outing, a party). It can be a re-enactment of your first date or a quiet evening at home snuggling on the sofa. Either way, your commitment is a daily choice as you experience life's challenges together. Your anniversary is a beautiful milestone celebrating your union and growth.

It's critical that no matter what difficulties you experience, you *choose* each other *every* day. Kelly engages in a quirky little ritual with her husband where they say: "We're still married—until 11:59 pm!"

> **REFLECTION**
>
> 1. What does commitment look like to you?
> 2. What are your ways of demonstrating your commitment to each other?
> 3. Are you and your partner aware of how you wish to celebrate your anniversary?

Meeting the Parents

It can feel daunting to meet your potential partner's parents (and siblings). We wonder if they will like us and vice versa and how we will fit in and get along. Family dynamics vary, as do cultural traditions. Some people are naturally emotionally close to their families. They enjoy spending time together and checking in with each other. Other people's families are so filled with tension and toxicity that it's difficult to occupy the same room, let alone form a positive connection!

Certain families appear to have no clear boundaries, which can make their close ties seem unhealthy to outsiders. There is so much dependency on family members that making any moves without consulting our parent(s) or siblings first feels wrong.

Remember that you are marrying (or moving) into a system established long before your couple. There will be adjustments, even if you adore your partner's family, which has quirks, personalities, and traditions that differ from yours, no matter how homogenous you are. Expect to have an adaptation period! You are getting to know each other and how you fit into this new dynamic.

During this adaptation period, approach the situation with an open mind and a willingness to compromise on things that do not affect your values. Embrace the differences and learn from each other's backgrounds and customs. Understand that it may take time to fully integrate into the established system, but with patience and understanding, you can create a harmonious blend of both your families' traditions.

Discuss with your partner your expectations, boundaries, and how you envision your roles within the new dynamic. This will foster understanding and prevent misunderstandings or conflicts. Also, remember that no family is perfect. Every family has its quirks and idiosyncrasies. Embrace these differences and find joy in the unique aspects of your partner's family. By doing so, you can build a solid foundation of respect and acceptance within your extended family.

In the next chapter, we discuss values, and this is where you must be honest with yourself (and your partner) about what you genuinely want as a commitment.

Reality Check

How things are:

How I would like things to be:

Red Flag(s):

Deal Breaker(s):

One action I can take:

Chapter 2

Compatibility

A prerequisite for couples: Build a ready-to-assemble piece of furniture together.

Compatibility means we can co-exist and work in harmony. When two people are compatible, they share similar values, interests, and goals. They get along and work well together, creating a spirit of collaboration, yielding mutual benefits for both partners. In a compatible relationship, there is a sense of ease and comfort. We embrace and celebrate each other's differences as they bring diversity and enrich our partnership. Each person's strengths complement the other's weaknesses, leading to a balanced, well-rounded dynamic.

We bring our unique personalities, temperaments, values, goals, wants, needs, and drives into our relationship. Our compatibility depends on how all the above fit together as we meld our lives as a couple. Love is not enough when there are major differences in values, interests, and goals.

Compatibility lays the foundation for harmonious relationships. It allows us to connect on a deep level, fostering understanding, support, and mutual growth. When we are compatible with our partner, we can achieve remarkable things together and create positivity in our lives and the world!

Values

Our values—something intrinsically valuable to us, which we hold dear—form the core of who we are. And our values rarely change. We must be clear about our values as we embark on a relationship with someone because these help us decide what we can and cannot accept. For what it is worth, values are priceless!

Examples of core values include:

- ❖ Wisdom
- ❖ Loyalty
- ❖ Respect
- ❖ Trust
- ❖ Action
- ❖ Ambition
- ❖ Honesty
- ❖ Integrity
- ❖ Reliability
- ❖ Perseverance
- ❖ Positivity
- ❖ Altruism

Our values shape our beliefs and behaviours and influence which causes and rights we fight for. But it is possible to change our beliefs and actions through new learning experiences, while maintaining our values. Examples of how our positive values translate into our actions include:

- ❖ Believing honesty is always the best policy.
- ❖ Putting family first.
- ❖ Prioritising work-life balance.
- ❖ Having empathy for others.
- ❖ Refusing an intimate relationship with a cigarette smoker.

Examples of negative core values that can affect our actions include:

- ❖ Believing we don't deserve good things to happen to us.
- ❖ Seeing everyone as untrustworthy.
- ❖ Viewing the world as a brutal place where only the toughest survive.

Choosing a partner means considering all aspects of that person, such as motivation, ambition, honesty, and other values we hold dear. We commonly believe that opposites attract, but that attraction can only last so long when your values are not in sync. Although you won't always share the same values or express them the same way, you must share enough of the major ones that form the fabric of your life as a couple.

The details people share on social media can provide insight into their lives. This is fertile ground for uncovering your partner's values. When you're attracted to someone, browse their social media to spot any potential concerns or intriguing aspects. Engage in a conversation about the topics you uncovered in their online profiles and gauge their reaction (See the Prelude to this book, The Dating Game).

Remember that we don't have to like everything our partner enjoys, and vice versa. We want to please our partner during the first phase of our relationship, so we may minimize our needs. Disliking baseball and attending a game to make our partner happy is an easy compromise, but suppressing our core values can lead to resentment and anger. Our values are integral to our identity, and they shape our beliefs and actions. They represent what we stand for and what is meaningful for us. We cannot change or love away our values since they are non-negotiable. Changing or ignoring our core values to please our partner is not sustainable and can damage the relationship.

> **EXERCISE A: Personal Values**
>
> Make a list of your top ten values. Ask your partner to do the same. Choose your top three values and rank them in order of importance. Compare your lists. What core values do you share?
>
> 1.
> 2.
> 3.
> 4.
> 5.
> 6.
> 7.
> 8.
> 9.
> 10.

Cultural Values

Our world has become a massive melting pot and continues to globalize. People travel and explore the world because they are curious to experience other countries and cultures. This interconnectivity has led to integrating and diffusing values and beliefs, creating a globalised cultural landscape.

Geopolitical alliances and conflicts directly influence how we perceive and accept diverse cultures, leading to adopting or rejecting certain values and beliefs. People seek asylum/refuge and immigrate from war-torn countries, bringing their ideologies to their new geographies, and these influence their values and how they partner. Kelly has a childhood friend whose life partner fled a war as a fifteen-year-old, and they have forged a successful relationship based on mutual understanding.

While geopolitical factors are key in shaping cultural values, they are not the only factors. Religion, family traditions, education, and individual experiences also contribute to cultural identity. Historical events and colonization have left a lasting impact on the cultural fabric of societies. Political decisions and policies implemented by governments can shape cultural values and beliefs. Trade agreements, multinational corporations, and information flow all facilitate the exchange of ideas and cultural practices between different societies. Immigration policies determine who enters a country and the diversity of its population.

While we may assimilate into a new relationship and location, we carry our history and culture, which rarely change because they are ingrained as our family and cultural backgrounds shape the customs we adopt and follow. Traditions, languages, and dialects of states/provinces vary. So, it's crucial to assess our shared values with a potential partner to ensure compatibility and prevent friction.

For example, a Canadian immigrant to the United States meets a Jewish American whose family hails from Europe. They must negotiate their backgrounds, cultures, religions, and customs regarding where to live and which rituals to practice. This is challenging, especially if one or both partners refuses to budge. And imagine what happens when they decide to have children. Let's say a couple lives in a community with a strict way of life, and one partner wishes to deviate from that. It can create problems for that couple and their child. Moving from downtown to the suburbs can cause issues for a partnership, so imagine relocating to another country. Dialogue and consensus must happen if one partner wants to move back to their country of origin or another country.

Historical legacies, political decisions, and economic globalization shape our cultural values and beliefs. Understanding that geopolitical factors influence diversity and cultural blending in our world can promote inclusivity, respect, and appreciation for the diverse communities in our partnerships and families.

REFLECTION

1. Were you born and raised in the same country?
2. Do you speak the same language?
3. How similar are your values and beliefs?
4. What are your reasons for staying in or leaving the country in which you live?
5. Where do you want to live once you are married and have children?

EXERCISE B: Navigating Cultural Diversity

Cultural, ethnic, and religious differences become crucial when you have children together.

1. How do you want to raise your children regarding religion and culture?
2. Are you or your partner expected to raise your children with the same religious values and practices with which you grew up?
3. How would raising your children according to your partner's religion affect you, your extended family, and the community in which you live?

Intercultural Unions

Intercultural unions are marriages or relationships between individuals from distinct cultural backgrounds. While intercultural relationships contribute to personal growth, cultural exploration, and a broader worldview, understanding the influence of ethnicity and culture on long-term relationships is important. Couples from distinct cultures may struggle with differences in language, communication, culture, and values. Our culture shapes our beliefs and family customs, such as rituals, births, weddings, and holidays. The differences in cultures and ethnicities may also cause significant upheaval when raising children. In this way, the absence of cultural compatibility may be a deal breaker when choosing a potential spouse from another ethnic or cultural background than yourself.

It is possible to embrace another culture and remain faithful to yours. Experiencing and respecting each other's ingrained beliefs, values, and customs is a beautiful way to expand your life. Intercultural unions thrive when both partners actively engage in communication, compromise when needed, and embrace the opportunity to gain experience and grow together. Sharing cultural traditions can strengthen the bond between partners. And society benefits from intercultural unions because they foster appreciation for cultural diversity.

REFLECTION

1. What ethnicity are you and your partner?
2. Where are your cultural differences?
3. Are you open to marrying someone of another ethnicity/culture? If so, what challenges might you face?
4. If you are in an intercultural relationship, do you plan to have children together? If yes, how will you navigate the diversity?

Spiritual and Religious Values

Going to church, temple, or Mesquite is practicing a religion. Going inward is practicing spirituality. We do not have to attend a house of worship to be spiritual. However, our spiritual and religious practices usually intertwine with our ethnicity and culture, founded on values often stemming from our upbringing and family traditions steeped in ritual and rites of passages. Examples of these include:

- ❖ Marrying or holding a civil/religious ceremony
- ❖ Baptising children or holding purification rites
- ❖ Sending our child to extracurricular religious studies (Christian Sunday School, Hebrew School, Catholic Confirmation Classes)
- ❖ Engaging in daily prayer rituals (e.g., Muslim Salah)
- ❖ Celebrating holidays by attending a house of worship (church, synagogue, temple)

When individuals come from diverse religious backgrounds, religion can become an obstacle in the relationship. This happens especially when certain religions hold more steadfastly to their convictions and rituals than others. The varying beliefs and practices can create challenges that may strain the bond between partners. Suppose your partner insists on their religious views, whereas you favour letting your children make their own decisions.

It requires open-mindedness, understanding, and compromise to navigate these differences successfully. By actively considering our partner's perspective, we can bridge the gap and find common ground, even amidst divergent beliefs. Compromise plays a crucial role in finding mutually beneficial solutions. It requires a willingness to meet halfway, to let go of absolute positions, and find a middle ground that respects the needs and desires of both partners. Embracing these qualities, we can navigate the complexities of our differences with grace and achieve harmonious resolutions.

> **REFLECTION**
>
> 1. Define religion and spirituality and what they mean to you?
> 2. Are you or your partner spiritual or religious (Or both)?
> 3. What level of importance would you assign to your religious/spiritual values?
> 4. Are religious differences a deal breaker for either of you?
> 5. If you have children together, how will you navigate your religious differences?

Hold an honest conversation about your non-negotiables regarding spirituality and religious practices. Remaining open and respectful will help you agree on how to honour both sets of your beautiful beliefs.

Traditions and Celebrations

Our traditions and how we celebrate them through holidays tie in with our values. Usually established in our family of origin, these derive from our ethnicity, culture, memories, and feelings, so if our partner refuses to share the joy of these with us, it can create tension.

When we become a couple, we merge two families' traditions. It's important to discuss and create unique traditions as a couple. For example, a couple decides not to take part in the Christmas tradition of family dinners and gift exchanges. Instead, they take a trip every December (and send the family a postcard of Froggie sipping a pina colada on the beach).

Besides holidays being stressful with all the extra cooking, gift shopping, and socialising, it's expected that we do it within a condensed time as we cram visits and celebrations into a one-week period! This can wear us down, making us feel irritable during a time of festivity and celebration.

When we factor children in, holidays and traditions may take on a new meaning. We want to raise our children with the same wonderful traditions we grew up with, and this can be difficult to manoeuvre if both partners have different traditions.

Celebrations can be a cause of disagreement for some relationships, especially if certain rituals are not a priority for our partner. If you treat your birthday like it's your coronation, you may feel hurt when your partner doesn't feel as enthusiastic. In contrast, your partner may go big on Valentine's Day and expect the same from you, while you feel it's overrated. Tension can arise if your partner doesn't acknowledge or celebrate holidays that are meaningful for you. You want to know that your partner will celebrate with you, even if they do not celebrate a specific holiday themselves. Nothing warms the cockles of your heart better than your spouse donning a Santa's hat while lighting a candle on your menorah. *Merry Chrismukkah!*

REFLECTION

1. What holidays do you celebrate, and what are your traditions surrounding those?
2. Are your partner's traditions and celebrations like yours?
3. What traditions would you like to pass on to your children?
4. Are you willing to honour your partner's traditional practices?
5. What new traditions would you like to create for your own family?

Arranged Marriage

In prearranged marriages, families or other influential individuals select the spouses before they give their mutual consent or knowledge. The couple usually has limited or no say in choosing their life partner. The arrangement is typically based on cultural, social, or economic considerations rather than personal compatibility or romantic love. Arranged marriage is common in certain parts of the world, particularly in South Asia, the Middle East, and some African countries. People rely on cultural or religious traditions to ensure compatibility and stability in couples and families.

Families or individuals rely on the help of a third party, such as a matchmaker, to arrange the marriage. The couple may or may not have had any previous contact or a relationship; the marriage is based on social status, wealth, education, and family values.

Arranged marriages can sometimes result in forced marriages and restrict a woman's freedom to choose her own partner. Forced marriages are illegal in most countries where people choose who they want to marry.

The practice of arranged marriage is a complex issue with benefits and drawbacks. It's crucial to approach the topic with cultural sensitivity and respect for independent choices and values.

Child Marriage

Child marriage is prevalent in certain parts of the world and refers to marrying a child (disproportionately girls) at an incredibly early age. Certain cultures have specific reasons for child marriage, but poverty and lack of education are the main ones. Marrying off minor children is a common choice for families to ease the economic hardship and the expense of raising them.

Child marriages are not relationships based on choice, compatibility, and equality between the partners. Instead, they are motivated by family finances or other factors. The effects of child marriage on young girls include a higher risk of early pregnancy, childbirth complications, and domestic violence. Completing their education becomes less likely for child brides, and they face coercion into roles as caretakers and homemakers.

Diverse groups are working together to raise awareness, fight child marriage, and help girls and their families. These efforts have contributed to declining child marriage rates in specific regions. But this global issue persists and denies children their rights to education, health, and opportunity, so we must unite against child marriage to stop it. Only through education, awareness, and advocacy can we create a world where all children can grow, learn, and reach their full potential.

We advocate for legal and consenting partnerships without casting judgement on couples' unions. However, if you are trapped in a child marriage, you may read this book to determine your next steps. Olson (2013) highlights those organisations dedicated to rescuing children from illegal unions (See Bibliography).

REFLECTION

Ask yourself:
1. Are you and your partner an arranged couple?
2. Were you given a choice in this arrangement?
3. Do you love and respect your partner?
4. Is pleasing your family or culture more important than loving your partner?

Money Values

We have all heard sayings about money that have formed our values. Consider how your parents taught you about money and the kinds of conversations that shaped your present thoughts toward finances. Sometimes, hearing phrases form unrealistic behaviours in our spending and saving habits. Other variables we experienced growing up may affect how we deal with money and resources.

Deep dysfunction could be the underlying factor behind the two extremes of spendthrift and cheap ass. Living in one of these extremes severely affects your relationship with money and how you share this resource with your partner. Pay attention because being overly cautious or generous with money can keep you from enjoying life and living authentically.

> **REFLECTION**
>
> Check all statements that apply regarding the messages you received about money and finances growing up:
>
> - ☐ Never a lender nor a borrower be.
> - ☐ Money doesn't grow on trees.
> - ☐ Easy come, easy go.
> - ☐ Money talks.
> - ☐ Time is money.
> - ☐ Money isn't everything.
> - ☐ Money and blood do not mix.
> - ☐ It takes money to make money.
> - ☐ Money can't buy happiness.
> - ☐ Money is power.
> - ☐ A penny saved is a penny earned.
> - ☐ Money makes the world go around.

> ☐ A fool and his money are soon parted.
> ☐ Money is the root of all evil.
>
> Can you think of any others?
> Next, have your partner do the same. How have these ideologies shaped your beliefs regarding money? Share your answers.

Although discussing money on the first date may be premature, you must know your partner's financial details before you fully commit. If you are interested in being exclusive with this person, this is the time to dive deep into their finances and money values. Avoid waiting until *after* creating a joint bank account to discuss your finances because you may uncover red flags or deal breakers regarding your partner's earning and spending habits. According to Sethi (2023), kick-start the money dialogue by asking critical questions outlined in the activities below.

EXERCISE C: Individual Finances

1. How much do you make (earnings and salary)?
2. How much do you owe (debts)?
3. What is in your bank account (savings and investments)?

> ### EXERCISE D: Show Me the Numbers
>
> Think about your financial transparency. While answering these questions together, consider how comfortable you feel sharing about your individual financial situations.
>
> 1. How will we make financial decisions?
> 2. What are our aspirations for our financial future as a couple? (How we want to use money as a couple.)
> 3. How will we budget and monitor our expenses?
> 4. How will we make major financial decisions together?
> 5. How will we manage financial obligations, such as student loans, alimony, child support, and shared debt like a mortgage and car payment?
> 6. What strategies will we apply to saving for emergencies (financial surprises or unexpected expenses)?
> 7. If we have a significant income difference, how will we manage financial contributions?
> 8. What are our separate and shared financial goals and dreams (buying a house, travelling, starting a business)?

These questions aim to foster productive conversations about shared financial goals. It can be challenging but worthwhile to work together on a fiscal plan that matches your values and goals, particularly in a relationship or marriage where you are establishing financial ties.

What if one partner has more money than the other? They come from significant money, stand to inherit an empire, or make more money than the other partner. You and your partner must discuss your beliefs about money before committing. Ask to see financial statements as proof of what your partner is telling you about their finances and be prepared to be transparent with yours. You do not want to share a joint credit card and be responsible for the debts your partner racks up. A person who claims not to have debts must prove it—especially if you are merging finances. Be careful with a partner who claims they gamble but never lose money. No one was born with a golden horseshoe up their butt!

Being fully transparent about your finances before committing can save you both from being legally bound to any debt incurred in the future. If you have financial and other assets, ensure a prenuptial agreement and a legal will to maintain clarity and provide protection.

Can you be with someone who has more money than you? This raises the idea of being a 'kept' spouse, which stigmatizes the lower earning partner who may contribute in non-monetary ways. People may unfairly judge you as a gold digger—a term commonly applied to someone who is only with their partner for financial gain. Your family and friends may become jealous and wrongly assume you do nothing while your partner works.

Society continues to judge and stereotype men and women who receive financial support as lazy and exploitative, even in the twenty-first century, and they persist despite advancements in gender equality. These stereotypes root deeply in traditional gender roles and societal expectations. While we've made progress in challenging these stereotypes, there is still work to do!

While one partner may contribute less monetarily, they contribute added value: home care, child and elder care, and life organisation. The higher earning partner may prefer to be the provider of material needs, while their spouse happily takes care of the home and hearth. The expression: "You make a living, while he/she makes the living worthwhile" applies here. When there are children and other obligations, ensure open dialogue to determine the financial responsibilities of the lower-earning partner.

An insurance sales agent once told a man that he should insure his wife for much more than he, to which he scratched his head, wondering. The agent explained that in the unfortunate event of his wife's death, he would need someone to help with childcare and household tasks. How much was that worth to him?

> **REFLECTION**
>
> 1. Are you willing to sign a prenuptial agreement to back up your intentions?
> 2. Can you live with your partner earning more money than you (or vice versa)?
> 3. What non-monetary ways do you contribute to the relationship?
> 4. How do your money values differ? How are they similar?
> 5. Can you allow yourself to feel deserving of the lifestyle your monied partner offers? And if you manage the home, which helps your partner focus on earning, can you accept the exceptional value you contribute?
> 6. Is there an inequity in your relationship—perceived or existing—because of the money situation of one partner?

Compatibility in Dollars and Sense

Compatibility is the degree to which two people's personalities, interests, values, and lifestyles align, and nowhere is this more critical than when we talk about our compatibility regarding money. According to Lorie Konish (online, 2022) money problems are a tremendous source of conflict in a relationship, so financial compatibility is key because:

- ❖ Sharing financial goals creates financial stability.
- ❖ Being open and honest regarding finances builds trust.
- ❖ Jointly deciding and managing finances reduces conflict and misunderstandings.

- ❖ Making financial decisions equally ensures a sense of shared responsibility.
- ❖ Having common financial goals promotes relationship growth.
- ❖ Preventing financial stress promotes a healthy, harmonious relationship.

Imagine one person who believes they work hard for their dollars, so they spend on themselves and their pleasures and live paycheck to paycheck. The other partner plans to amass one million dollars by the time they retire, even if it means they have less fun now. They meet, date for a while, then marry. Imagine the conflicts related to money that they will face!

Discussing money values is integral to a couple's relationship. There are specific questions you can ask your potential partner to understand their attitude towards money. Listen actively to your partner's responses during these conversations without judgement or criticism. Understanding each other's money values can help you build a solid foundation for a healthy financial future together.

REFLECTION

1. What is your approach to budgeting and saving money?
2. How do you feel about debt?
3. Do you have any significant debts?
4. What are your long-term financial goals, and how do you plan to achieve them?
5. What are your thoughts about credit cards, and how do you use them?
6. Do you believe in joint or separate bank accounts?
7. Do you have any financial obligations (such as child support or alimony) which could affect your future together?

Political Values

Our political beliefs often shape our worldview, influencing choices related to family, career, and personal values. When we share similar political values, our relationships may be more harmonious. Having aligned political values may allow us to navigate important societal issues as a couple, such as social justice, human rights, and the environment. We can work collaboratively to support causes we both believe in, which not only strengthens our bond but also creates a sense of purpose and shared goals.

It is crucial to engage in open and honest conversations about political values early in a relationship to ensure compatibility and pre-empt potential conflicts. Significant differences in political values can lead to conflicts and tension within your relationship, making it difficult to create a unified path forward. These conflicts may extend beyond political discussions and seep into other areas of the relationship, causing emotional distance and resentment.

While partners don't absolutely need to have identical political values, remember that values are important in relationships. Laurie and her partner's father have differing political views. Laurie is anglophone and her father-in-law is francophone. Both were born and raised in Quebec. When Laurie and her father-in-law discuss politics, they embrace this as a chance to learn something new from each other. It allows for productive discussions, compromise, and growth, and connection.

This holds for most couples. Even if you disagree, you can see things from each other's perspective and appreciate diverse viewpoints. When we engage in meaningful conversations about difficult topics, we foster empathy and mutual understanding.

> **EXERCISE E: Political Orientation**
>
> To find out how your political views are similar or dissimilar, discuss these questions with your partner:
>
> 1. What political party or ideology do you identify with, and why?
> 2. What are the most critical issues to you politically, and why do they matter?
> 3. What is your stance on social issues, such as abortion, health care, LGBTQ+ rights, and gun control? Do you lean more towards traditional values or progressive change?
> 4. Are there any specific politicians or political figures you admire or align with? If so, what qualities or policies do you appreciate about them?
>
> Remember to approach these questions with an open mind, respect differing opinions, and engage in constructive dialogue.

Conflicting Values

Sometimes we meet someone we feel inexplicably drawn to who is the opposite of us. This happens because they may have a trait we value and wish we had. For example, a wallflower feels attracted to the 'life-of-the-party' because being outgoing is a personality trait they wish they had.

The universe guides us to what we need to learn. Dating someone with opposite traits may seem exciting at first, but it can lead to resentment. Imagine that your partner is outgoing and authoritative while you are shy and reserved. Despite loving how your partner owns a room, entertaining a crowd, you are a wallflower and feel abandoned.

You could force yourself to join in the fun. Or, since your partner knows you are shy, they catch your attention and call you over to join in. When you have distinct personalities, it's crucial to pay attention to your partner's emotions and prioritise their happiness.

The lines blur as we combine two people's lives. Sometimes, we get sucked into our partner's unhealthy values, desensitising us to our environment. For example, we prioritise our health by avoiding junk food, while our partner enjoys chips and candy bars, believing life is too short to eat lettuce! At first, we think our healthy habits will influence our partner, but eventually we eat chips once a week while watching TV together. Three years in, we are buying chips and candy bars, and our partner still hasn't touched a salad! We have gained weight and feel awful in our skin, then resentment rears its ugly head. We make snide remarks about their eating habits and secretly blame our partner for our weight gain and unhealthy diet (We can relate). This can generate deep feelings and resentment. Understanding your partner's values and discussing 'What might happen *if...?*' is crucial.

> **REFLECTION**
>
> 1. How might holding similar values affect your future as a couple?
> 2. What might happen if you do not share core values with your partner?

Needs Versus Wants

'Needs' and 'wants' are two distinct categories that help us understand our priorities and decide how we allocate our resources. A need is a non-negotiable vital for our basic functioning and well-being that we must have to survive and thrive. A want is a nice-to-have but is not essential for survival. For example, a frog needs water but doesn't require a crown to survive!

Abraham Maslow developed a five-tier model of human needs called Maslow's Hierarchy of Needs (1943), which motivates our behaviour:

1. **Physiological** - food, water, and shelter
2. **Safety/Security** - physical and financial
3. **Love and belonging** - friendship and connection
4. **Self-esteem** - feeling good about oneself
5. **Self-actualization** - finding meaning in our life

For us to address and fulfill our higher-level needs, it is imperative that we first meet our basic needs for food, water, and shelter. These fundamental requirements are crucial for maintaining our existence and quality of life. Fulfilling our psychological needs brings security, belonging, and personal growth. If we cannot provide for ourselves, our self-esteem may take a massive hit. Our basic universal needs include:

- *Food and water*: We need sustenance to survive and maintain our health.
- *Shelter*: We require a safe and secure place to live that protects us from the elements and provides privacy.
- *Clothing:* We need clothes to protect our bodies from environmental factors.
- *Healthcare:* Access to medical care and essential treatments for our physical and mental well-being.
- *Education:* Basic literacy and numeracy skills and the opportunity to learn, gain experience, and develop knowledge.

Wants are desires and preferences beyond our basic needs. We may wish to have these things, but they are optional for survival. Personal tastes, cultural factors, and individual goals influence our wants. Examples of wants include:

- *Luxury goods*: expensive items such as high-end cars, designer clothing, and luxury vacations.
- *Entertainment:* non-necessary activities like movies, concerts, or sporting events.
- *Technology:* the latest gadgets, gaming consoles, and smartphones.
- *Travel:* visiting exotic locations and going on leisure trips.
- *Hobbies:* pursuing recreational activities and collecting items based on personal interests.

Wants are subjective and vary significantly from person to person. They encompass various non-essential desires that go beyond basic survival needs, like food, shelter, and clothing. Our wants contribute to enriching our lives, providing enjoyment, pleasure, and fulfillment. While they enhance our lives, wants are not required for survival or well-being.

Understanding the difference between needs and wants is crucial for managing our resources effectively. When starting our life together, we must rethink our goals in different areas like personal life, career, finances, and family. Expectations influence how we perceive these.

EXERCISE F: Needs Versus Wants

Refer to Maslow's Hierarchy of Needs (See Bibliography):

1. What are your wants in a relationship?
2. What are your needs in a relationship?
3. What are your partner's needs and wants?

Interests

Self-interest motivates our behaviour, as every action is a function of our personal/professional intent in fulfilling our wants and needs. We do this by deciding and acting to benefit ourselves. This instinct drives us to prioritise our own well-being and happiness. While we may think this behaviour is self-centred, it plays a pivotal role in our survival, personal growth, success, and overall happiness.

Self-preservation is one key reason for acting in our own interests because we feel naturally inclined to protect ourselves from harm and ensure our safety. Making decisions that prioritise our personal security, financial stability and emotional well-being includes actions such as searching for a well-paying job, pursuing hobbies and passions that fulfill us, and finding a compatible partner.

Not to be confused with selfishness, acting in our own self-interest is foundational for our happiness. When we strike a balance that lets us fulfill our needs, we can contribute positively to our intimate relationship and better care for our partner. Self-interest becomes negative when our sole focus on our interests leads to greed, exploitation, and disregard for the rights and well-being of our partner. We see this in the scenario of marrying for money, social status, engaging in destructive behaviours that affect our intimate relationship, or other reasons not related to love.

Goals

We set goals based on what we value as meaningful.

If our goal is to own a big house, but our partner wants to live in a tiny home, we may buy a house with a vast backyard, build a tiny home, and hold conjugal visits! Like values, knowing how your goals compare with your partner's is critical. Considering your values and how they relate to your wants and needs, you must define your short-term and long-term goals.

Short-term goals are tiny steps towards your destination or 'plan,' which is your long-term goal. Small steps help you achieve your long-term objectives. For instance, you could set a goal of completing your highest education level (e.g., a Ph.D.) by age forty-five. Creating steps, such as saving tuition money and finishing your undergraduate degree, are necessary to achieve these goals.

If you know your objectives, you will better understand your 'why' when you move in with someone or marry them. Starting your life together means redefining your personal, career/studies, financial, retirement, relationship, and family goals.

Smart Goal-Setting

Setting goals can help you clarify what you want to accomplish and create a plan to achieve it. The acronym SMART, developed by George Doran, Arthur Miller, and James Cunningham and explained in their 1981 article (online), helps us plan for success while setting individual and couple goals. MindTools (2003) elaborates on these:

> *Specific (Significant and straightforward)*: The goal should be clear and specific, answering the questions: What do I want to achieve? Why is this goal important? Who is involved? Where will it take place?
>
> *Get specific on this: What is your goal? Why choose this goal?*
>
> *Measurable*: The goal should have specific ways to measure progress and success.

How will you know when you have reached your goal? How will you measure your progress?

Achievable (/Attainable): The goal should be challenging yet attainable and require effort and commitment while being easy to achieve.

Is this goal realistic? Is it in your control to achieve your goal?

Relevant (Makes sense): The goal should relate to your overall objectives, aligned with your values, and meaningful to you.

Is the goal worthwhile in your situation? Does the goal match who you are and what you can do?

Time-sensitive (Time-bound): The goal should have a specific deadline. This helps create a sense of urgency and motivates you to work towards the goal.

When do you want to achieve this goal by (six or twelve months from now)?

An example of a SMART goal is: "I train every day to run a 5K race in under 30 minutes by June 1st of this year." This goal is specific (running a 5K race), measurable (under 30 minutes), achievable (with training and effort), relevant (to personal fitness and health goals), and time-bound (by June 1st). When you establish a SMART goal such as this, you develop a comprehensive plan that includes measuring your progress and achieving your aim.

Individual Goals

Individual goals are objectives people set to achieve in their personal or professional lives. They can be short-term or long-term goals and vary in complexity and difficulty. Setting separate goals is an integral part of personal growth and development. It helps individuals to identify parts they want to improve and gives them a sense of purpose and direction in their lives.

Personal goals can include improving fitness (See example above), learning new skills or languages, advancing in a career, or achieving financial stability. Other goals might focus on personal development, such as improving communication skills, building self-confidence, or developing stronger relationships with family and friends.

Setting goals helps us focus and make progress towards what truly matters, leading to a more fulfilling life.

Relationship Goals

Common goals are the short- and long-term goals we want to achieve together. An example of a long-term goal is purchasing a home. Saving one partner's paycheck and attending open-house events are examples of short-term goals to accomplish buying a home.

Other common goals are travelling, having children, adopting a pet, or starting a family business. As a couple, we aim to accomplish what we both desire and put in the effort to achieve.

Couples must have common goals to create a sense of team within the relationship. This develops safety, trust, and a feeling of unity. When we work together towards shared goals, respecting each other's needs and wants, we form a strong and supportive partnership. Anything we choose as a couple reinforces our 'Team WE.'

Challenges arise when one person in the couple does not buy into the common goal and instead fosters separate goals. Communication is vital and requires regular check-ins because plans, like life circumstances, change.

Achieving a Balance

Your goals may differ; your partner wants to retire in the country, whereas you dream of retiring in a modern condominium downtown. Life rarely unfolds as planned, so you must closely examine and compare your long-term goals before committing. Having similar objectives forms the foundation of your relationship. Imagine you are in a canoe paddling one way, and your partner is paddling the other. You will be a power couple if you remain motivated and move in the same direction!

For example, a couple invests in real estate to build a nest egg for when they retire. One partner purchases several properties, and they jointly buy a home to live in. They plan to buy one investment property every two years. But it never happens and the dream fizzles. The couple doesn't communicate their desires. They stop investing in additional real estate, leaving their goal of building wealth together unaccomplished.

> **EXERCISE G: Balancing your Individual Goals**
>
> Consider your values and interests as you reflect on your personal goals.
>
> 1. Write a list of your top five.
> 2. What are the similarities?
> 3. What are the differences?
>
> Ask your partner to do the same. Compare your lists and discuss.

Other Aspects of Compatibility

Learning about each other's goals helps you see if you are compatible regarding future endeavours. During the honeymoon period, hormones can overshadow everything, and even if you have the same goals, you may face diverse obstacles. You must go deeper and look at those other areas that can challenge your compatibility.

Introverts Versus Extroverts

Introverts gain energy from within, focusing on their inner thoughts and ideas rather than external events. Introverts need time to refuel their stores before re-engaging socially, and when they do, they would rather be with one or two people than in large groups. The introvert, often mistaken for shy, sits back and observes the scene.

Extroverts are warm, positive, social, and excited, making them the centre of attention at parties. Social situations energize extroverts since they draw their energy from being in the company of others and find satisfaction externally. While two extroverts can have fun together, they may compete for the stage.

The introverted husband sometimes texts his extroverted wife when there's something important to share. She prefers to share what is on her mind via conversation. He often 'shushes' her because she is noisy to him, and she feels unheard.

The key is to respect each other's differences and needs. When the extrovert overwhelms the introverted partner with information, realize that your partner needs alone time to recharge. Conversely, the extrovert needs the stimulation of being around people, so the introvert may have to make concessions regarding group gatherings. Consider how you can healthily meet your individual needs without jeopardising the other.

> **REFLECTION**
>
> 1. Check all that apply:
>
>   ☐ One of you is an extrovert, while the other is an introvert.
>   ☐ Both of you are introverts.
>   ☐ You are both extroverts.
>
> 2. How will you reconcile these differences?

Givers, Takers, and Matchers

While researching, we discovered there are three types of people: givers, takers, and matchers, instead of only givers and takers. The giver focuses on and pays attention to what others need while the taker is usually self-focused and evaluates what others can give to them. According to Ness Labs (n.d.), the matcher seeks to create an equal balance between giving and receiving.

The giver and taker form an opposites-attract pair. Not that the giver never takes and vice versa. However, often the dynamic entrenches and drains the giver while the taker appears oblivious to the one-sidedness. Matchers believe in reciprocity or the even exchange of favours.

The key questions are: Do we aim to gain as much as possible or give freely without expecting reciprocity? And how does this shape our relationship?

> **REFLECTION**
>
> 1. Are you a giver, a taker, or a matcher?
> 2. Is your partner a giver, a taker, or a matcher?
> 3. How does your established dynamic work for you?
> 4. Are you preoccupied with your partner's self-centeredness and selfish behaviour? Is it a point of contention?

Age and Generational Differences

You have fallen in love with your partner. Everything feels fitting and beautiful. You have much in common and you enjoy your time together—despite the thirty-year age difference! Okay, so it's only twenty years (Celine Dion made it work)! Age and generational differences can affect your relationship. Do the math. In your twenties, a 40-year-old partner sounds fun and mature. When you are in your forties, your partner will be 60 or 70 years old (or young). They may be the same age as your parents while you are younger than their adult children.

When there is a significant age gap, getting to know each other's friends may prove challenging, as one of you may not fit in generationally. Tastes in culture, music, art, lifestyle choices, and social interests may differ and conflict. The younger partner may still have a desire for adventure and exploration, while the older partner may prefer a more settled and comfortable lifestyle. This disparity in preferences can create tension and lead to dissatisfaction and over time, the age gap can become more apparent because of your differing life stages.

While you are starting out as a couple, the possibilities are endless as your relationship blossoms, and the future becomes even more exciting and full of potential. When the years pass and both partners age, the dynamics of the relationship can change. You will be in your prime while your partner is winding down, potentially facing health issues.

When you plan to enjoy common goals and interests, the younger individual may take on the role of caregiver as the older partner faces health issues and the effects of aging. This unexpected shift in responsibilities can strain the relationship and require significant adjustments.

Despite love being a beautiful union and powerful bond perceived to overcome all obstacles, the reality is usually more complex than the idea. Be realistic about the potential difficulties that can arise. Open and honest communication about expectations, desires, and concerns is vital for navigating the complexities of your diverse ages.

Evaluate whether your age difference might pose challenges. The decision to proceed with a relationship despite an age gap rests with the individuals involved, but it requires a deep understanding of each other's needs, a willingness to adapt and compromise, and a commitment to facing any challenges that may arise. By approaching the relationship with clarity and foresight, couples can strive to overcome the obstacles presented by an age gap and build a strong and fulfilling partnership.

Sexual Fit

The level of sexual attraction and satisfaction between two people is crucial for the success or failure of a romantic relationship. Sexual compatibility includes physical attraction, emotional connection, communication, and sexual preferences. Before you pass yourselves off as sexually incompatible, consider whether you have communicated your sexual needs and desires with your partner. It is amazing how two people can get naked together yet feel shy to talk about the act and what they each like. Open and honest communication is crucial for partners to express their sexual needs and find a compromise for satisfaction.

As a couple, you can enjoy exploring new sexual experiences to keep your relationship exciting. Ask your partner to wear a French maid outfit while he does the housework! Seriously, though, sexual compatibility requires high trust, respect, and intimacy between two individuals. When partners satisfy each other sexually, it increases intimacy, bonding, and fulfillment.

Neurodiversity

Romantic relationships for neurotypical people come with inherent difficulties, so when you add neurodiversity, relationships can present specific challenges. Neurodiverse couples refer to romantic partnerships where one or both have neurodevelopmental conditions such as autism spectrum disorder, attention deficit hyperactivity disorder (ADHD), or other neurodivergent traits where their brains are wired differently. Couples where one or both have differing cognitive and social abilities face unique challenges and opportunities in their relationships. The greatest challenges include regulating emotions, social awkwardness, anxiety, sensory sensitivity, and increased frustration levels.

In the Netflix series, *Love on the Spectrum U.S.* (Holden & O'Clery, 2022), neurodiverse individuals seeking love are followed through their attempts at couple relationships, highlighting the raw feelings and obstacles each faces in their search for romantic connection. This poignant series gives a compassionate glimpse into the realities that neurodivergent people face in all aspects of life, and especially in intimate relationships.

It's already difficult to be in a couple relationship, so while both neurodiverse and neurotypical couples experience similar challenges in relationships, these may be amplified for neurodiverse people. Communicating effectively allows both partners to express their needs and expectations. And as we must do in any relationship, celebrating our partner's strengths fosters connection, growth, and love.

Inter-abled Couples

An inter-abled couple is where one partner has a physical or mental disability and needs support from their partner or someone else. A beautiful example is Squirmy and Grubs, an inter-abled couple chronicling their journey on their YouTube channel (See Bibliography). They cover diverse topics about their lives and the realities of being an inter-abled couple, from daily issues to caregiving and intimacy. This couple is loving and interdependent, displaying a wonderful example of connection and intimacy.

Perhaps you are the partner of a disabled person. Non-disabled people might ask personal questions about your relationship, especially about intimacy and sex. Understand that people may be naturally curious, and even rude. They may expect a response because the inter-abled couple differs from what they're used to. But you don't owe anyone an explanation and need not give any answers if you are uncomfortable. As most would refrain from inquiring about others' sex lives, we must respect that inter-abled people can have fulfilling intimate relationships. In layperson's terms, MYOB (mind your own business)!

Inter-abled couples may appear rare, but anyone can experience illness or accidents that change their lives and physical/mental abilities. If your partner is in a high-risk profession like the police or military, there's always a chance of a condition that alters your lives as a couple. If your soldier partner returns from war with post-traumatic stress disorder (PTSD) or a missing limb, this makes your couple inter-abled.

The myriad of health concerns that occur as we age may mean that we become inter-abled as a couple (See Life Transitions in Chapter 15). For instance, when a spouse develops Alzheimer's disease, they become dependent on their partner, creating an inter-abled relationship. Empathy and patience are key when we realize the truth of those wedding vows: "In sickness and in health."

> **REFLECTION**
>
> If you are in an inter-abled couple, do you feel:
>
> - ☐ Accepted
> - ☐ Respected
> - ☐ Loved
> - ☐ Considered an equal partner
>
> Does your love for your partner extend to wanting the best for them, even if they become disabled?

Truly Knowing Each Other

It takes a lifetime to know ourselves and, thus, our partner. We never know how we will deal with an experience until it arises, so how can we know how our partner will react? It's impossible to know and foresee how someone acts or reacts until we live together and experience life's trials and tribulations. Life transitions test our grit and our relationship. We learn a lot about ourselves and our partner as we progress through the various ages and stages, facing life challenges and changes together (See Life Transitions in Chapter 15).

Communicating, spending quality time together, being vulnerable, accepting each other, sharing goals and values, respecting boundaries, forgiving, and celebrating differences are all hallmarks of the deep understanding that helps us truly know our partner. Regularly checking in and being open to growth and change are necessary for building a strong bond and lasting connection.

Relationship Tests

When the world's woes weigh on you, you may unintentionally take it out on the person closest to you. When you feel angry, let down by outside forces, and displace this onto your partner (e.g., Kicking the dog because you feel frustrated or angry with your boss). Just because your partner is your soft landing doesn't mean that you should take your anger out on them. Over time, this behaviour can damage your relationship.

It's not whether we get along, but how we *commit* to getting along when faced with challenges. Also called tests because they test you, they test your relationship, and they test your staying power! It is tempting to give up on a relationship when you face obstacles. You may have heard: "When the going gets tough, the tough get going."

The goal is to highlight the difference between relationship tests and your well-being within your couple, not to guide you through a relationship that endangers your safety (See Abuse in Chapter 4). If you are reading this book, you are likely committed to collaborating in the best interests of your couple—and that means riding the choppy waters of adversity.

Effective couples see themselves as a united front against the world and have one another's backs. They ride the waves of good and terrible times together. And in doing so, they come out stronger and more connected.

Defining your Non-Negotiables

Relationship non-negotiables are the fundamental values, qualities, or boundaries individuals establish with each other. These are the fundamental aspects of a healthy and fulfilling relationship. While the specific non-negotiables can vary from person to person, here are typical examples:

1. **Trust:** Trust is the foundation of any strong relationship. It involves being transparent and having faith in one another. Trust is non-negotiable for most people, as a lack of trust can lead to insecurity, doubt, and relationship breakdown.
2. **Respect:** Mutual respect is crucial for a healthy relationship. It involves valuing other's thoughts, opinions, boundaries, and individuality. Disrespectful behaviour is non-negotiable.
3. **Communication:** Effective communication is vital for understanding and resolving issues in our relationship. To have a healthy partnership, we must communicate openly and honestly, listen actively, and express our needs and concerns.
4. **Emotional support:** Being emotionally supportive of our partner during good times and challenging times is vital for relationship well-being. Emotional support is non-negotiable because it involves being there for the other, providing comfort, and offering a safe space for vulnerability.
5. **Shared values**: Having compatible values is crucial. While not all values must align perfectly, having core values in common can help create harmony and reduce potential conflicts.
6. **Common goals**: Sharing goals can contribute to a solid foundation in our relationship.
7. **Boundaries:** Establishing and respecting boundaries is crucial for personal autonomy and our healthy relationship dynamic. Non-negotiable boundaries include physical boundaries, emotional boundaries, or the expectation of personal space and privacy.
8. **Compatibility:** While compatibility is a complex concept, it refers to the harmony between both partners, including similar

interests, lifestyle preferences, long-term goals, and a shared vision for the future.
9. **Supportive of personal growth**: Supporting each other's personal growth and individual pursuits is critical for maintaining a healthy relationship, including encouraging the other's passions, respecting personal development goals, and allowing space for self-improvement.

Non-negotiables vary based on individual needs and values, which we will not compromise for our relationship to work (More about boundaries in the next chapter). Examples of non-negotiables include being with a partner who:

- Takes care of themselves and their health
- Has shared religious values
- Puts family first
- Is financially stable
- Has clear goals
- Is well-organised
- Wants an open relationship/wants a monogamous relationship

There are means to meet our partner's needs through kindness, love, and mutual respect—even if we don't always accept or agree. We have the right to our wants and needs and can choose what we will and will not accept. Openly discussing our non-negotiables can build a sound foundation for a healthy relationship.

Reality Check

How things are:

How I would like things to be:

Red Flag(s):

Deal Breakers:

One action I can take:

Chapter 3

Self-Care

Expect to have your limits tested!

It is paramount to look after ourselves, not only for our well-being, but for our happiness in relationships with others, and particularly with our intimate partner. Self-care is all about taking care of our physical, emotional, and mental well-being. It includes how we self-manage and nourish our life and relationship with ourselves, our partner, and others:

- ❖ Cultivating self-awareness and understanding ourselves and our values (See Values in Chapter 2).
- ❖ Regulating our emotions and developing coping strategies for stress and frustration.
- ❖ Communicating our thoughts and feelings openly and honestly while actively listening to others (See Communication in Chapter 7).
- ❖ Taking responsibility for our actions, so we own our mistakes and learn from them instead of blaming others.

- ❖ Exercising self-discipline in achieving our goals (perseverance, procrastination, motivation).
- ❖ Striving for autonomy and independence in our personal growth and pursuits as we encourage our partner to do the same.
- ❖ Staying flexible and adaptable to new circumstances and facing challenges together (See Life Transitions in Chapter 15).
- ❖ Setting healthy boundaries and communicating these to our partner.
- ❖ Resolving conflict, applying a problem-solving mindset (See Chapter 7).
- ❖ Engaging in continuous self-improvement, remaining open to feedback, and recognising that personal growth is an ongoing process.

Caring for Ourselves

Self-care is fundamental. On airplanes, the crew instructs adults to put on their oxygen mask before helping their child or fellow passenger. This reality underpins our entire life because we cannot properly care for others if we do not first take care of ourselves.

We have diverse needs for self-care, including everything from spa treatments, monthly haircuts, regular medical and dental check-ups, sleep hygiene, and diet, to how we manage our baggage, expectations, respect ourselves, and set healthy limits.

Expressing our need for self-care depends on a wide range of factors, such as personality, lifestyle, and individual circumstances. Self-care is a crucial practice that allows us to prioritise our mental, emotional, and physical well-being. What works for one person may not work for another, and we must recognize and respect these differences, particularly with our partner.

One aspect that influences self-care needs is personality. For example, introverted individuals may need more alone time to recharge and restore their energy, whereas extroverted individuals thrive on social interactions and regularly need to connect with others. Some people may find solace in creative activities, such as painting, writing, or playing an instrument, while others may prefer more physical outlets, like exercising or practicing yoga. These differences in personality result in various self-care approaches that are unique to individual preferences and needs.

Lifestyle is another factor that affects self-care needs. If our work schedule is hectic, we may require more time-management strategies and stress-relief techniques to maintain a healthy work-life balance. Individuals with flexible schedules might have more opportunities to engage in extended self-care practices, such as taking vacations or participating in leisure activities. Parenting responsibilities, financial constraints, and other life circumstances can also heavily influence the type and amount of self-care we need.

Individual circumstances play a crucial role in determining self-care needs. People dealing with chronic illnesses or disabilities may require specific self-care routines that prioritise physical health and address unique challenges. When we face mental health issues, we may focus more on therapy, meditation, or self-reflection as self-care. If we experience significant life transitions, such as illness, grief, or career change, we may have heightened self-care needs during these times of change.

Recognising and accommodating each other's diverse needs for self-care promotes our overall well-being in our relationship. By supporting and respecting our individual preferences, we cultivate an environment that encourages each other to prioritise self-care that serves our unique needs and lets us be together healthily.

Let's look at the areas where we take care of ourselves…

Regular Health Checks

Visiting the doctor is vital to maintaining our physical health. Woe is the person who brags about never being sick a day in their life, never going to the doctor, then falls ill in their senior years and wonders why. Getting regular medical care is part of self-managing one's health and wellness. It is vital to see your family doctor regularly and visit the dentist every six months or yearly.

Diet and Exercise

Food and eating are extremely personal and often cultural. We grow up eating a particular way, which shapes our food preferences and eating habits. Yes, we can change. The meat-eater can become a vegan. It is challenging to change long-standing food attitudes. So when we meet and marry, there may be differences. And that's fine, but respect is key.

What to do when one partner is a clean eater while the other insists on eating meat, potatoes, cheese, and bread or binges on sugar and junk food? This can cause friction in a relationship. We may become defensive and self-righteous as we face questions about our choices. One partner may disregard, insult, or belittle another person for their decisions. Or the person having problems losing weight may be resentful that their partner eats French fries every day and does not gain an ounce.

Obesity can lead to diabetes and is on the rise as our population opts for processed and fast food. And as Happy Hour becomes Happy Multiple Hours, heavy drinking is taking a toll on our health. Having a drink, smoking pot, or eating junk food occasionally is moderate, but if we engage in overconsumption of these things, we risk issues related to addiction, liver damage, cholesterol, and obesity. Think about what could happen if our partner has health problems and continues with unhealthy eating habits.

One partner may exercise daily while the other does not. If you love playing a sport, such as tennis, and have suggested your partner join and they refuse, consider how to resolve the feelings and challenges. It's valuable to seek activities you can both enjoy together that don't rely on expensive gym memberships that go unused. Gardening, taking a walk after dinner or a nature hike on the weekend are excellent ways to stay active. Doing simple activities together helps spend quality time, balances the differences in interests, and fosters connection.

Sleep Hygiene

Why is it called beauty sleep when we wake up looking like a troll? While we need eight hours of Zs nightly, our sleep habits and needs change over our lifetime according to what is happening with our bodies and in our lives. Everything affects the quality and quantity of our sleep—from staying out late as a twenty-something party-goer to two a.m. baby feedings and tossing and turning during illness or menopause.

Consider the amount of sleep you require versus what your partner needs. One of you is a morning person while the other is a nighthawk. Your partner likes to sleep late on weekends and you're champing at the bit to go out and do things. How do you reconcile these differences? This is key when you are sharing a home and a bedroom, and more so when you are raising children. Having a routine that includes healthy sleep habits sets the tone for everything from how you feel to how you manage your day, especially if you do not sleep enough and become irritable.

Personal Hygiene

It may seem odd to discuss personal hygiene, but it can happen that one partner does not shower often. Your partner doesn't believe in showering more than once a week. Or they are the opposite and must shower more than twice daily. You may feel dirty if you do not match the same amount of personal hygiene as your partner. It can be delicate if one of you doesn't shower enough and has a noticeable odour.

If you need to talk with your partner concerning their hygiene, do so with utmost care and respect, and try to discern if it is a habit or a value. It may simply be a habit of laziness of not wanting to get into the shower after a long day at work or the belief that daily showering removes healthy oils and causes dry, itchy skin. Unhealthy habits are variables you can work on, but values are deep beliefs that are challenging to change.

If it's a belief for your partner and a deal breaker for you, you may need to find someone with the same standards. But remember that a pig is a beautiful creation of the universe, loyal and loveable—so what's a little mud?

REFLECTION

1. What are each of your self-care habits?
2. Do you or your partner butt heads with how each of you engages in self-care?
3. Are there any self-care practices you would like to see your partner adopt?
4. What are your non-negotiables? List and discuss them with your partner.

Each person has the right to determine and take charge of their own bodily care, while also accepting the corresponding responsibilities and consequences. While we may want to push our partner to be healthier or insist they relax, we must remain aware of the fine line that exists between wanting someone to be healthy out of love and wishing to control them because of our desires. People who live hard and neglect their health have a higher risk of severe health issues as they age and may come to depend upon others to care for them. Taking care of our body and health is an act of self-respect and valuing ourselves.

> **REFLECTION**
>
> 1. How would you rate your health on a scale of one to ten?
> 2. Do you and your partner support and want the best for each other?
> 3. Are you or your partner trying to control the other regarding personal habits (e.g., Tell the other not to eat cake because *you* are trying to lose weight)?
> 4. Does your partner have any medical issues that worry you?

Baggage

Airlines limit the amount and weight they allow onto their airplanes because excess baggage weighs the flight down and increases the risk of a crash. We all have our own baggage—from our childhood, past relationships, life events, and everything that's shaped us up to now. What might happen if we let all this baggage weigh us down? If we're not whole, we won't attract someone who is. Trying to fill a void in ourselves through a relationship can totally backfire when we realize it doesn't make us happy or satisfied. We might never feel fulfilled. (If you want to fill the void, it's cheaper and less heartbreaking to get Poly-fil for $9.99!)

How Baggage Affects Connection

Entering a relationship to solve your problems may make things worse if you don't address your issues first. There is a risk that you will assume the role of fixer. For example, a person from an abusive or alcoholic home often repeats the dynamic with a romantic partner. If you do not actively break the pattern, you risk continuing it. People may say: "Well, that is all I know." And to a degree, this is an enormous factor. But if you work on yourself, pay close attention to red flags, and honour your values and deal breakers, you can avoid history repeating itself. You must be what you want to attract in a partner. Do the work—there are no shortcuts!

Let's explore the critical aspects of baggage and how it can affect our connection.

Self-Sabotage

We sometimes undermine or sabotage ourselves, often unintentionally, which hinders personal growth, success, and overall well-being. When we engage in behaviours, thoughts, or acts that are counterproductive or harmful to our goals, relationships, or happiness, this self-defeating pattern can manifest in various areas of life, such as career, relationships, health, or personal development.

For example, we love our partner and can't wait to see them, but we create high drama, undermining our relationship and pushing our partner away. We make a self-fulfilling prophecy, and the connection fails. This can be self-sabotaging. Kelly knows someone who complained at every turn that their partner abandoned them whenever they did something alone or did not help with a chore. Eventually, the story became true when the partner left the relationship.

The reasons behind self-sabotage can be complex and rooted in factors, such as experiences, traumas, low self-esteem, fear of success, or a lack of self-confidence. It can be a defence mechanism to protect oneself from potential disappointment, rejection, or vulnerability. However, self-sabotage perpetuates a cycle of self-limitation and prevents us from achieving our goals and living a fulfilling life—with ourselves and our partner.

Denial

When we see or know something is happening, and we choose to ignore it by denying it exists, this is denial. This approach helps us minimize the pain—if we don't see or acknowledge a challenging situation or event, it cannot hurt us. An example is a husband whose partner spends substantial amounts of money, and he tells himself the problem is not so serious—she shops the sales. Meanwhile, their financial resources dwindle.

Dissociation

We feel separated from our conscious awareness, and this disrupts how we integrate our thoughts, feelings, sensations, memories, and sense of self. When we dissociate, we disconnect ourselves, cutting ourselves from the world. It is a feeling of intense detachment that may involve memory loss, detachment from our emotions, the perception that people around us are distorted and unreal, and a blurry sense of our identity. We may lose touch with our awareness and our surroundings. And this is a normal reaction, as dissociation can unconsciously save us from painful thoughts, providing a coping mechanism in response to trauma or overwhelming stress. Dissociative disorder is a more complex set of behaviours requiring a trained professional's intervention.

Let's suppose a wife becomes the primary breadwinner because her partner lost his job. She notices he spends countless hours on the computer and assumes he is job searching. She is unaware he has a porn addiction, and she dissociates from the possibility that he has no intention of finding work. Working all day to support someone who isn't looking for work would be too painful to contemplate, so it becomes her blind spot.

Commitment Phobia

A phobia is an intense, debilitating, irrational fear that keeps us stuck and unable to act. A partner who fears commitment may avoid taking the relationship past the dating stage or does not want to marry (out of fear that it won't last). Fear of committing to someone or something can result from baggage. For example, failing to launch (See Chapter 4) can cause fear of committing. Sometimes, we hold unrealistic expectations of our partner and how our lives must unfold as a couple and family. These expectations may lead to resenting our partner for not caring for us in the way we want. Hence, we cannot commit.

Reasons for avoiding commitment are fear of the relationship failing, feeling vulnerable, and not feeling we are good enough. Some people choose not to commit, waiting for someone or something better to come along, believing it is better not to 'put their eggs in one basket.' Others are afraid to commit based on their family relationships and the trauma they experienced. And still others hold commitment like a dangling carrot until their partner changes a habit, and *then* they promise they will commit.

Sometimes we decide to settle down with someone at an early age, without experiencing the freedom of being single and independent (travelling, completing studies, living alone, and playing the field in dating). We risk waking up one day, wanting to explore the world, and regretting our commitment.

Rescuing and Fixing

We unrealistically believe we can change another person by doing whatever we can to minimize the consequences of their behaviour. A partner may call in sick for their hungover spouse, dispose of alcohol, conceal bottles, and make excuses to others about their partner. They cover for their partner's escalating behaviour to mitigate the negative results of the addiction.

When we rescue another person, we prevent them from facing their reality. We erroneously believe that by controlling another person's actions, we can effect change. And what occurs is the opposite: we stand in the person's way of hitting their bottom and realising they must make a change for themselves.

Not only do we want to jump in and take full responsibility for rescuing someone else for *their own good,* but sometimes we do it for ourselves and our need to feel 'special.' So, when our partner hits rock bottom, as the 'fixer,' we blame ourselves because we didn't do enough or weren't special enough for our partner to change their behaviour.

> **REFLECTION**
>
> On a blank page, list:
>
> 1. What you will not tolerate in an intimate partner and relationship.
> 2. All the things you want in an intimate partner and relationship.

Do not restrain yourself as you write, even if it feels like you're being too picky.

When you get to know yourself, you learn what you like and what you won't accept from your partner. Let yourself be alone for a time as a starting point to determine what you need and want in your couple relationship. And when you choose an intimate relationship, allow it to develop naturally before getting physically intimate or setting up a home together. It's difficult to extricate yourself once you've invested—and sex and living together are two massive emotional investments.

> **EXERCISE A: Life as Taking a Trip Together**
>
> Imagine your cohabitation/marriage as a trip you're taking together. Consider what you want to bring and the baggage that weighs you down. List these in two columns.
> In my suitcase, I pack…
>
> Next…
>
> 1. Choose from your list the top items you want to pack. Why do you want to take these items on your journey, and what purpose will they serve?
> 2. Can you identify any self-sabotaging or other behaviours that may impede your relationship?
> 3. Are there any issues you are ignoring?

Boundaries

We often assume our partner knows what we want, so we don't communicate it. Then we feel bewildered and resentful when we cannot meet our needs! Exploring and communicating expectations is critical for a relationship because it helps us create and express healthy boundaries.

According to TherapistAid.com (2016), there are three ways we express our personal boundaries:

1. ***Rigid***: You live at Alcatraz. No one gets in; no one gets out. Your boundaries are so stringent that there is no wiggle room. It is your way or the highway.
2. ***Porous:*** You soak up everyone else's stuff and disregard your values to make others happy. You are a doormat, and people walk all over you.
3. ***Healthy***: You empathize but always honour your values and opinions. You set healthy limits for yourself and others.

Remember this fundamental idea: We teach people how to treat us.

Types of Boundaries

Our boundaries fall into six major categories according to TherapistAid.com (2016):

Physical refers to our personal space, that zone around our physical self where we let someone enter and at what distance from us (usually two arms' length for strangers).

Intellectual refers to our mental space for thinking, communicating, and cultivating ideas. Violating this boundary occurs when someone belittles or dismisses our beliefs and ideas, undermining our intellectual autonomy and respect for our thoughts.

Emotional refers to our feelings, what we choose to share, and with whom. When someone emotionally abuses us through criticism or invalidates our feelings, they violate this boundary.

Sexual refers to all aspects of our sexuality regarding the physical, emotional, and intellectual. When someone leers at us, touches us inappropriately, and pressures us into unwanted sexual attention or acts, this violates our sexual boundaries.

Material refers to our money and possessions, which we disburse and share according to our desires. When someone steals these from us, pressures us to lend or give money or resources, or damages our belongings, they violate our material boundaries.

Time refers to how we use our time to have enough time for work, play, and personal time and how others respect this. When someone tries to monopolize our time, they violate this boundary.

These boundary types can help us navigate the doubtful situations we regularly encounter that test us. Our boundaries relate to our values and this understanding can improve our decision-making. Our relationships benefit when we assert our limits, allowing us to enjoy authentic connections with others.

REFLECTION

Think about the different personal boundaries above.

1. Where are my boundaries most:

    ❖ Rigid
    ❖ Porous
    ❖ Healthy (What *is* currently working?)

2. How can I set better boundaries for myself? What strategies can I apply to do this?
3. Plan for Change - How can I ensure I am honouring my boundaries?

Consequences

Your partner has not given you an answer to confirm their interest in plans you proposed earlier in the week, (despite that you reminded them once in-between without receiving a response). At the last-minute, when they finally call to ask about the meeting time and place, you tell them you've made other plans.

Again, because it bears repeating: We teach people how to treat us. Natural consequences for behaviour that goes against our values and disrespects us is critical for healthy functioning in relationships. For example, your partner often arrives late when you have plans to meet. By tolerating and making allowances for this behaviour that violates your time boundaries, you send an obvious message that you are okay with your partner's unreliability. And this goes for any behaviour we tolerate or accept. So, when we finally have enough, blow a gasket, it comes as a shock. By this time, we may feel so fed up we want to end the relationship.

By giving consequences, you can effect genuine change and help your partner modify their negative behaviour. Remember, people may test us to see what they can get away with. So, taking the instance of showing up late, you leave after waiting a reasonable amount of time (say 15 minutes). This tough love approach teaches your partner how to treat you. And you can apply this formula to most situations where you feel taken for granted or dishonoured.

Applying natural consequences for errant behaviour is not a spiteful act, but honours your boundaries by sending a coherent message. There is no need to beg, cajole, nag, or yell. State your truth and observe how your partner reacts—if they change their behaviour. Then you can decide how to move forward.

Expectations

Expectations are our powerful beliefs about what we think will happen. The longer we are in a relationship, the more we expect our partner to know what we want. We hope our partner will remember that we take cream and two sugars in our coffee, and we feel hurt when they forget and bring us sugarless, skim milk coffee. Our immediate reaction is: *What the hell?* An argument ensues, and we are off to the races!

Expectations are standards we set in relationships. When partners have conflicting beliefs or values, it can be challenging for them to meet each other's standards, resulting in a sense of unrealistic expectations and potential conflicts.

Expectations Versus Reality

Awareness of what we expect forms the foundation of all our relationships. Creating boundaries results from the natural merging of our expectations with our values. The key is to be aware of the expectations we hold for our relationship. Your ideal life of sitting around eating bonbons while your partner works sixteen-hour shifts may not coincide with your partner's expectations, so you must communicate your expectations.

Unrealistic expectations can stop a relationship in its tracks. And reality never quite measures up and can be disappointing. (Plastic surgery is fantastic, but it can't turn the Hunchback of Notre Dame into Brad Pitt!) When we're too demanding and don't leave any room for compromise, we risk pushing our partner away because they can resent us. We cannot authentically connect when we erect insurmountable walls around us. Relationships thrive on give and take, so we must be fair and realistic.

Self-awareness and a willingness to explore the expectations you hold for yourself are your starting point.

> **REFLECTION**
>
> 1. What are my expectations of myself in terms of personal growth, career, and overall fulfillment?
> 2. How do my expectations of myself align with my values and long-term goals?
> 3. Are my expectations of myself realistic and achievable, or do they set me up for constant disappointment or feelings of inadequacy?
> 4. How do I handle setbacks or failures in relation to my expectations of myself? Do I practice self-compassion and resilience, or am I overly critical?
> 5. Have I created a healthy balance between striving for excellence and allowing myself to be imperfect?
> 6. How do I prioritise self-care and mental well-being amidst my expectations of myself?

> **EXERCISE B: Personal and Shared Expectations**
>
> Use the following questions to lead a conversation with your partner about personal and shared expectations:
>
> 1. What are my expectations of a romantic partner in terms of communication, emotional support, and shared responsibilities?
> 2. How do my experiences and upbringing influence my expectations in intimate relationships?
> 3. Are my expectations of a partner realistic and fair, or do they stem from unrealistic ideals or societal pressures?
> 4. How do I communicate my expectations to my partner, and am I open to negotiating and compromising when necessary?
> 5. Do I hold my partner to higher standards than I hold myself? If so, why?
> 6. How do I respond when my partner's actions or behaviours don't meet my expectations? Do I communicate openly and assertively, or do I withdraw or become passive aggressive? (See passive-aggressive behaviour in Chapter 7)
> 7. Do I recognize and appreciate when my partner exceeds my expectations, or do I take it for granted?
> 8. How do I balance my needs and desires with the expectations within the relationship?

When we enter a relationship expecting the other person to change, we hold false hope and set ourselves up for disappointment. If your partner drinks every night and this bothers you, don't expect this behaviour to change and bother you less once you live together. It will only magnify and drive a wedge in your relationship. If your partner is mean and disrespectful to you when dating, this will only worsen when you share a home.

These behaviours are red flags because they alert us to the danger of getting involved and investing together in the future. Your partner's behaviour will eventually amplify, becoming a deal breaker, especially if you live twenty-four/seven with the consequences of their behaviour. We may put up with someone's inappropriate actions because we are not respecting our boundaries.

Managing Expectations

If you are a planner, your partner may view you as controlling. Conversely, if you are spur-of-the-moment, your partner may see you as flaky or flighty. Sometimes, a planner/organiser who comes from chaos ends up with a more spontaneous partner. We may balance each other out.

We must strive to accept our partner as they are—but within limits. Certain habits we can brush off and live with, so long as our partner's behaviour does not hurt or put us in danger. We can't expect someone with substance abuse or workaholic tendencies to change. If we try to fix them, thinking they'll change once we live with or marry them, we're setting ourselves up for a lifetime of disappointment. This can become a serious sticking point in our relationship.

Key is managing expectations by expressing our clear boundaries. If we know we need something to happen, we must plan for it by telling our partner what we expect. We remain flexible because we must also consider our partner's needs and wishes. By sharing our expectations, we are setting our healthy boundaries. For instance, if we usually eat dinner at six pm and our partner eats at 8 or 9 pm, we can set a clear expectation and offer to meet halfway—say 7 pm—so we can meet both our needs. We can let our partner know in advance that dinner will be on the table, and we will eat at 7 pm. They can choose to join or eat later. In this way, we have managed an expectation and respected our limits.

By communicating our needs and desires, finding common ground, and respecting differences, we can manage our diverse expectations lovingly. This will strengthen our bond as a couple, creating a lasting and fulfilling connection.

> ### EXERCISE C: Great Expectations Part 1
>
> I expect:
>
> 1. List all your expectations of your partner and your future life as a couple. Do not censor yourself—fill out the page.
> 2. Review your page. Circle your top must-haves. Put a question mark beside the ones that may be unrealistic.
>
> For example:
>
> - *Respect*: I expect my partner to respect my parents.
> - *Affection*: I expect my partner to know when I need a hug.
> - *Money/Income*: I expect my partner to pay more because he is a man.
> - *Pets*: I expect my partner to understand my need to adopt refuge animals.
> - *Life Balance*: I expect my partner to know automatically when to stop working and give more attention to our family.
> - *Children:* I expect my partner to change diapers and care for our kids every weekend while I am with my friends.

> **EXERCISE D: Great Expectations Part 2**
>
> 1. What is one expectation of your partner that causes friction? Does your partner have an expectation of you that causes friction?
> 2. Do you expect your partner to change based on living together, marriage, babies, time, your help (i.e., rescuing)?
> 3. Does your partner expect you to change?
> 4. On a scale of one to ten, with ten being the most likely, what is the chance you or your partner will change?
> 5. What would happen if you or your partner were not open to change?

When we have clear boundaries based on well-managed expectations that align with our values, we can better care for ourselves and our needs. When we care for ourselves, we make sound decisions in our relationships. So, it does not matter what happens because we trust ourselves enough to know that we can manage whatever arises in our relationship with another person.

Mirror, Mirror on the Wall

A relationship is usually a mirror. Intimate relationships highlight our strengths and weaknesses as they provide valuable insights into our true selves. So rebound relationships can be challenging because we've gone right back out and found that mirror!

Here are ways relationships can function as mirrors:

- ❖ **Self-Reflection:** Relationships provide a mirror through which we see ourselves more clearly. How we react to situations, our emotions, and communication often mirrors back to us by our partners, friends, and family members. If we pay attention, these reflections can offer valuable insights into our behaviour and emotions.

- ❖ **Projection:** Sometimes, we project our insecurities, fears, and desires onto others. For example, if we are overly critical of our partner, it might reflect our self-criticism. Recognising these projections can lead to self-discovery and personal growth.
- ❖ **Personal Growth:** Healthy relationships can challenge us to grow and become better versions of ourselves. The way we manage conflicts and the lessons we learn can be a mirror reflecting our emotional maturity and communication skills.
- ❖ **Emotional Support:** Relationships can also mirror our capacity to give and receive love, empathy, and support. If we find it challenging to express emotions or accept help, our relationships might suffer, reflecting our struggles in these areas.
- ❖ **Patterns and Triggers:** Over time, patterns in our relationships become clear. These patterns can mirror previous experiences, childhood dynamics, or unresolved issues. Recognising these patterns can be the first step toward breaking unhealthy cycles.
- ❖ **Strengths and Weaknesses:** Relationships can highlight our strengths and weaknesses. A supportive partner reflects our inner strength, while a controlling relationship reflects our vulnerabilities and the need to be assertive.
- ❖ **Personal Values:** The way we navigate relationships reflects our core values. For example, if honesty is essential to us, we are likely to be honest in our relationships. If loyalty is a core value, we seek loyalty in return.

While relationships can function as mirrors, they are not a one-to-one reflection of who we are. People are complex, and many factors influence relationships. Pay attention to the lessons relationships teach, as they can improve self-awareness and lead to healthier connections with others.

> **REFLECTION**
>
> 1. In which ways on the above list do you and your partner mirror each other?
> 2. How does this help or hinder your relationship?

Reality Check

How things are:

How I would like things to be:

Red Flag(s):

Deal Breaker(s):

One action I can take:

Chapter 4

Red Flags and Deal Breakers

The deal breaker is the red flag!

We have already introduced the concepts of red flags and deal breakers in the Introduction. In this chapter, we delve deeper and explore those behaviours that may cause you pain, frustration, and sadness in your relationship. Our goal is not to be cynical toward couple relationships; instead, we want to highlight where you must pay attention.

Let's start with two key questions:

1. Do you feel stressed regarding your relationship or partner?
2. Do you feel less than others or question your self-worth in this relationship?

Check in with yourself using the material below.

Distinguishing Red Flags and Deal Breakers

Here's a table outlining the distinctions between red flags and deal breakers in common relationship issues:

Red Flag One or both of you…	*Deal Breaker*
Consumes addictive substance(s) regularly.	Shows reliance on substance(s), with mood and behaviour changes that negatively affect your interactions or put your life in danger.
Prioritises other relationships (friends, family).	Is absent from your couple and shared activities, spending time and energy with others instead.
Engages in gaslighting, name-calling, put-downs, controlling behaviour, blaming, and shaming.	Engages in physical, emotional, or verbal aggression toward the other.
Likes to shop or spend money.	Constantly overspends, trying to play catch-up with bill payments.
Has mental health issues (either diagnosed or undiagnosed).	Has difficulty emotionally engaging because of depression, bipolar disorder, schizophrenia, or narcissism.
Accumulates possessions and hangs onto unused, unwanted items that clutter living space.	Hoards items and makes living spaces crowded and hard to move around in.
Displays jealousy and possessiveness.	Checks the other's personal items, phone, and email, and tries to separate you from loved ones, cutting off your support system.
Displays a lack of consistency (not with bowel movements) paying bills and keeping promises.	Is unreliable; it feels like a parent-child relationship with constant cajoling or nagging.
Engages in lots of public displays of affection.	Love bombs (as they want to bond prematurely), showering the other with excessive attention and affection, resulting in them feeling overwhelmed and controlled.

Asks you to lend them money.	Suggests you borrow money if you do not have the amount they want. This giant red flag often becomes a deal breaker when it's too late and damage to your finances occurs.
Constantly fight and have trouble getting along.	Wants the other to change—even contemplating attending couple's therapy early in the dating process.
Can't commit to the relationship long-term; there are significant differences in your values.	Constantly break up and make up—love is not enough glue to sustain your relationship.
Has frequent lapses in employment.	Is chronically under—or unemployed.
Senses the other person has a hidden agenda.	Is clear that the partner has an ulterior motive for being in a relationship.

Red flags can escalate into patterns that become entrenched. Unchecked and untreated compulsions like drugs and alcohol risk becoming full-blown addictions. Untreated mental health can degrade. Anger management issues escalate. A partner who lies or protects a double life doesn't suddenly become honest. *Leopards do not change their spots*, as the saying goes. Suppose red flags appear throughout the honeymoon phase. You have the power to change course by setting boundaries and communicating clearly or end the relationship. Remember the sage words of Maya Angelou: "When someone shows you who they are, believe them the first time." (X—formerly Twitter, online). Past behaviour is a predictor of current and future behaviour.

Abuse and Coercive Control

Intimate partner violence, domestic abuse, and coercive control include any act that violates your safety, security, and well-being. According to the World Health Organisation (2021), one in three (30%) women worldwide experience physical assault or sexual violence, a staggering statistic. This presents a major health issue and human rights violation that negatively affects a woman's physical, mental, sexual, and reproductive health, and in some settings, increases the risk of AIDS/HIV.

Males can also fall victim to physical and emotional abuse. Typically, society views men as powerful because of their size and stature, which makes it more difficult for them to admit someone is abusing them, let alone convince others. Kelly knows a man whose spouse physically and emotionally abused him. He felt ashamed about being abused by a woman. He left the relationship when his children were toddlers because it became unbearable. No matter your gender or status, you may still be vulnerable to abuse.

Abuse is insidious and involves a pattern of behaviours in an intimate or familial relationship where one person tries to dominate the other through diverse tactics aimed to scare, hurt, isolate, humiliate, harass, monitor, take away freedom, or unreasonably control their day-to-day activities. It can include physical violence and sexual abuse, but not always.

Psychological manipulation makes it more challenging to address and clearly label abuse. Sometimes, the lines blur between the diverse abuse listed below as they overlap or merge. Controlling behaviour is often one of the earliest warning signs of abuse, which includes criticising your choice of clothing and devaluing your friendships. The abuser may try to isolate you from the people you love. Over time, the abuse worsens, particularly when the abuser successfully cuts you off from your family and friends. By this time, your self-esteem is sufficiently low to make you more vulnerable to the abusive partner's actions.

Abuse is cyclical because it often follows a predictable pattern that begins with a period of calm and gradually escalates until a violent episode occurs, the time between episodes becoming shorter, according to psychologist Lenore E. Walker (1979). Based on her seminal work documenting The Cycle of Abuse, a social cycle theory, and writing about battered woman syndrome, the following graphic adapted by Howarth (2020, p. 54) depicts the circular nature of intimate partner violence:

Cycle of Abuse

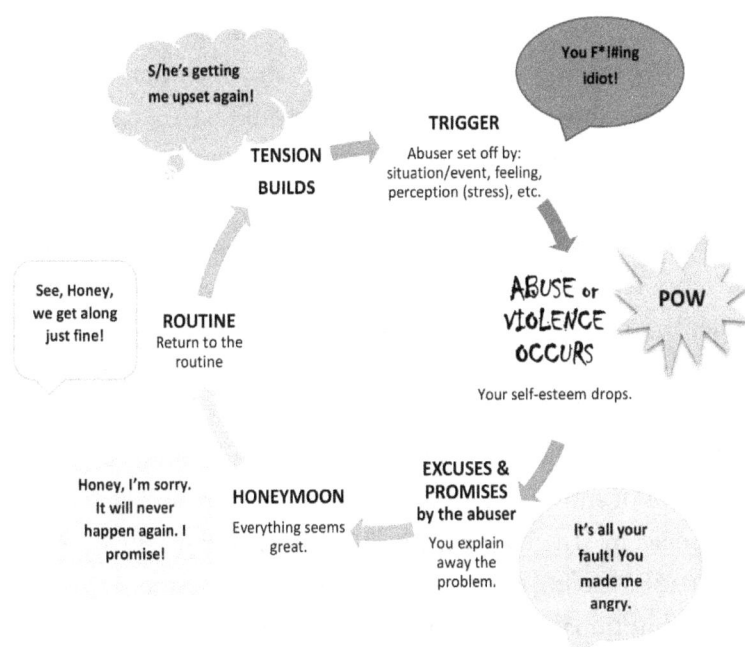

Figure 1: Adaptation of Dr. Lenore E. Walker's Cycle of Abuse

The *Cycle of Abuse* model has been analyzed and updated, specifically by psychologist Dr. Josephine Serrata (2017), suggesting "…It takes the relationship out of its social context, which may include marginalization and oppression based on race, ethnicity, gender identity and expression, and geographic location, among other factors…." This shift is considered more representative of the changing social context, realities, and increasing awareness of how much of a growing problem intimate partner violence is. We highlighted the cyclical nature of the model despite it being fifty years since Walker proposed her theory because when we are in an abusive relationship, there are repeating patterns, which may be beyond our control to change because of other mitigating factors and the circumstances and dynamics surrounding abuse and coercive control.

Throughout her childhood, Kelly witnessed this cycle play out as her father physically and verbally abused her mother. Her father would often say: "Sorry, it won't happen again," to which her mother would reply: "I know," but she felt scared. They would have a calm period and then something would set him off and the violence would recur. This pattern usually followed the trajectory of the graphic above. Her mother's chronic illness, her father's alcohol abuse, and the overall lack of social support reinforced the circular nature of violence that persisted until her mother eventually succumbed to her illness.

Treating this topic aims to help you understand the nature of every kind of abuse, including:

Physical: hitting or assaulting you, causing physical harm. Your partner slaps or shoves you, then says they are sorry and that it will never happen again. The reality is physical violence typically escalates into severe assault, leaving marks on your body. While the physical marks heal, the emotional scars they leave are devastating. You may cover up the bruises, making excuses (such as bumping into something) to hide the truth to protect your abuser. You might wonder what you have done to deserve this treatment, and if only you had done x or y, this would not have happened. Shame drives you crazy, leading to an uncontrollable cycle. It's reasonable for you to be afraid because your life is at risk.

Physical abuse can lead to death, jail, or murder (or a combination of all three). You must leave to protect yourself (and your children, pets, or any dependents). Tell a trusted person, get a restraining order, go to a shelter, and protect your privacy. Disable tracking on your phone and avoid social media. Never take chances with your physical safety and security.

Verbal: lashing out with words—swearing, yelling, name-calling, and put-downs. At first, it may be a nasty remark or assault on your character that you brush aside as a one-off comment during a heated exchange. It then escalates into consistent and harmful verbal attacks, leaving you feeling degraded and humiliated.

Arguing intensely and regretting what you say is one thing, but constant verbal attacks are not acceptable. Set a boundary early in the relationship that you will not tolerate this behaviour and walk away from verbal disrespect from your partner. Attacking someone's character undermines trust and security in the relationship.

An unwillingness to communicate is another form of coercive control, as it prevents the other person from understanding the issue, instead, forcing them to figure it out on their own (hence, the crazy-making aspect of it).

Emotional: using manipulation to chip away at someone's confidence, perception, and sense of reality. Gaslighting involves denying or distorting facts to make you doubt your memory or perception of events, making light of the abuse and not taking your partner's concerns seriously, i.e., "That didn't happen—you're making that up." or "You're the crazy one." Also in this category is blaming the victim by shifting responsibility and saying he/she caused the abusive behaviour.

If your partner tries to control the activities you do, who you see, where you go and for how long, and even your physical appearance, this is *abuse*. Controlling your activities and isolating you from family and friends cuts you off from your support system and makes it difficult for you to seek help and validation.

Emotional abuse is a complex mix of behaviours that result in one thing: your partner makes you question your sanity. It is challenging to identify emotional abuse because it is insidious as it catches the victim unaware. Abusers chip at your self-esteem, so you feel more deserving of their anger and less confident about leaving the relationship. Even minute instances of abuse can escalate and wear you down, and you may not realize it's happening until something violent or more extreme occurs.

It may feel good at first that your partner wants your attention and wants to share everything (sometimes even a social media account), but it can morph into abuse when your partner monitors your activities, including phone calls and private messages. It escalates by a partner taking actions to gain control over you. Your partner may threaten physical violence and harm your loved ones or belongings.

A person may treat us in ways we might never consider abusive. Examples of emotional intimidation include locking you out of your shared home, taking your car keys from you (when you are drunk notwithstanding), harming your pet, and turning friends and family against you through lies and falsehoods. Accusations that attempt to malign or manipulate you can be emotional abuse. Teasing can cross the line of making fun versus humiliating or shaming someone.

Sexual: non-consensual intercourse, withholding sex and affection, or forcing unwanted sexual acts. This type of abuse affects your vulnerability in the one area you need to trust and feel safe. Any time someone coerces or forces you into sex represents abuse. If your partner withholds sex, leaving you feeling undesired and unloved. You may wonder what is wrong with you, when it may have nothing to do with you at all.

Your partner's lack of interest in sex may result from a medical issue, addiction, resentment, or cheating, among other issues. For example, if your partner avoids discussing how their sex drive stems from depression or sexual problems, it can leave you feeling isolated, ashamed, and guilty. Know that none of this is your fault; there may be a coercive control element to your partner's refusal to talk about sexual issues.

Financial: a significant issue that can trap individuals in unhealthy relationships. It often starts with seemingly innocent intentions, like sharing a bank account to simplify bill payments. However, it can quickly escalate into controlling behaviour, limiting your access to money, or even stealing from you. This financial dependence can make it incredibly difficult to break free from the relationship.

If you notice your partner trying to control your finances, decide for you, or manage your money without your consent, it's important to be cautious. They may manipulate your emotions, appearing desperate or even proposing marriage solely to gain access to your funds. DO NOT GIVE YOUR MONEY to a prospective partner without careful consideration.

If you decide to proceed with joint finances, document and legalize all financial decisions involving money. This will help protect your interests and make it easier to navigate any potential disputes in the future. Maintain your financial independence by keeping your own bank account and credit rating so you have control over your finances and to protect yourself from potential abuse.

Remember: Financial abuse is control and can have dire consequences for your overall well-being. If you suspect you are experiencing financial abuse, seek support from trusted friends, family, or professionals who can help you navigate the situation and ensure your safety.

> **EXERCISE A: Movie Night**
>
> Watch one or all of the following films (See Bibliography) to learn more about abuse and financial fraud:
>
> - *Dirty John* (Cunningham et al., 2018)
> - *The Tinder Swindler* (Higgins, 2022)
> - *Bad Vegan* (Smith, 2022)

Criminal: when someone forces you to take part in illegal activities as a witness or unwilling participant and you feel trapped out of fear of retaliation. If your partner engages in illegal activities, this affects you. You are an innocent bystander at the least, and at the most, are abetting their criminality. It circles back to your values. Consider the following crimes: driving while impaired (DUI), pedophilia, voyeurism, and embezzlement. Do you want to be associated with someone who breaks the law?

Even small criminal acts are illegal, and can lead to more illicit activities, potentially harming you and your family. For example, a teenager grows marijuana at home and later engages in voyeurism. While they may seem unrelated, there are indicators of dishonesty and a hidden life as the person continuously pushes boundaries and engages in illegal behaviour.

Neglect: depriving someone of necessities like food, attention, and intimacy. Negligence by your partner can be part of any other type of abuse. When a partner leads a double life or has an affair, they prioritise other things and neglect the relationship. It may be subtle at first, but over time, negligence can extend to other facets of your couple and family relationships. Be aware of how your partner's neglect of you makes you feel.

Coercive control is part of intimate partner violence, and its effects can be long-lasting and detrimental to your mental and emotional well-being. Many districts recognize the various layers of domestic violence. We must do more work to understand the complexities of abuse, keep victims safer, and give harsher penalties to perpetrators.

REFLECTION

1. What is the difference between someone being concerned for you versus controlling you?
2. Are there any instances where you feel your partner is trying to control you?
3. In what ways does your partner create a safe space for being vulnerable?

Creating a Safety Plan

When you are in an abusive or exploitative relationship, the significant potential danger to you is just before, during, and after leaving. You must carefully extricate yourself. If you are already cohabiting or married, you need a safety plan that involves having a:

- ✓ Hidden bag packed with your essentials and personal documents (medical card, birth certificate, passport).
- ✓ Phone number of a safe house where you can go during an escalating crisis.
- ✓ Way to alert your loved ones so they can support you when you leave.
- ✓ Quick, safe exit plan, time, place to stay, and mode of transport.
- ✓ Reserve of cash tucked away.

If you feel you are in immediate danger, dial 9-1-1 (or the local emergency number in your country).

Research shows that it usually takes an average of seven attempts to leave an abusive relationship. The abuser often tries to lure you back with professions of undying love and promises of changed behaviour—their desperate last effort to keep you. Please do not fall for these manipulative words that tell you what you most want to hear (because we desire that Happily Ever After).

Her emotionally abusive common-law partner begged Kelly not to leave, dangling the promise of marriage after two decades—it was too little too late. While she felt tempted, she knew that change was not imminent; it was over. If the person does not marry you when times are good, you must not expect nor want to marry them when the relationship fails! Be aware of Band-Aid solutions because they rarely work. Say what you mean and mean what you say. Watch for your rescuing tendencies and behaviours that make you hope and want to restore peace.

Safely exiting is the first and most challenging step. It may require weeks or months of planning to leave your abuser. Plan with someone you trust, which may require changing your name, city, province, or country. Do not reveal your intentions until you have safely exited. Sometimes, when an abused partner (often the woman) declares her intention to leave, her partner becomes panicked and wounds (or kills) her.

Abusers sometimes adopt a loving behaviour to manipulate you when they see you are distancing yourself, which can be extremely dangerous. Separating from an abusive partner can lead to violence affecting your loved ones. You may need to take legal action and get a restraining order to restrict contact and protect yourself from harm by your partner.

Consult a trained mental health professional who specializes in intimate partner violence to escape your abusive relationship. Specific hotline numbers for Canada and the United States appear in the Bibliography at the back of this book. Use the Internet to find domestic abuse crisis hotlines, centres, and resources near you.

Mental Illness

A partner's mental illness can take a massive toll on your relationship, especially if it goes undiagnosed. Consider schizophrenia, bi-polar disorder, psychopathy, and sociopathy, chronic depression—these are common mental illnesses we may encounter in a partner. Although these can severely affect your relationship, how you navigate and manage mental illness in your partner is vital for successful outcomes. Be aware of the ways mental illness can affect your couple:

- ❖ Effective communication is challenging as mood swings, emotions, and misunderstandings occur.

- Withdrawal by you or your partner can lead to feelings of isolation.
- Changes in sexual intimacy can reduce libido caused by medication, side effects, and fatigue.
- The partner without the mental health condition may feel obliged to take on more responsibilities and caregiving, which can lead to stress and burnout.
- Social stigma may cause self-esteem issues as you feel judged by others because of societal misconceptions, and this can affect how you relate to each other.
- Daily routines and activities are disrupted, and plans are changed, which can lead to frustration and tension.
- Financial strain of treatments, such as therapy and medications, can cause stress, especially if the mentally ill partner cannot work or maintain steady employment.
- Resentment and frustration can mount over the constant demands of supporting someone with mental health challenges, also resulting from unrealistic expectations.
- Family dynamics are affected, particularly if you have children who may not understand their mentally ill parent's behaviour, leading to challenges in co-parenting.

Narcissism

When discussing selfish behaviour in a partner, popular media often highlights narcissism. Consider all the TV shows, such as *Gossip Girl* (2007) and *Pretty Little Liars* (2010), which cast self-centeredness as a positive trait. No wonder we apply the label 'narcissist' to anyone who appears self-centred.

The American Psychiatric Association (2022) describes narcissists as grandiose, attention-seeking, admiration-seeking, and lacking empathy. It bears mention here because an intimate relationship with a narcissist can blindside you. Their pattern of behaviour combines with abuse, and this presents a huge red flag. You don't see narcissistic behaviour until you are deep into the relationship and affected by the train wreck of dealing with it.

The *Diagnostic Manual of Mental Disorders* (*DSM-5*) (2022) highlights the characteristics of someone with a narcissistic personality disorder (NPD) as they:

- Show off or boast their inflated sense of self-importance.
- Are preoccupied with their fantasy of greatness, power, and beauty.
- Feel they are unique, only recognised by other notable people who have achieved notoriety or greatness.
- Need constant admiration, becoming falsely charming to get this.
- Have a massive sense of entitlement, expecting to be first and served quickly.
- Exploit others for their gain, often taking all the credit.
- Lack of empathy, whereby they cannot see another's point of view or relate to how others feel.
- Are envious or outright jealous and belittle other people's efforts: *How dare they achieve X, Y, or Z!*
- Are haughty, arrogant, and condescending—especially with those whom they perceive as inferior.

None of these traits *alone* points to narcissistic personality disorder (NPD). Someone diagnosed with NPD consistently shows at least five of the listed behaviours without improvement.

Suppose you are in an intimate relationship with someone who has NPD. You may experience their overt controlling, manipulative behaviour and feel frustrated by their lack of compassion and caring for you. Everything is usually about them. According to Dr. Lisa Firestone (online), narcissists have difficulty loving their partners because they see them as only valuable because they fill a need. At first, the narcissist draws you in with their big personality, charm, and likeability. But this changes over time:

> *This is why many people who have been in a long-term narcissistic relationship initially describe a very passionate and exciting honeymoon period. Then a sharp decline as the likability decreases and the self-centred behaviours increase. Narcissists are prone to falling madly in love with someone instantly and are very quick to commit. However, this initial love and commitment [are]… not easily sustained* (Firestone, online, n.d.).

Narcissists struggle with criticism, relationships, and risk-taking. The situation can turn abusive as the narcissist tries to fuel their need for control; they become aggressive, isolating, demeaning, gaslighting, and manipulating. You may feel lonely, not good enough, and angry. Your self-esteem may plummet. The probability is high that the relationship—fraught with chaos—fails.

Also, consider that this trajectory is not unique to relationships with narcissists; any untreated mental health issue in your partner can be abusive and detrimental to the relationship. Whether your partner receives a mental illness diagnosis, do a self check-in about your ability to stay the course. If you cannot manage your partner's escalating behaviour or are being abused physically or emotionally, you may decide to leave the relationship—especially if your partner refuses to consult a professional and manage their symptoms.

> **REFLECTION**
>
> 1. Has your partner been diagnosed with NPD or any other mental illness?
> 2. If so, what attracted you to your partner?
> 3. Do you have a parent diagnosed with NPD (or other mental health issues) or who is self-centred?
> 4. Do you equate your self-worth with how you are loved?
> 5. Do you often try to rescue or fix others?

Asking yourself if you feel good in your relationship may seem odd, but you must check in with yourself regularly. You will sense if your partner values you and your time together. When knowingly respected, you feel good in your skin, loved unconditionally, and safe. Being open to subtle signs and listening to your gut will help you be aware of where you are at. (Mind you, we all have our blind spots!)

Your partner showing affection should feel comforting, not anxiety-producing. Negative feelings can manifest in ways that will alert you. Think of your 'fight or flight' system response to stress. If seeing your partner incites dread or makes you feel you are walking on eggshells around them, this signals you are not well in the relationship. When physical symptoms affect your health, it's a sign of feeling threatened. You may need to seek help.

There is no place for abuse in your relationship. Your partner's unacceptable behaviour is not your fault. You are not making them angry, violent, or mean; you cannot control their outbursts. Intimate partner violence rarely resolves without serious intervention. Abusive behaviour is a pattern that often escalates. Besides wearing you down as it chips at your self-esteem, abuse risks harming or killing you. You might say it's *only* emotional or verbal abuse; understand that these types of abuse can become physical, with detrimental and sometimes fatal outcomes.

> **REFLECTION**
>
> If you are in an abusive relationship:
>
> 1. How is your partner abusing you?
> 2. Why do you stay?
> 3. What is stopping you from leaving?
> 4. What is the worst that can happen?

Addiction and Compulsion

Typically, we view substance abuse as consuming alcohol or drugs. Consider the substances people use—sometimes in moderation, and other times, heavily or outright abusively:

- Alcohol
- Cigarettes
- Drugs/prescription drugs
- Gambling
- Gaming
- Food
- Money
- Power
- Work/Studies
- Spending money/shopping
- Sex (porn, affairs)

Addiction is influenced by a combination of genetic, environmental, and neurobiological factors. Addiction and compulsions affect the prefrontal cortex, the region of the brain responsible for impulse control and decision-making, altering the brain's reward system, and leading to compulsive drug or substance use despite the negative consequences.

When we engage in addictive behaviours, such as substance abuse or compulsive gambling, our brain undergoes significant changes that make it incredibly challenging to stop the behaviour. The repeated exposure to addictive substances or behaviours triggers a surge of dopamine, a neurotransmitter associated with pleasure and reward. This flood of dopamine reinforces the connection between the addictive behaviour and the pleasurable feelings it produces, making it more challenging to resist cravings and make rational choices. This results in the vicious cycle of addiction, where individuals struggle to quit or may even move from one addiction to another, despite being aware of the negative consequences.

A key indicator of addiction is when someone's sole focus and interest revolves around their addiction, leaving no room for other activities. For example, your partner likes to relax by drinking or smoking marijuana, especially after a long, hard week. You notice how compelling the habit is for your partner and their behavioural changes. Over time, you observe that:

❖ Your partner uses alcohol or drugs (or another substance) compulsively. They may often talk about their substance use and try to quit.
❖ The substance takes up space in your relationship.
❖ Your partner's personality or behaviour drastically changes when they drink (or use their chosen substance).
❖ Life feels chaotic as it revolves around your partner's substance abuse.
❖ You cover up for or rescue your partner from the consequences of their 'using.'

The difference between using drugs or alcohol recreationally and developing a substance abuse habit can be subtle. When someone hides their compulsion, combined with our blind spots, we may miss the signs. When our partner compulsively consumes substances, this can lead to various problems: financial, relationship, social, legal, and personal. These are the red flags.

You can gauge how your partner's use of these substances affects you and your relationship by how it makes you feel. If you focus on the behaviour, instead of diagnosing your partner as a person with a substance use disorder (because that is the authority of a qualified professional), pay attention to how you behave considering your partner's substance use. Heed the chaos that might result from your partner prioritising their compulsion over your relationship and family.

Substance abuse is a waving red flag you must heed because it can be a deal breaker. The problem is that compulsively consuming an addictive substance often escalates. It can lead to misuse of money and other resources, mistreatment of you and your children, lack of trust, poor decision-making, health, legal, and social problems that affect your well-being and relationship. You may tell yourself that your partner only drinks on weekends. This is a sizable chunk of your week! Experiencing a drunken partner two days a week can be intolerable and unacceptable. Over time, your weekends become defined by your partner's drinking. And this behaviour often spills into the week. Trying to separate your partner's weekend behaviour is impossible and may frustrate you.

Be wary of your need to enable, rescue, or change your partner, which can involve twisting yourself into a pretzel for your life to run smoothly. It's not your job to pick your partner up and dust them off or make them whole. You cannot do for someone what they can and must do for themselves. For example, you may not want to date a smoker but choose a partner who smokes and swears they will quit. This bait-and-switch tactic makes it unlikely for the smoker to stop smoking (after many failed attempts) because they are addicted. Sometimes, you let things slide that go against your values because you feel so attracted and become invested in the relationship. Imagine being with a partner who wears a portable oxygen mask and still smokes.

Heavy substance use can lead to a destructive cycle that drains your relationship of energy, time, and resources, causing an abusive situation. It becomes the focus of your couple and family life. And when you put up with it, you are tolerating the abuse. Remember, this will not change with marrying your partner.

Understanding addiction as a disease and medical condition helps to shift the focus from blame and shame to empathy and treatment. Therapy, medication, and support groups are all treatment options that can be more effective when individuals are not burdened by guilt and shame. It is crucial to promote education and awareness about addiction to foster a supportive environment that encourages individuals to seek help without judgment. For more information about addiction, please visit the Canadian Centre for Addictions (See Bibliography).

People are not their *addictions*. Addiction is a complex and chronic disease that affects the brain and behaviour of individuals. It is important to dispel the misconception that addiction is simply a lack of willpower or a moral failing. This misguided belief perpetuates stigma and prevents individuals from seeking the help and support they need. By recognising addiction as a disease rather than a personal failing, we can foster understanding, empathy, and effective interventions to help individuals overcome their struggles and regain control of their lives. Treating both the physiological addiction and the person's underlying belief system is necessary to help them. Some people successfully overcome their addictions and thrive!

> **REFLECTION**
>
> 1. How would you define addiction/substance abuse?
> 2. How would you know if your partner has an addiction?
> 3. How do you feel about being around your partner when they are intoxicated?
> 4. What would be your reason for staying with a partner who has an addiction?

Failure to Launch

You've been dating the man of your dreams, and he still lives at home. Wait, it's not an issue because he does chores around the house. Upon closer inspection, you notice he acts like a grade sixer, cannot hold down meaningful employment, spends his day playing video games, and cannot commit to building a life with you. You wonder if he is commitment-phobic.

"Failure to launch syndrome" is a colloquial term often used to describe a situation where a young adult, typically in their late teens or early twenties, struggles to transition into independent adulthood. It is characterised by a failure or delay in taking on responsibilities, such as finding employment, pursuing further education, or establishing independent living arrangements. It is also associated with Peter Pan Syndrome/Cinderella Complex—people who find it difficult to grow up.

The 2006 film (Dey) by the same name explores Failure to Launch Syndrome. Tripp, a 35-year-old slacker, prefers to stay home and be cared for by his mom. However, his parents have had enough and apply subtle methods to make him leave. They engage Paula, who uses her feminine charm to get Tripp out of the family home.

If you suspect your partner struggles with taking on adult roles and responsibilities, especially after age thirty-five, consider these behaviours:

- ❖ Unmotivated to move out of their parents' home
- ❖ Lacking a meaningful career or cannot hold down a job
- ❖ Dependent on parents for financial and emotional support
- ❖ Acting childlike
- ❖ Unwilling to do basic household chores
- ❖ Holding unrealistic expectations of the relationship
- ❖ Hiding behind excuses regarding advancing your relationship
- ❖ Engaging in immature and self-destructive behaviours
- ❖ Feeling frightened of commitment

One or several of these behaviours do not mean failure to launch. Other underlying reasons may exist, such as addiction, trauma, and lack of compatibility. If this sideshow makes you feel nervous, disappointed, or frustrated, it might be time to rethink your commitment to your partner. Remember, it is not your job to change or rescue them.

Encouraging self-exploration, setting achievable goals, and providing practical support can help individuals overcome barriers and transition into independent adulthood. Therapy, career counselling, skill-building programs, and financial planning can also be valuable resources for addressing this issue. You must ask yourself how invested you are in this relationship to the point of sticking it out, waiting for change.

Difficult In-laws

Even when they are friendly, there will be snags in your relations with your partner's family. Mother-in-law might have an opinion on how to raise the children. Or there is a genuine tension between your partner and your parents for whatever reason. The key is to present a united front. You chose your partner, and your parents and siblings must know they must respect your choice. It's one thing if they are witnessing abuse, but another if they are the originators of abusive behaviour for selfish reasons. If your partner's family feels more like outlaws, saddle up and hold tight to that horsey—yeehaw, you're in for a wild ride!

Observe Behaviours

Families aren't perfect but be aware of behaviours your prospective in-laws (parents or other close family members) may exhibit while you are dating because these can present red flags and even deal breakers. Pay attention to in-laws:

- ❖ Refusing to let go of their adult child (often call or show up unannounced)
- ❖ Applying manipulative, controlling behaviours
- ❖ Having addictions that affect their child and your relationship
- ❖ Engaging in meddling behaviour where they pit you and your partner or your children against you
- ❖ Displaying abusive behaviour toward your partner or you
- ❖ Treating your partner like their spouse (especially if their spouse is absent or deceased)
- ❖ Excluding you from family functions or not making you feel welcome
- ❖ Acting controlling or needy and attention-seeking
- ❖ Demonstrating martyrdom accompanied by guilting you

When you marry within your culture, you share a collective understanding of its inherent mores and customs. If you marry outside your culture, your way of relating to close family members may differ. For example, if a business involves generations of family members living and working together, roles and boundary lines can blur. Later in life, Kelly married into a culture different from hers, where the family had an established business. In the beginning, she felt annoyed because the lines between personal and professional lives blurred, causing family members to mix their personal and work lives. The challenge was to carve out alone time to decompress and be a couple.

A red flag that can become a deal breaker if one of you puts your parents and family ahead of your relationship. No matter the family constellation, in-law problems can place a wedge between you and your partner. Communicating openly with your parents about your perceived or actual grievances is vital. Setting clear boundaries and presenting a united front can help maintain peace (See Baggage, Boundaries, and Expectations in Chapter 3).

Estrangement

You've gone no-contact with a toxic family member, and you feel badly about it. Plus, there is pressure from others to reconcile for the benefit of harmonious family relations (that do not feel so harmonious to you). Should you? That depends on your relationship and the nature of the conflict between you.

Whatever the reason for cutting ties with a family member (or anyone else) is yours and yours alone to decide. Ask yourself whether maintaining a relationship with this individual causes chaos and disruption in your life. If you are constantly spinning in an unhealthy dynamic with a substance abuser, for example, then you are completely justified in limiting or cutting contact altogether. And if this person has been abusive toward you, the rule of exiting the cycle of abuse applies (See Chapter 4).

It's not because you share genes, history, or social connection that you must tolerate the unacceptable. First, trust your feelings and your decision to not engage with the person. Recognize that guilt is unproductive, and that you have done nothing wrong if you are the one constantly dealing with the negative consequences of their destructive behaviour.

Guilt, sadness, anger, frustration, resentment, and other emotions may play on you because they often reflect shared history or the values you hold dear about family. Work through your feelings with a trusted friend or therapist. Estrangement—whether forced or by choice—poses complex challenges. You get to choose to re-engage with this person, and if you decide to remain no-contact, honour your feelings. It takes courage to say what you mean and mean what you say as you exercise your healthy boundaries!

> ### EXERCISE B: Family Dynamics
>
> Hold an honest conversation with your partner regarding your respective families, their dynamics, and how you fit into those dynamics. This conversation can provide valuable insights into each other's backgrounds, values, and expectations. Begin by expressing your desire to understand each other better and create a solid foundation for your relationship. Approach the conversation with an open mind, ready to listen and share about:
>
> 1. How have your own family dynamics shaped you? Talk about your parents, siblings, and any significant experiences or traditions that have influenced your upbringing. Share your feelings, both positive and negative, about your family and how they may affect your relationship. Encourage your partner to do the same.

2. What are the similarities or differences in your family dynamics? How might these differences affect your relationship?
3. How do your respective families handle conflict, communicate, and show love and support?
4. What concerns or challenges do you have about blending your families?
5. What family dynamics do you wish to create for yourselves as a couple? Discuss your shared values, goals, and expectations for your future family. How can you build a supportive and loving environment that incorporates the best aspects of both of your families?

Remember that everyone's family is unique, and there is no right or wrong way to navigate family dynamics. The goal is to gain a deeper understanding of each other's backgrounds and find ways to support each other in the contexts of your respective families. This might include differences in cultural or religious backgrounds, conflicting values, or challenging relationships with certain family members. Together, brainstorm strategies to navigate these potential obstacles and support each other through them.

Chronic Under or Unemployment

Not having a decent job or settling for low-paying jobs when you're qualified for higher-paying positions can contribute to failing to launch. Still, it could also signal a broader issue. While job loss can be tough, most people use it to their advantage and find better employment. The red flag is when someone who *can* work chooses not to, and you disagree with your partner's lack of employment as a couple. Their unemployment poses a threat to your shared goals of saving for travel, property, and more.

Kelly experienced her previous partner's prolonged unemployment. This added stress to their relationship because she resented the reality that as a graduate from a master's level university program, he was fully employable. She took on more contract work while home-educating their child, and he took a four-year hiatus and burned through his savings.

When Your Relationship is a Secret

If your partner has not told their friends or family about you after dating for a while and things between you are serious, this is a red flag. Strongly consider asking them why. People only hide things when there is something they wish to keep secret for fear of getting caught! This does not include meeting your partner's children. It is customary and wise to wait before introducing a new relationship until it is severe enough to warrant involving the children. Be cautious about introducing your children to new partners, as it could cause trauma if the relationship doesn't last. Be safe and give it time before you expect a close bond between your kids and your new partner.

Being a secret can mean:

- ❖ Your partner is already in a relationship, and you are their side piece.
- ❖ Your partner feels embarrassed dating you. This could be because of your status in society, your job title, or other reasons.
- ❖ Your partner can't, won't, or is afraid to commit for reasons you cannot understand (See Failure to Launch above).

It's also possible that your partner's family of origin is so dysfunctional that they have cut all contact. You will never likely meet your partner's family, even if you express your willingness to. It would be best to respect your partner's wishes, trusting their judgement.

Kelly went no-contact with her father over twenty years ago because their relationship was toxic and caused her pain and stress. Friends and family pushed the idea of reconciling, but she deemed it in her best interests not to re-engage. We don't choose our toxic family members, and although we often hear "Blood is thicker than water," sometimes we must withdraw from the relationship. It feels emotionally wrenching but necessary for our sanity and well-being.

> **REFLECTION**
>
> 1. Do you or your partner keep your relationship a secret from key people in your life?
> 2. What is your or your partner's reason for secrecy?
> 3. What would happen if others discovered your relationship?

When Your Partner Leads a Double Life

There is nothing quite as unsettling as realising the person you love and trust is living a double life. When a partner is secretive, it feels like you no longer know them. You may question everything you thought you knew about them and wonder if any part of your relationship is genuine.

You must approach the situation cautiously if you suspect your partner leads a double life. Gather evidence to understand what's happening. Confronting them before you have all the facts could lead to more secrets and lies.

It is important to take care of yourself; don't blame yourself for your partner's actions and don't allow yourself to be manipulated or gaslighted. Seek support from friends and family and consider speaking with a therapist to help you process what's happening.

You must decide what to accept in a relationship. If your partner leads a double life that includes cheating or other forms of betrayal, it may be time to end the relationship. If they are hiding something that is less hurtful but still concerning, talk openly and honestly with your partner to see if you can move forward. Whatever you decide, know that you deserve honesty and respect in your relationship. Don't settle for anything less.

When You Love a Prisoner

And we don't mean when you tie your lover to the bedpost! There are pen pals who write to, then fall in love with incarcerated individuals. And there are relationships where it all started well and went horribly wrong as our partner strays down a criminal path. An intimate relationship with a convicted felon often presents huge waving red flags as it rests on a tenuous foundation fraught with profound challenges.

There are diverse factors that could have led to your partner's incarceration, including the possibility of wrongful imprisonment. Bias within the criminal justice system, inadequate legal representation, false testimonies, or even mistaken identity can all lead to wrongful imprisonment. So, it is crucial to approach the situation with an open mind and thoroughly evaluate the circumstances of your partner's incarceration. By considering multiple factors, you can better understand the potential flaws in the legal process and work towards seeking justice and exoneration if you believe this is the case (especially if you want to uphold your wedding vows "For better or for worse").

If you choose to pursue a relationship with someone behind bars, whom you technically don't know, be mindful that you may only see the side of them they want you to see. Usually, they will be on their best behaviour during visits—visits that are controlled and monitored. You don't have any real-world dating experience with each other, unless your partner gets day passes and conjugal visits (But still...). And the honeymoon phase is especially deceiving in this circumstance because you may not clearly know what you are dealing with.

Be aware of the manipulation prisoners may use when they feel desperate. Since they have nothing to lose, the risk of them love bombing (See Chapter 5) you is greater. Therapy, honesty, and accountability for their actions may show rehabilitation. Pay attention to your own need to rescue and fix someone (See Rescuing in Chapter 3). Although you may believe in the cause, you must remain vigilant about the reality that this person stands accused (or convicted) of a crime. It is critical to ask yourself what the attraction is and why, when you can have someone on the outside, you would choose a complicated relationship with a person in prison.

If your incarcerated partner ever gets out of prison, you will be their safety net because it is in their best interest to have a stable, loving partner ready to receive and host them on the outside. By showing corrections officials how solid, dependable, and reformed they appear, they may be granted an earlier release.

Consider the complications. Physical intimacy will lack, often causing frustration and loneliness. You may have different expectations and goals for your future together, making it challenging to plan long-term. You are signing up for an enormous responsibility to support your incarcerated partner as they rebuild their life when released from prison. There is also the social stigma as family and friends may pass judgment and harbour negative perceptions, which can be isolating, especially if they choose to estrange themselves from you.

If you contemplate marriage, know that it may be more beneficial for your incarcerated partner than it may be for you. For the jailed person, marriage offers practical advantages upon their release (to secure housing, find employment, and reintegrate into society). Some organisations and programs prioritise housing and job opportunities for married individuals to make transitioning from prison to freedom smoother.

Also, a massive consideration are the legal implications. Being married to an incarcerated partner involves complex legal processes and responsibilities, including visitation rights, financial arrangements, and navigating the legal system for potential appeals and parole hearings. The financial burden on you will be overwhelming. Remember: Marrying someone is tying yourself to them legally and financially. (Let that sink in.)

If you are seeking a romantic connection with a prisoner because you think it may be easier, considering the captive audience (pun intended), think again. Be mindful of your potential need to rescue and fix someone. There are healthy ways to meet and fall in love with like-minded people who are not behind bars and have their freedom. You are worthy of love from someone who comes with less baggage.

If you are hell-bent on dating a prisoner, approach your relationship with critical thinking and realistic expectations for each of your well-being. Consider postponing marrying your incarcerated prince/princess until they have settled into their new life as a free citizen. Married, you will be responsible for your partner's actions. Living under the same roof, you risk being charged as an accessory to illegal activity if your partner relapses. Carefully weigh all the above before making such a life-changing commitment. Each case is unique; it is crucial to consider all factors before embarking on a fairy tale romance with a prisoner.

Kelly and Laurie take no responsibility for a reader's choice to engage in an intimate relationship and partner with a convict because we do not condone this type of 'couple relationship' as healthy or wise.

REFLECTION

Consider your motivations and the potential consequences of being romantically involved with an incarcerated individual:

1. Am I of mental and emotional sound mind?
2. What attracts me to this person?
3. Might the incarcerated person be manipulating me for their own purposes?
4. What are the emotional and logistical challenges of developing a healthy relationship with someone who may have limited communication and visitation rights?
5. What are my long-term expectations for this relationship? Are they realistic given the reality of the situation?
6. Am I aware of and willing to accept the social stigma and potential judgement of others regarding this relationship?
7. Am I equipped to support someone with mental health issues or trauma related to their criminality and incarceration? How might it affect my well-being, including potential stress, anxiety, and emotional strain?
8. What are the legal and financial consequences of my involvement, such as legal fees, potential restitution, financial support, or the effects on me and my life if my partner relapses?
9. Do I have a support system to help me navigate the challenges of being in a relationship with someone incarcerated?
10. Have I weighed the benefits and risks of pursuing this relationship, considering both the emotional fulfillment and potential hardships?

Scams and Shams

Someone may have an ulterior motive for pursuing a relationship with you. Intimate relationship scams and shams refer to fraudulent activities involving deception and manipulation to exploit romantic partners for financial or personal gain. Relationship fraud encompasses various deceptive practices. These include presenting a false identity during in-person encounters or on online dating platforms with the goal of committing romance fraud, a scheme designed to swindle you out of your money, personal information, and other valuable belongings.

Intimate Relationship Fraud

When she was twenty years old, Laurie's work colleagues introduced her to a gorgeous model-like God from another country. Her co-workers expected her to fall madly in love and marry their friend so he could immigrate to Canada. Despite the tempting possibility that this gorgeous hunk of a man could be her husband, Laurie had a weird feeling in her gut that something wasn't right. She was relentless in her pursuit of her co-workers' reasons for choosing her, like a dog with a bone, questioning their motivation. They confessed their friend was seeking asylum in her country, and by marrying him Laurie would help the imposter immigrate faster. Laurie further tested her colleagues by insisting on a ridiculous sum of money if they expected her to engage in their scheme. However, once she explained she would only marry for love, they retracted their offer, and Laurie walked away from the scam feeling she had dodged a bullet.

Another type of intimate relationship fraud involves grooming vulnerable individuals online where scammers portray themselves as potential partners. They gradually build trust, love, and romantic attachment with their targets. Once they have earned the person's confidence, they may start asking for monetary help, often citing financial emergencies or other reasons that tug at the victim's emotions.

Another scam involves catfishing, where imposters create fake profiles, posing as desirable partners. Scammers use stolen photos from other social media sites to create attractive profiles and trick people seeking love and looking for relationships online.

Then there are love-bombing (See Chapter 5) experts, dangerous scammers who use excessive compliments and attention to deceive their victims to gain trust and gradually access their finances and other resources. Some love fraudsters enlist the help of unsuspecting romantic partners to flow money to their operations, such as money laundering, drug trafficking, and other illegal activities.

Falling with a Safety Net

While there are lovely people in the world, there are also shady characters. Most of the time, we can weed them out, and sometimes not. We get lonely and feel the need to connect. Our dream is to find that someone special who sees us, hears us, and loves us. Falling in love is wonderful—so long as you fall with a safety net!

Imagine you have just started a new relationship with someone and you're excited about the special connection you have with your fling, online partner, long-distance love, or vacation acquaintance. You continue your contact online and engage in regular video chats. It feels like this is turning into a bona fide relationship.

Insert safety net here: Examine and consider the motivations of the person you love before you rush into a committed relationship, especially when it involves sponsoring or marrying someone to immigrate. Examples are:

- A hookup in a tropical paradise, leading to an online relationship, where the person eventually asks you for help (to give them money)
- An older person looking for a young plaything
- A young person looking to exchange caregiving for financial support
- Someone you met in an online chat room or dating site, who wants to move the relationship quickly, and relocate to your country
- A prisoner with whom you correspond who believes they were wrongfully charged
- Someone who is not available to take your calls or can only connect with you during odd hours
- A person with whom you have been chatting for a year, and declaring love, you send sexually explicit photos to each other. Next thing you know, you receive an email threatening to post your naked pics all over the Internet unless you pay up. This is 'sextortion.'

Not all people you meet are scammers, but be vigilant to flush out these imposters and thieves. Laurie always verified the person she chatted to by typing their name into an Internet search. Remember to keep yourself safe: people usually act in their self-interests. If someone is overly generous or intense and pressuring you for quick decisions, they want something from you. When the circumstances and dynamics of the relationship are suspicious, you must ask yourself (and your partner) questions.

Your safety net is your intuition. Usually anything that niggles at you or makes you question the motives of someone is your intuition telling you to be careful. It also means to take what they have said and cross-check it to ensure their actions match their words. While this isn't always possible, doing your research is critical. Let's say your online boyfriend tells you he volunteers in the evenings at a homeless shelter. Ask him to video chat while he is there! Ask for licenses, criminal background checks, or whatever you need to verify the person is who they say they are. This is not being paranoid—it is the new rule for online dating!

And if you fall victim to a catfish scheme, know that you are not alone. Even the most intelligent and conscientious people make mistakes. Devious people can be difficult to weed out. Never let your shame stop you from talking to a trusted friend, family member, or professional about your concerns. No matter what your mistake (even sending naked pictures)—because you are only human—it shouldn't stop you from contacting the police.

It's always vital to watch for red flags and be clear about your deal breakers. Dating experts agree on and propose the significant deal breakers listed below.

EXERCISE C: Deal Breaker Checklist

Part A: Please check any that apply.
Your partner...

- ☐ Engages in abuse (physical, verbal, sexual, financial, emotional, criminal) in your relationship or has a history of abuse with someone else.
- ☐ Keeps your relationship secret.
- ☐ Cancels plans at the last minute.
- ☐ Is not over their ex.
- ☐ Refuses to address critical issues.
- ☐ Shows no interest in the other or the relationship.
- ☐ Appears to have no goals or a vision.
- ☐ Abuses substances, including sex, drugs, alcohol, gambling, marked by denial and refusal to seek help.

- ☐ Is unfaithful and commits acts of cheating (openly flirts with others).
- ☐ Lies (untruths or omissions) or acts secretively.
- ☐ Fights dirty (name-calls, applies the silent treatment and personal attacks, or gaslights you) and excessively.
- ☐ Wants different things.
- ☐ Avoids standing up for the other when in-laws do not respect your boundaries.
- ☐ Does not share the same beliefs regarding finances.
- ☐ Is a taker who is highly selfish and self-serving.
- ☐ Does not share the same values.
- ☐ Disagrees about wanting to have children.
- ☐ Is jealous or possessive of you.
- ☐ Isolates you from friends and family.
- ☐ Does not trust the relationship process and tries to rush it.
- ☐ Changes their mind on significant agreements you've made together.

You have a sense that the relationship doesn't feel right (anxiety concerning the relationship, questioning your self-worth).

Part B: List your Deal Breakers

Have you uncovered any deal breakers, i.e., non-negotiables you refuse to live with that make you want to leave the relationship? If so, list them here:

1.
2.
3.
More:

> **REFLECTION**
>
> 1. Have you noticed any red flags in your relationship, and are you able to discuss these with your partner? If not, why?
> 2. Are any of the red flags deal breakers for you?
> 3. Do you ever feel your safety is at risk?
> 4. Has anything about your relationship made you feel misled?
> 5. If you read this book and discover your relationship isn't what you thought it was, what happens next?

Reality Check

How things are:

How I would like things to be:

Red Flag(s):

Deal Breaker(s):

One action I can take:

Chapter 5

Sex and Intimacy

I love Intercourse… Pennsylvania (Yup, it's an actual place—right next to Bird in Hand, Lancaster County, USA)!

Imagine having sex with someone yet feeling afraid to clarify questions regarding their values as they relate to yours. Countless people do this! They are afraid to ask someone direct questions for fear of turning them away or off. Newsflash! This makes the intimacy foundational in building a meaningful and hopefully lasting relationship.

Sex and physical affection are not intimate despite people often equating the two. While sex can be part of intimacy and stems from intimate bonding, you don't need intimacy to have sex. Hence, the one-night stand or hookup sex (later in this chapter). And you can have a close relationship with someone that does not involve sex. Either can be enjoyable! There is a fine line between physical love, sex, and intimacy. Sometimes, the three intermingle and feel similar, but they are not. Regarding sex, think of intimacy as foreplay and sex as action!

Sex can also be mistaken for intimacy by people with baggage, and that's most of us! A person may crave love and intimacy, so they sleep with someone to fill a void. Intimacy happens when two adults feel safe and cared for while sharing their bodies. Sex is a way to express intimacy and trust in a committed, monogamous relationship where you are honest about your wants, needs, and expectations.

Intimacy is the bond of closeness between two people in an interpersonal relationship. Author Taylor Jenkins Reid explains that people often misunderstand intimacy as only being about sex: "But intimacy is about truth. When you realize you can tell someone your truth, show yourself to them, stand in front of them bare, and their response is 'You're safe with me.'—that's intimacy." (2018).

Types of Intimacy

Psychologist Helene Brenner (2004) suggests four types of intimacy that contribute to a stronger connection with your partner:

1. **Emotional Intimacy** - telling your partner how you feel and what you want from the relationship. Openly sharing your feelings fosters emotional intimacy.
2. **Intellectual Intimacy** - communicating your thoughts and beliefs. Watching a movie together and discussing it promotes intellectual intimacy.
3. **Experiential Intimacy** - enjoying shared experiences, such as training and running a marathon, taking a class, or travelling. Doing these kinds of activities as a couple creates shared memories. Embarking on fresh adventures fosters experiential intimacy.
4. **Spiritual Intimacy** - taking part in devotional practices and attending religious events together. Appreciating a sunset can also foster spiritual intimacy.

Being Vulnerable

A huge part of being in an intimate relationship is allowing ourselves to be vulnerable with our partner. When we express and share our authentic selves—the good, the bad, and the ugly—we allow true intimacy. Think of it as "Into me you see." We let our partner see all of us, and in that seeing, we can feel loved for who we are and without pretense. If we fear letting someone in, afraid of rejection, we can never experience the vulnerability that leads to deep connection with our partner. And part of that is being willing to experience hurt and disappointment.

Intimacy is a vulnerability you share with chosen people and your partner. Connecting and understanding one another is the foundation for building healthy relationships. The more vulnerable you are, the deeper the connection, and the more likely you feel safe and respected. Conversations are complicated, especially when you expose yourself to someone else. But with tough conversations where you let yourself be vulnerable, a relationship can become manageable. More intimacy equals more connection between you.

In a 1987 study, psychologist Dr. Arthur Aron developed thirty-six questions to speed up closeness between two strangers and lead to love. The following exercise is the 36 Questions for Increasing Closeness, which you can also find online (UC Berkeley, n.d.). You can do this questionnaire with your partner as you get to know them. You can also revisit the exercise to rekindle the romance in your relationship. This activity is not limited to intimate partnerships; you can do it with anyone with whom you are seeking greater connection.

EXERCISE A: Increasing Closeness

36 Questions for Increasing Closeness

TIME REQUIRED: Forty-five minutes every time you do this practice.

HOW TO DO IT

Identify someone with whom you'd like to become closer. It could be someone you know well or are getting to know. This exercise has a reputation for making people fall in love. It's also helpful for anyone you want to feel close to, including family members, friends, and acquaintances. Before trying it, ensure you and your partner are comfortable sharing personal thoughts and feelings.

Find a time when you and your partner have at least 45 minutes free and meet in person.

For 15 minutes, take turns asking one another the questions in Set One below. Everyone should answer every question in alternating order so that a different person goes first every time.

After 15 minutes, move on to Set Two, even if you haven't yet finished the Set One questions. Then, spend 15 minutes on Set II, following the same system.

After 15 minutes on Set Two, spend 15 minutes on Set Three. (Note: The next set of questions is more probing than the previous one. The 15-minute periods ensure you spend an equivalent amount of time at every level of self-disclosure).

Set One

1. Given the choice of anyone worldwide, whom would you want as a dinner guest?
2. Would you like to be famous? In what way?
3. Before making a telephone call, do you ever rehearse what you want to say? Why?
4. What would make up a "perfect" day for you?
5. When did you last sing to yourself? To someone else?
6. If you could live to ninety and keep either the mind or body of a 30-year-old for the last 60 years, which would you want?
7. Have you ever had a hunch about how you will die?
8. Name three things you and your partner have in common.
9. For what in your life do you feel most grateful?
10. If you could alter your upbringing, how would you change it?
11. Take four minutes and tell your partner your life story in as much detail as possible.
12. What would it be if you could wake up tomorrow having gained any one quality or ability?

Set Two

1. What would you want to know if a crystal ball could tell you the truth as to yourself, your life, the future, or anything else you desire?
2. Is there something you've dreamed of doing for a long time? Why haven't you done it?
3. What is the greatest accomplishment of your life?
4. What do you value most in a friendship?
5. What is your most treasured memory?
6. What is your most terrible memory?

7. If you knew you would die suddenly in one year, would you change how you live now? Why?
8. What does friendship mean to you?
9. What roles do love and affection play in your life?
10. Alternate sharing something you consider a positive characteristic of your partner. Share five items.
11. How close is your family? Do you feel you had a happier childhood than most other people?
12. How do you feel about your relationship with your mother?

Set Three

1. Make three factual "we" statements. For instance, "We are both in this room feeling...."
2. Complete this sentence: "I wish I had someone I could share...."
3. If you were to become a close friend of your partner, please share what would be vital for them to know.
4. Let your partner know the specific qualities you appreciate in them; be very honest this time, saying things you might not say to someone you've just met.
5. Share with your partner an embarrassing moment in your life.
6. When did you last cry in front of another person? By yourself?
7. Tell your partner something that you like about them.
8. What is a no-joke topic?
9. If you were to die this evening with no opportunity to communicate with anyone, what would you regret not having told someone? Why haven't you told them?
10. Your house, containing everything you own, catches fire. After saving your loved ones and pets, you have time to

> make a last dash to save any one item safely. What would it be? Why?
> 11. Of all the people in your family, whose death would you find most disturbing? Why?
> 12. Share a personal problem and ask your partner for advice. In addition, ask your partner to reflect on the feelings you just expressed regarding that issue.

You can try this practice with anyone you want to develop a profound connection with. If your answers don't feel deep or reflective of your relationship, consider devising your own list of questions that become increasingly more personal.

Sexual Myths and the Media

We must pay more than lip service to having sex because we are all sexual beings. Films, porn, and societal generalizations contribute to the myths surrounding gender roles and wreak havoc with what is normal. If you are unsure of your wants and needs, you may get caught up in the myths and lose out on discovering what great sex is for you.

Common myths regarding sex and sexuality include:

- ❖ Good girls don't.
- ❖ Guys want to score.
- ❖ If you masturbate, you will go blind.
- ❖ Using a vibrator means you are unhappy in your sex life.
- ❖ The bigger the shoes, the bigger the organ (and not the one in church).

The media portray women as thin, big-boobed, hairless (apart from their heads), and airbrushed. None of these women have cellulite or acne, and their hair could stay in the same style for days. They cast men as buff, tall, and muscular. Often, people pay more attention to someone's appearance and performance rather than their qualities as human beings. This scripted, acted, well-marketed lie snows us into believing we must look and act in a prescribed way to enjoy sex and entice and excite others.

Sex Across the Lifespan

Sex is only fifteen to twenty percent of a relationship, but it feels like more. So, while that percentage doesn't seem high, it's an equally important subject for partners. Any sex act begins with consent from both partners. Open communication, respect, and care are the emotional precursors to physical bonding. Feeling safe helps us be vulnerable with our partner.

Our attitudes and preoccupation with sex vary according to the stages of our lives:

In our teens to twenties: Marked by exploration, sex is new and exciting, yet scary. Not knowing what to do or assessing what is 'normal,' we are body conscious. Raging hormones make us ready for sex anytime and anywhere! Condoms, menstruation (not wanting to disgust a partner), and social media influence our sex lives. Feeling ashamed and striving for perfection are common in sex, especially when we compare ourselves to others if our ideals are based on pornography and the media. Girls seek attention, and sometimes, by using their physical attributes. Guys want to score (Some girls want to score, too).

In our twenties to thirties: In this self-discovery and personal growth stage, the hookup culture with no strings attached sometimes prevails. We settle into our careers and living situations, finish our studies, and may still live with our parents as we strive to save money and build a stable foundation. This marks a significant period of transition and decision-making where we balance the exploration of our personal desires, ambitions, and relationships with the recognition that our biological clock is ticking.

In our thirties to forties: We know what we want and how to get it. More comfortable with our body and how it functions, we are unashamed of our imperfections. If we want children, we may consider that our fertility may be dwindling. *Psychology Today* suggests that couples have the best sex in their thirties and forties if they don't have kids living with them (online, n.d.).

In our forties to fifties: We reassess our lives and priorities and plan our future. Perimenopause for women and mid-life crisis (*Is this as good as it gets?*) can occur for both men and women. If we have children, sex can be another chore, as life stressors lead to diminished sex drive and sometimes difficulty connecting with our partner.

In our fifties to sixties: Use it or lose it! Physiological changes can hinder the act of sex. Too tired for sex? Scheduled sex? Bodily functions may present issues. (Releasing a turd or urine: I once had an orgasm that was an organism!) Bodily functions can be funny instead of embarrassing, depending on your relationship and comfort level.

In our sixties and beyond: Cognitive, psychological, and physical decline may occur. Intimacy changes and relies on a deeper connection with our partner (although sex is still on the table—not literally perhaps). Touch and physical affection remain vital, such as massaging, caressing, and handholding.

Sexual Orientation

We extend this book to any couple, irrespective of sexual orientation, but we cannot speak on behalf of the LGBTQIA+ community. We hope the information, questions, and situations presented here resonate with all readers.

> **REFLECTION**
>
> 1. Are you both out to your friends and family?
> 2. What support do you have for your couple?
> 3. Do you want to have and raise children together? If so, how will you proceed?
> 4. Would your partner be supportive if you were to change the status of your pronoun?
> 5. Does your state law recognize same-sex couples and allow gay marriage?
> 6. What are your rights if your partner suddenly fell ill or passed away?

Virginity

Let's define what makes up sex. Some people say sex is full-body nudity and sexual intercourse. Others say any intimate act, from kissing and petting to fondling. Preferring to only engage in sex once married ties to your values. You hold a strong ideal of purity, virtue, and the notion that you will only have sex with the person who commits to you. Or you never found someone you wanted to have sex with, so you never did it.

Do you believe in saving yourself for marriage, meaning you do not engage in sexual activity until you are married? We often see this compatibility in people of deep religious faith—once again, tied to their values. To position this topic (pun intended!), consider these questions:

> **REFLECTION**
>
> 1. Is your virginity vital to you? Are you saving yourself for marriage?
> 2. What are your thoughts on older virgins who have not dated and never married?
> 3. What is your responsibility if you have sexual experience/history, and your partner is a virgin?
> 4. Can you wait? Or do you want a partner with sexual experience and prowess?

No matter the circumstances, dialogue is critical. You must be able to discuss with your partner all your motivations regarding sex. And you both must respect the other's stance. If you value abstinence until marriage and your partner tries to force you into sex before your wedding night, this is a major issue and could be a deal breaker that ends the relationship.

The Hookup Culture

Sex outside a committed relationship, also called casual sex or friends with benefits (FWB), means getting together for a fun time with no commitment. Social media idealizes the hookup culture popular with teens and young adults, positioning sex as urgent. Ours is a culture of consumerism, and sex is a hot commodity. How often have you heard "Sex sells"? If people seek immediate connection, two problems arise:

- ❖ When you sexually engage without delay (the hookup), trust, confidence, and love are all freely given before learning about each other. You are handing over the keys to the castle—what more is there to discover?
- ❖ The energy you spend hooking up with multiple people may prevent you from finding a long-term intimate partner.

Kelly heard from a 31-year-old how a friend in his circle regularly engages in casual sex: "He's wasting his time and energy. Hooking up is distracting him because he always has that high from hooking up. It's not sustainable."

The problem with hooking up is that it can stir profound feelings of attachment, blurring the lines between casual intimacy and emotional connection. We may find it challenging to recognize and accept the arrangement as nothing more than a friends-with-benefits situation.

The hookup culture is here to stay, and the sexual hookup applies to people of all ages and stages. Younger people often mistake physical attraction for love, so waiting for an emotional connection may not make sense to them. Often, young adults don't have the experience that makes them sensitive to red flags in a partner and will insist that they are sexual beings with physical needs for connection and fulfillment. So, we walk that fine line between imposing our morality and acknowledging the social trends. We're opening a can of worms here (By the way, frogs eat worms).

Often, instant gratification leads to a 'try-before-you-buy-attitude.' You may enjoy the hookup now. Sleeping with someone you met at a club while under the influence of alcohol is not a good foundation for a lasting relationship. Having sex with a stranger poses an immediate risk to your health and safety because a drunk person is not of sound mind to consent to sex. Dangerous behaviours and legal consequences can result, especially if your alcohol or drug level is over the limit, and you pass out or accidentally overdose.

Getting naked with someone we don't know is like over-sharing on social media, a behaviour commonly observed in today's youth. A hookup's unscrupulous recording may lead to our sexual images being shared with the public, potentially ending up on Internet sex sites. Videos and pictures posted on social media platforms can haunt individuals indefinitely, leading to the destruction of their lives, an unfortunate reality that we must not overlook.

Older people have an edge when starting new relationships because they have experienced hurt and learned unhealthy love patterns do not work. Preferring to wait before having sex with someone they've just met may be considered a value of self-respect. Older adults, who are potentially more vulnerable, can become victims of online dating scams and lose their hard-earned savings.

You want to stack the chances of finding intimacy in your favour. So, if you seek connection, you must challenge your choice of hooking up—with the option of getting to know someone on a deeper level. There will be plenty of time to enjoy sex. Why not invest in learning about one another by doing activities? We can learn so much about someone when we take the time to play together. Channel your sexual energy into shared interests, which sets the tone for fun and enjoyment. If the end goal is a lasting connection, set the foundation for a stable relationship while peeling back the emotional layers.

While hookup sex can be exciting and fulfill physical needs, it may not be beneficial for those seeking a long-term, stable relationship. We know examples of people who met and slept together the first night, moved in within a month and are still going strong twenty years later. These examples are not the norm; sometimes, it simply works out. Hooking up does not create a clear end goal. True intimacy relies on communication and trust, foundational for fostering connection. Knowledge is power, and our goal is to present the scenarios so you can make informed choices. Ask yourself if your actions are leading you in the direction you want to go. (If all you want are hookups, that's okay because chances are, you won't be reading this book!)

> **REFLECTION**
>
> 1. Do you presently hook up with others?
> 2. Why choose casual flings over a committed relationship?
> 3. Does hooking up feel more like a compulsion?
> 4. Do your hookups involve alcohol/recreational drugs?
> 5. Are you hooking up, hoping your sex partner will fall madly in love with you?
> 6. Have you read racy novels or watched sexually explicit films and want to try everything in them?
> 7. What can 'hooking up' teach you about your preferences?
> 8. Is hooking up taking energy and time away from what you want to achieve in a relationship?
> 9. Do others judge you for choosing casual sex over a relationship?
> 10. Are you using hookup sex to avoid a committed connection?

Love Bombing

A date who comes on strong may be a love bomber. Love bombing is a manipulative tactic used in romantic relationships to gain control over you and is a form of emotional abuse. Love bombers shower you with attention, compliments, gifts, and trips. They try to monopolize your attention by bombarding you with phone calls and texts.

According to Healthline (online, n.d.), love bombers are needy and do not respect your boundaries. They push for early commitment and overwhelm you with their intensity. There is a manipulative and controlling intention in love bombing, and this behaviour is not genuine.

Instead, it intends to manipulate the person into feeling compelled to reciprocate or do what the love bomber wants. The goal is to create a deep emotional bond that will make you dependent on the attention and affection of the love bomber.

Once the love bomber has gained your trust and dependence, they may use this to control you. They might threaten to withdraw love or attention or make demands to keep the relationship intact.

According to August McLaughlin (2022), these five red flags can help you identify a love bomber:

- They often employ grandiose gestures to impress you (and others).
- The relationship becomes serious too quickly.
- The love-bombing partner has low self-esteem, trying to cover up a huge flaw, and their behaviour may be associated with narcissism.
- You want to return to the beginning when things were simpler and more romantic.
- The love bomber leaves you when you no longer suit their purpose.

For these reasons, the relationship can feel abusive. McLaughlin (2022) states that the love bomber may break off the relationship if you stop praising them or giving them free housing.

Love bombers may appear this way because of their lack of relationship experience, immaturity, or trust issues resulting from past hurt. Here, it is innocent, often called 'puppy love.' If you feel there is potential with this person, test it out by holding an honest conversation. Explain what you need and want for your couple to work. If the person is genuinely a love bomber, they may act hurt, defensive, and unreasonable while continuing the behaviour. Time for you to run the other way!

Recognising signs of love bombing is crucial, such as when someone tries too hard to win you over or makes you feel obligated to them. Mutual respect, trust, and love that grow over time form the foundation of healthy relationships, not manipulative tactics.

> **REFLECTION**
>
> Consider the five points above and answer the following questions:
>
> 1. Does your partner's attention feel overwhelming?
> 2. Is your partner prematurely pushing you to give more or be all-in?
> 3. Do you feel respected and happy?

Your Healthy Sex Life

A healthy sex life can vary as individuals have unique needs, desires, and preferences. With all the messaging swirling around us, how do we know if our sex life is happy and normal? There are specific aspects that contribute to a healthy and gratifying sex life, according to Linda Rodgers (2023), and what's normal depends on you and your partner. Keep in mind that open communication and mutual consent are crucial in any sexual relationship.

Here are the key components of a healthy sex life:

- ✓ **Communication**: Open and honest communication is essential. Discuss your desires, boundaries, and concerns with your partner. This includes talking about what you enjoy, what makes you uncomfortable, and any fantasies you have. Communicating enables consent.

- ✓ **Consent:** All sexual activities must be consensual, meaning that all involved willingly and enthusiastically agree to engage. Consent is ongoing and we can withdraw it any time.
- ✓ **Respect and Trust:** To build a trusting relationship, we must feel respected in our boundaries. We must allow ourselves to experience pleasure when we decide to have sex with someone.
- ✓ **Emotional Connection**: Emotional intimacy can enhance the physical aspects of a sexual relationship. Feeling emotionally connected to your partner can lead to a more satisfying and meaningful sex life. This usually comes (pun intended) with feeling safe with your partner.
- ✓ **Variety and Exploration**: Trying new things and being open to exploring various aspects of your sexuality can add excitement to a long-term relationship (See Kink or Spice below). This may involve experimenting with different activities, locations, or even introducing sex toys if both partners are comfortable with it (Batteries not included).
- ✓ **Safe Sex Practises**: Knowing your partner's history and practicing safe sex protects both partners from sexually transmitted infections (STIs) and unwanted pregnancies. Using contraception and regularly testing for STI's are vital.
- ✓ **Physical Health**: Being in good physical health can positively affect your sex life. Regular exercise, a balanced diet, and adequate sleep can contribute to overall well-being, including stamina for those long nights of passion. (Wear a helmet to bed!)
- ✓ **Spiritual and Mental Well-being:** A healthy sex life links to overall well-being. Stress, anxiety, and mental health can influence sexual satisfaction. Mental and emotional health can contribute to a positive sexual experience. Past traumas or mental illness (diagnosed or not) can affect a couple's sex life.
- ✓ **Mutual Satisfaction**: A healthy sex life involves both partners feeling satisfied and content. This may require a balance

between giving and receiving pleasure and being attuned to each other's needs.

There is no one-size-fits-all definition of a healthy sex life. What works for you may not work for another. It's crucial for partners to communicate openly, respond to each other's needs, and continuously work together to maintain a satisfying and respectful sexual relationship. If issues arise, seeking the guidance of a healthcare professional or a certified sex therapist can help.

> **REFLECTION**
>
> Consider the following questions to gauge where you are in your sex life:
>
> 1. Is there mutual trust and respect?
> 2. Do you feel loved and cared for?
> 3. Are you shy or assertive when talking to your partner about sex?
> 4. Do you have preconceived notions about sex caused by your upbringing (i.e., Having sex with someone before marriage can hinder your chances of getting married)?
> 5. How do you resolve sexual issues and is there anything sexual that turns you off?
> 6. How often do you like to have sex and how do you like to initiate it (or have it initiated)?

How Much and How Often

One partner may want sex more than the other. Consider life events, stressors, changes, and where you are in your lifespan, as these affect your sex drive and opportunities for sex. We can't seem to get enough of each other when we are newly dating. Sex is hot, heady, and marked by the endorphins surging during the honeymoon period.

How many times per week are couples having sex? Is there a norm? This ties in with the various life stages. Refer to *Sex Across the Lifespan* earlier in this chapter to see where you are with sexual desire and frequency. What are the factors that contribute to wanting more/less sex? For example, society perceives eighteen-year-old men as notoriously horny. During pregnancy, a woman may want more sex, but her desire may decrease while raising children and during menopause. Why is this? Hormone fluctuations, lack of sleep, and pain during intercourse all contribute to the loss of libido. Refer to the *Holmes Rahe Life Stress Inventory* (See Bibliography) because life transitions can affect your sex drive.

REFLECTION

1. What turns you on about your partner?
2. What does consent (verbal and non-verbal cues) mean to you?
3. Are conversations regarding sex difficult for you?
4. How often do you have/want to have sex?
5. How will you navigate fluctuations in your sex drive and sex life?

Kink or Spice

Toy boxes are not only for kids! You can explore and express your sexuality through different activities, like role play, toys, and games. Your sex life is an opportunity for enjoyment and freedom. Some people believe in pushing the boundaries of their sexuality by testing different activities. So long as you both consent and no one is harmed, everything is on the table (or bed, if you prefer).

Discussing this point of sexuality might seem strange when you are young, vibrant, and open to trying new experiences. Yet, it would surprise you that with all this sex talk (and everyone thinking everyone else is having great sex), there is the need to venture into ramping up your sexual game.

In the beginning, sex can be exciting and adventurous, but life events can make us lose that spark in our relationship. There is no shortage of things to distract us from having sex. When we are dating, we cannot imagine not having sex. Over time, we must get out of our heads and into the sheets. And this is where adding spice—and a bit of kink—comes in handy!

Some couples engage sexually with other people to spice up their relationship. Consenting adults must communicate openly and honestly and agree. Swinging or polyamorous relationships should only happen if both partners consent. (Disclaimer: We do not suggest using this book as a reason to consider having an open relationship with your partner. Our goal is to support couple relationships without judging open or polyamorous relationships.)

REFLECTION

1. How easy or difficult is it to discuss what turns you on?
2. Are you open to 'talking dirty' with your partner?
3. What might hold you back from being playful or free in expressing your sexuality?
4. What boundaries are you willing to push to spice up or add kink to your sex life?
5. Do you have a sacred space dedicated to enjoying fantastic sex?

> **EXERCISE B: Sex-Talking**
>
> Watch the series *How to Build a Sex Room* (Rose, 2022) with your partner. Engage in a candid conversation about:
>
> ❖ What you like
> ❖ What you dislike
> ❖ What you find helpful
> ❖ What you may be open to trying

Sexy Seniors

As bodies age, become out of shape, and develop aches and pains, sex becomes less like an expression of unbridled passion and more like a gymnastic feat. And who wants to think of two dried-up frogs getting it on, anyway? Newsflash: If you live long enough, you will grow old and may still want to get it on! The good news is that you have many freedoms with sex that you never had:

❖ More self-confidence
❖ Experience with sex
❖ You know what you like and dislike
❖ No risk of pregnancy
❖ No need to tiptoe around young children or family members
❖ More time to fulfill your sexual needs and fantasies

But there are caveats, too! STIs or sexually transmitted infections are rising amongst seniors, so use a condom, especially since your health may be more fragile as you age. Privacy may be an issue if you live with your children or in a senior's residence (Payback—remember when you sneaked around your parents to have sex). Failing health, such as one partner with dementia, may create the need for a new consent. For example, the policy statement of a closed ward in a senior's residence states that sex between residents is allowed so long as your partner is lucid and can consent. Can a person with diminished cognition consent to sex? If you've always enjoyed a healthy sex life with your partner, there is no reason this cannot continue.

If you don't use it, you lose it! As we age, our bodies lose natural lubricants (Think skin dehydration), and sex can become painful, especially for women who are pre, post or menopausal. We must be open to using all available resources, such as hormones, lubrication, and electrical stimulation. Remember that it might seem easier to avoid having sex altogether, but that is not ideal. Self-care includes consulting with your physical health practitioner (gynecologist, urologist) versed in the latest sexual health treatments.

Physical affection becomes vital as we age. Sex may rely more on touch and massage but does not exclude sexual intercourse. Those caring for seniors must respect their need for touch and intimacy and create a safe space for residents to have sex if they desire and consent to it.

According to Michael Castleman in *Psychology Today* (2017), seniors' residences are moving from a policy of policing and 'don't' to finding ways of facilitating sex and intimacy. 'Do not disturb' signs, respecting the closed door by knocking before entering, and maintaining an attitude of openness, are vital for caregivers of older adults. People must not assume that just because someone is a senior, they are not sexually interested or sexually active.

> **REFLECTION**
>
> 1. How do you imagine dealing with sex and intimacy as you age?
> 2. As you age, is there particular self-care you want to do to enhance your sex life?
> 3. If you have an aging parent, are you open to discussing their intimacy needs (Would you pack their vibrator when moving them to a residence)?
> 4. If they are in a residence, what accommodations would you make to maintain your parent's sexual health and well-being?

Sexual Disorders

The term sexual dysfunction covers a range of issues that prevent a person from enjoying sex. It can affect either partner and can be physiological and emotional/psychological. With age comes myriad issues that can cause sexual dysfunction. For example, menopause can be incredibly challenging, with debilitating symptoms such as a dry vagina, mood swings, and hot flashes. Sex may be the last thing she wants to engage in, yet her partner still finds her attractive and wants to get naked. Men with diabetes commonly experience erectile dysfunction. Sometimes, men experience premature ejaculation. Physical challenges such as lack of flexibility, painful joints, trouble moving, and aging can affect both partners.

First, understanding sex's importance to you in a relationship and having compassion is critical. If your partner suddenly experienced sexual dysfunction, would you leave your partner and the life you created together? Would you see this as another challenge, or buy a vibrator or stocks in Viagra?

In *Psychology Today's* article, "The Fundamentals of Sex" (online, n.d.), a sexual disorder is prevalent if it causes distress, harms others, or becomes compulsive. This segues into our next topic.

Sexual Deviance

Sexual deviance, also called sexual perversion, is "… any sexual behaviour, such as a paraphilia, that is regarded as significantly different from the standards established by culture or subculture," according to the *APA Dictionary of Psychology* (2023). Deviant sexual behaviours include voyeurism, fetishism, bestiality, necrophilia, transvestism, sadism, and exhibitionism. Specific examples of deviance include peeing on someone (golden shower), dirty Sanchez, anal sex, sexual asphyxiation, filming sex, bondage, sadomasochism, and pedophilia.

Sex must always be between two consenting adults. While one person may consider an act deviant, another might embrace it and be willing. You have the right to say no, refusing any sex act that makes you feel uncomfortable, such as non-consensual or coercive activities. Consent and comfort are essential components of healthy and consensual sexual experiences. It is important to prioritise open communication, establish boundaries, and respect each other's limits to ensure a positive and enjoyable sexual encounter for all parties involved. When we act on our sexual proclivity to engage in a deviant (violent) sex act that can harm another, it is coercive behaviour that is an outright deal breaker.

Deviant sexual behaviour requires a higher level of consent to engage in the specific sexual act. Your values and comfort level drive your willingness to consent. The act must not be illegal. For instance, peeing on someone with their consent is legal, but engaging in sex with a minor is pedophilic and unlawful. This is the fine line between deviance as a red flag and deviance as a deal breaker.

> **REFLECTION**
>
> Questions concerning deviant sexual behaviour:
>
> 1. Does this sex act fit with my values? Is there consent?
> 2. Am I comfortable doing this act (Is there a 'yuck' element that turns me off)?
> 3. Is this a one-time or occasional occurrence versus a compulsion? (See Addiction and Compulsion in Chapter 4.)
> 4. Am I feeling coerced? Is it safe?
> 5. Is it legal?

Applying the above questions, take the example of your partner photographing or videotaping you naked or having sex. We never recommend this for obvious reasons (mentioned earlier), but let's spell it out again: There is ALWAYS the possibility that these photos will end up online. If your relationship tanks, an acrimonious split could cause the misuse of your photos. Safety depends on the trust between you and your partner that you will both keep the recording for your eyes only (but still). If being photographed nude or recorded during sex makes you uncomfortable, then it's automatically non-consensual. If this is a prerequisite for your partner, and you feel pressured or coerced, the red flag has become a deal breaker. And if someone takes pictures or videos of you without your knowledge or consent, this illicit act is outright betrayal.

You can apply this formula to any sexual activity when deciding how to proceed. Always listen to your inner voice. If it tells you something feels off or uncomfortable and goes against your values, heed it. Someone who loves you will not try to coerce you into going against your values. And if they do, take your value elsewhere!

Reality Check

How things are:

How I would like things to be:

Red Flag(s):

Deal Breaker(s):

One action I can take:

Chapter 6

Infidelity

Oops, I cheated (Again)! It was an accident.

Cheating is one of the most damaging betrayals in a relationship. If you have agreed to a monogamous relationship and one of you breaks the agreement, this signals a significant issue that you must resolve. Infidelity is a formidable red flag, if not a complete deal breaker! Cheating is the same as lying, and once may be enough to cause such a trauma that it never happens again. Or it can create an addictive effect and become a slippery slope. If your partner cheated, consider whether you could genuinely forgive and trust in your relationship again or end it.

Excuses! Excuses!

The cheating partner may present a lame reason for having an affair. Consider the following excuses as rationales for infidelity:

- ❖ Oops, I tripped and fell into her vagina/onto his penis!
- ❖ Oops, I got drunk and had a hook-up.
- ❖ Oops, my parent(s) always did it, so I thought it was okay.
- ❖ Oops, I wanted to sow my wild oats.
- ❖ Oops, I was feeling lonely, and you had a headache.
- ❖ Oops, I wanted revenge sex.
- ❖ Oops, the battery died on my vibrator.
- ❖ Oops, I wanted to try some kink, and you didn't want to.
- ❖ Oops, I wanted to see the difference between you and someone else.
- ❖ Oops, I was depressed.
- ❖ Oops, it was only once, and it meant nothing.
- ❖ Oops, the devil made me do it!

Can you think of any others?

There is no excuse for cheating on your partner! Remember: People behave according to their values. Someone may say they believe in monogamy, but their cheating actions show their values do not match their words.

Two Types of Infidelity

There are two types of infidelity: physical/sexual and emotional. Both types can occur separately or simultaneously and are equally damaging.

Physical/Sexual Cheating

Cheating is when one person has sex outside a monogamous relationship without their partner's consent or knowledge. One or both partners might engage in a physical affair for diverse reasons, including that they:

- Feel unhappy or unfulfilled in their current relationship but do not want to leave.
- View an outside relationship as a lifeboat out of a troubled relationship.
- Want to validate themselves—they have ego issues or crave attention and the feeling that others find them attractive.
- Have a compulsion or addiction to sex and seek to fill a void.
- Want to explore kink, but their chosen partner is uninterested.
- Feel their relationship lacks emotional connection, so they try to replace it with physical sex.
- Are curious to explore sex with someone of the same or opposite gender, culture, or community.
- Want to have their cake and eat it too—stay married while cheating.

If your partner has an extramarital affair and it leads to a pregnancy, the consequences become more complex. This represents a huge red flag and an outright deal breaker, if you're planning to marry someone who cheated and got their fling pregnant/or became pregnant themselves. The child will be a constant reminder of the infidelity, and your partner will have to divide their attention and resources between two families. Marrying a cheater, especially one who has a child from their infidelity, means you're taking a risk and setting yourself up for heartbreak.

Emotional Cheating

Emotional infidelity occurs when we share our emotions in an intimate exchange and form an emotional bond with a person who is not our partner. It may result because we cannot emotionally connect with our partner. A simple lunch with a friend/co-worker becomes more personal, not simply 'shop talk.' Or we engage in online chatting or gaming and develop a connection with someone else. (Did you know there are online games where avatars can have sex? It gives a whole new meaning to the word 'joystick'!)

Over time, you may increasingly seek this kind of connection because it feels so good. And the risk is that the connection will turn physical/sexual. "…Emotional affairs are more common than physical affairs, with 45% of men and 35% of women admitting to having an emotional affair…" (*Gitnux*, 2023). People may not see how insidious and damaging this type of infidelity is. Emotional infidelity is hugely hurtful and can prevent the couple's primary relationship from moving past the pain of such a trauma.

Myths About Cheating

Let's explore and debunk common myths about cheating:

> **Myth:** Infidelity always occurs because of a lack of love or attraction in the relationship.
>
> **Reality:** Relationship dissatisfaction can contribute to infidelity, but it's not the sole reason. Personal insecurities, a craving for excitement, emotional dissatisfaction, or unresolved issues can all contribute to cheating.

Myth: Emotional cheating is not cheating.

Reality: Relationship *gold* is to connect emotionally with someone. We delude ourselves into thinking we are not truly cheating. A relationship has the potential to lead to a full-blown affair *because of* the deep emotional connection. Every time you check in with someone else, you are checking out of your relationship.

Myth: Men are more likely to cheat than women.

Reality: Studies show that all genders are unfaithful, though their motivations and behaviours may not be the same. Studies have found that the gender gap in infidelity is narrowing, with women engaging in extramarital affairs at similar rates to men. It's crucial to recognize that infidelity can affect individuals of any gender.

Myth: Once a cheater, always a cheater.

Reality: While certain people may engage in serial infidelity, they can still learn from their mistakes and change their behaviour. Labelling someone as a cheater can underestimate their ability to grow and mend relationships. Open communication, counselling, and personal commitment help to restore trust.

Myth: Infidelity is the ultimate betrayal; there is no way to recover.

Reality: While infidelity hurts a relationship, it's not always impossible to fix. Couples can successfully rebuild their relationships after infidelity, often through therapy or counselling.

It calls for commitment, open communication, forgiveness, and a genuine desire to resolve the root problems. Healing is gradual, and the outcome depends on the individuals involved.

Myth: Monogamy is unnatural, and humans are not designed to be faithful.

Reality: While people have different relationship preferences, monogamy is a common and valued commitment. Many couples successfully maintain monogamous relationships built on trust, love, and mutual respect. People have diverse relationship dynamics, and it's crucial to distinguish between personal preferences and societal norms.

Myth: Infidelity is the sole responsibility of the cheater.

Reality: While cheaters are at fault, relationships and circumstances also play a role in infidelity. Relationship issues, communication problems, and unresolved conflicts can contribute to infidelity. Understanding the broader context can help address the underlying issues and prevent future occurrences.

REFLECTION

1. What would you do if you discovered your partner was cheating?
2. What beliefs would keep you in an intimate relationship with someone who cheats?
3. By tolerating infidelity, how are you dishonouring your values?

4. What outcome (end-goal) would you like to see? How realistic are your expectations?
5. What would make you consider ending the relationship?
6. Why would you stay with your partner after their infidelity?

The Other Woman/Man

Perhaps you're reading this book because *you're* having an affair with a married person. You are the 'side piece.' Sometimes, limiting beliefs dictate our behaviour. A limiting belief is a story we tell ourselves that may or may not be accurate and holds us back from becoming who we are meant to be. An example is the other woman who says: "There are no available men to date."

Here are common motivations for engaging with a cheater:

- ❖ You are on a power trip to profit from conquering someone else's territory.
- ❖ You have low self-esteem and feel unworthy of a fully committed, functional relationship.
- ❖ You feel excited by the thrill of the chase and sneaking around (forbidden fruit).
- ❖ You cannot commit to one person.
- ❖ You do it because you *can* (It's easy).

If you're reading this book because you are in a relationship with a cheater, it's more likely that you're the other woman or man. And it all sounds so romantic—you're hoping he will leave his wife or partner for you. He says he's not happy in his primary relationship, flattering you by saying he's happy with you, and sharing:

- ❖ He was young when he married, but he has matured and now knows what he wants.
- ❖ She nags too much, and you don't.
- ❖ The relationship is humdrum, but this one is novel and fun.
- ❖ Sex is boring with his wife/partner but feels exciting with you.
- ❖ His wife/partner doesn't understand him, but you do.

Guess what? The expression that a man never leaves his wife holds. Why should he? He has the best of both worlds—someone to keep the home fires burning while he stokes them in his loins with someone else because it's more exciting. If he monkey-bars from one relationship to another, chances are he will do it to you when the relationship becomes humdrum.

When you start a relationship as a '*sidepiece*,' you may become heartbroken to learn your partner will not leave their primary relationship. If your partner, who cheated on their spouse, leaves them to be with you, you may worry about them having another affair if they become unreliable or work late. After all, he/she did the same while dating you. Either way, you irresponsibly trade one set of problems for another or a similar set. (Besides, do you want to be a stepparent to teenage children?)

The guilt, heartbreak, and home wrecking can come back to haunt you in unimaginable ways when you are in so-called love. This book is not for those involved in infidelity, since its purpose is to assist people in genuine relationships. Without sounding harsh, we implore you not to be that other woman/man.

> **REFLECTION**
>
> 1. What if you or your partner were unhappy or unfulfilled in the relationship?
> 2. What are the downsides or benefits of staying in an unhappy or unsatisfying relationship?
> 3. What is an alternative to infidelity?

Coming Clean

The honest cheater is someone truthful enough to tell you, but not honest enough to avoid cheating. This person feels so guilty that they must unload and come clean with their partner. Think hard and long before 'fessing up' to your partner. If you decide to tell your partner, you must be clear about your reason:

- ❖ Your guilt is too much to bear. Unburdening yourself of guilt is selfish and transfers the weight onto the other person—it intentionally hurts them.
- ❖ You decide your affair is not worth causing further harm to your partner or relationship. So, you keep it a secret. However, secrets often get exposed. Decide whether you should come clean to your partner or risk they will hear it from someone else.

Work with a professional therapist to process your baggage before you decide whether to tell your partner about your infidelity.

> **REFLECTION**
>
> Does your partner:
>
> 1. Engage in sexual or emotional relationships outside your couple?
> 2. Become defensive or downplay your concerns when you question their outside relationships?
> 3. Promise to stop having sexual affairs, but continue to do so?

What Motivates us to Stay

What makes us stay when we feel betrayed by the person we love and trust (aside from ourselves)? Whether our partner cheated once or is a serial cheater, we tell ourselves a story that keeps us in a relationship fraught with cheating. This story is a myth based on fear and anchors us in an unhappy, unchanging relationship that doesn't serve our needs and goes against our values. Motivations for staying include:

- ❖ I love them/They love me.
- ❖ They will change.
- ❖ They made a mistake.
- ❖ It would cost too much to divorce.
- ❖ This was a one-off occurrence.
- ❖ I'm not _____ enough (pretty, intelligent, sexual).
- ❖ I cannot financially provide for/support myself and my children.
- ❖ Better the devil I know (for convenience).
- ❖ I have nowhere to go/no way out—I feel trapped.
- ❖ Splitting up would destroy the kids' lives, so I'm staying for the children.

- ❖ My parents, family, friends, or community would never understand.
- ❖ No one else will have me because I have children.
- ❖ What affair?

> **REFLECTION**
>
> 1. Do any of the above motivations resonate?
> 2. What are the stories behind these statements, and how true are they?
> 3. Could any of these stories be a limiting belief stopping you from moving past your partner's infidelity?

If you checked any of the above boxes, it's time to bust those myths!

Myth: Love can conquer all, including infidelity.

Reality: Love is often the base of any relationship, but it's not always enough to overcome the breach of trust caused by infidelity. Rebuilding trust takes time, effort, and willingness from both partners. Dealing with cheating involves open communication, professional help, and addressing the underlying issues. Love alone cannot magically fix all the problems caused by infidelity.

Myth: The cheating spouse can change, and the couple can repair the relationship.

Reality: Rebuilding trust and repairing a relationship after infidelity is challenging and complex. It requires genuine remorse, consistent effort, and a commitment to personal growth from both partners. However, some cheating spouses may refuse or lack the ability to change, and certain relationships are irreparable. Once someone breaks trust, it may be difficult to fully regain it, and you must assess if it is workable to rebuild a healthy relationship. If you expect your cheater to have a moment of clarity, change, and stop cheating, please review Rescuing and Fixing in Chapter 3.

Myth: The cheating was a one-time mistake and won't happen again.

Reality: While someone can betray their partner once, we need to look at the context and reasons behind it. Cheating can be symptomatic of deeper relationship problems or individual character traits. Rebuilding trust after infidelity takes time and effort from both partners. You must address the root causes and implement measures to prevent recurrence. Only as a couple can you decide whether and how you can move past an indiscretion.

Myth: Financial stability justifies staying with a cheating spouse.

Reality: While financial stability is a valid concern, it should not be the sole reason for staying with a cheating spouse. While financial stability is a valid concern, individuals should not stay with a cheating spouse solely for the sake of money. We need to consider how the relationship affects our mental and emotional well-being, as financial stability alone may not bring long-lasting happiness. One of the author's finances dramatically improved once she left.

Myth: Staying with a cheating spouse is better because divorce is too expensive and troublesome.

Reality: While divorce can involve financial costs and legal complexities, consider the potential toll of staying in a relationship where your partner has broken your trust and there is ongoing emotional distress. Take a step back and think about your well-being. Are the downsides of staying in the relationship worse than the challenges of getting a divorce?

The financial consequences of divorce can vary based on district, assets, and individual circumstances. Getting advice from professionals like divorce attorneys and financial planners can help you make better financial decisions and informed choices.

We should not overlook the emotional and psychological toll of staying in a relationship after infidelity. Continuously dealing with the aftermath of betrayal and mistrust can affect one's self-esteem, mental health, and happiness. Taking steps toward healing and personal growth can bring more happiness and fulfillment—and set you up for a healthier next relationship!

Myth: You stay with your cheating spouse because you do not feel you are enough.

Reality: Infidelity can profoundly affect a person's self-esteem and make them question their self-worth. However, recognize that cheating does not reflect the betrayed partner's value or worthiness. A cheating spouse cheats because of their own circumstances or unrelated factors. But here is the thing: you must be enough on your own. No one can ever make you feel less than without your permission. Don't give your cheater that power! Consider how your partner's infidelity equates with love, respect, and all those values you hold dear.

Myth: Staying for convenience or familiarity is the easiest option.

Reality: The fear of change or the unknown drives your decision to stay in a relationship for convenience or familiarity. Sticking with an unfaithful partner can have lasting detrimental effects on your emotional well-being and self-assurance. Choosing convenience over personal well-being may not be the healthiest option. You can do better!

Myth: You stay with a cheating spouse because you have nowhere to go.

Reality: Feeling trapped or having limited options can contribute to the decision to stay with a cheating spouse. However, it's crucial to recognize that resources and support are often available in these circumstances. Friends, family, and support organisations can help you find alternative living arrangements. Exploring options and reaching out for help can be vital in breaking free from having nowhere else to go. There is always someone or somewhere to welcome you and help you re-establish yourself.

Myth: Others would never understand or accept your decision to leave.

Reality: The fear of judgement and lack of support from others can be a significant factor in deciding to stay with a cheating spouse. Remember, everyone's circumstances are unique, and you don't owe anyone an explanation for your choices. Seeking guidance from trusted individuals or professionals offering a non-judgemental perspective can be helpful. Prioritise your well-being and make choices that align with your values and happiness, even if others may not fully understand or accept them. If you live for others, your life is a sham. Consider your values—these are all that matter!

Myth: Staying together for the children is always the best option.

Reality: It's not better to stay in an unhealthy relationship for the sake of maintaining a stable environment for children. Witnessing ongoing infidelity and a lack of trust can negatively affect children's emotional well-being. Children benefit from seeing their parents in loving relationships, whether together or apart. This is a massive myth to bust! Read on.

Staying for the Sake of the Children

Partners may choose to stay together for the sake of their children, even after infidelity. If your child is aware you are staying with the cheating partner, what values are you modelling? Staying in an unhealthy relationship sends as powerful a message as leaving. If you leave, you must contend with your child's resentment of breaking a family apart, and if you stay, *you* end up feeling resentful. Your children do not experience their cheating parent the same way you experience your cheating partner. It was only when Laurie was old enough to understand, did she wonder why her mother stayed with her adulterous father.

Whenever a parent removes their energy from their couple and family, this can be detrimental to the children's safety and security. It can cause a lack of presence, attention, time, love, and honesty. Children see everything; even when we don't think they are aware, they usually know something is happening and may hear things meant for adults only. Children, especially younger ones, aren't aware of all the complexities of relationships. The child must confront adult realities while still in the throes of childhood fantasy. When a child learns that their trusted parent is hiding an affair, it can severely affect their emotional wellbeing. The child may blame themselves for their parent's actions.

When Laurie was five years old, she experienced the effects of her father's infidelity. A neighbour informed her mother that her father was seeing another woman during his work lunch hours. To confirm the information, Laurie and her mom took a taxi to discover where her husband spent his lunch breaks. Laurie lay on the cab floor while her mother, disguised with sunglasses and a headscarf, kept watch as the taxi followed the cheater from his workplace. Laurie's mother confirmed her suspicions when she saw her husband enter the home of someone who would be his mistress. What's worse, the woman he was having an affair with was his wife's best friend! Laurie remembers the outing as an extraordinary adventure—like something out of the movies—as a child would! Her experience left a lasting mark, making her believe all men cheat and she should be ready for it.

The cheater cannot simply apologize away their infidelity. Cheating damages trust, self-esteem, and the spirit of both partners and children in a relationship. As role models, consider what you want your child to learn and imitate as they grow into well-adjusted adults in healthy relationships.

Staying for Other Reasons

Your decision to stay or leave is yours if you remain true to yourself and your values. It's one thing to deal with infidelity, but the fallout includes sexually transmitted diseases (STDs), betrayal, and broken trust. It can be difficult and sometimes impossible to recover from your partner's external affair(s). Infidelity can cause such deep wounds that it creates dysfunction and baggage (See Baggage in Chapter 3). The partner who experienced cheating may feel a range of emotions, including:

- Resentment
- Anger
- Fear
- Guilt
- Lack of self-esteem/feeling not good enough
- Mistrust
- Sadness/Depression
- Grief and loss
- Hypervigilance

Can infidelity create a stronger couple bond, or does it destroy a partnership forever? This situation is not black or white—only what suits your relationship. If you both choose to move past the infidelity and stay together, you must first re-establish trust. Without trust, you cannot move forward. Cheating partners must work hard to regain your trust, and if you decide to stay, you must be open to giving them a chance to prove themselves. Know that the healing process will be emotionally challenging; there will be triggers as you work through the trauma.

When to seek professional help:

- If you both decide to work things out.
- The person cheating has troubling fantasies involving minors, animals, and sexual violence against others (Then again, this may be an outright deal breaker).
- When the person's infidelity creates chaos in your couple and family relationships.

- When you want to end the relationship—but feel trapped.
- When you have worked things out, and still feel mistrustful and triggered.

> **REFLECTION**
>
> 1. Would you stay with the cheater for the sake of your children?
> 2. If your kids begged you to stay, would you?
> 3. What would you do if your community would ostracize you for leaving your partner?
> 4. Would you tell your children why you are leaving their other parent?

The Hit to Your Self-Esteem

It's crucial to differentiate between the actions of the cheating spouse and your self-worth. Feelings a cheating partner brings out include betrayal, rejection, and insecurity, and you may question your worth and desirability. Your partner's infidelity may trigger a lack of self-confidence about your appearance and personality. You may compare yourself with the person your partner cheated with, feeling like you do not measure up, doubting your attractiveness, intelligence, and ability to meet your partner's needs.

Your experience of infidelity shatters your trust—not only in your partner and the relationship—but also in yourself and your judgment in choosing a trustworthy partner. All this can lead to blaming yourself for your partner's actions. The emotional fallout can lead to feelings of sadness, anger, and humiliation—all taking a toll on your self-esteem. Not all these feelings are universal because each of us responds differently based on our personality, coping mechanisms, and relationship dynamics.

You may worry about being rejected again in future relationships, and opening to trust others can cause challenges in forming new connections. No one deserves to be betrayed. Rebuilding self-esteem and confidence after infidelity involves getting support from loved ones, taking care of yourself, and working on personal growth. Staying in a relationship out of insecurity can harm your emotional well-being.

Consider counselling or therapy to heal feelings of inadequacy and develop a healthier self-worth. It's crucial to remember that you deserve to be in a relationship where you feel valued and treated with loyalty. You are enough, and the actions of others do not determine your worth. You deserve a loving and fulfilling relationship that respects and honours you.

Earning Back Trust

Infidelity is a significant breach of trust in a relationship; rebuilding it can take time and effort. The cheating partner bears a greater responsibility for rebuilding trust. Here are tips for the cheating partner to earn back trust after infidelity:

1. **Take responsibility for your actions:** Acknowledge that what you did was hurtful and be accountable for your actions. Your remorse must be genuine.
2. **Be patient:** Rebuilding trust takes time and won't happen overnight. Be patient with your partner—they have every right to take their time and space and heal in the way they need to.
3. **Openly communicate with your partner:** From now on, be transparent about your actions, feelings, and where you are. Transparency is critical for rebuilding trust.

4. **Show consistency:** Commit to changing your behaviour and show your partner you are trustworthy.
5. **Listen to your partner:** Hear your partner's concerns and needs. Be empathetic and acknowledge and understand the pain you have caused.
6. **Seek professional help:** Seek individual therapy to work through your underlying issues that led to the infidelity and to improve your communication and relationship skills.
7. **Give your partner space:** Don't pressure your partner to forgive you or move on too quickly after your infidelity.
8. **Keep your promises:** You must show your partner you are serious about making things right, and this is the only way to help rebuild trust.

REFLECTION

1. What boundaries must you establish to move forward in your relationship?
2. How might your cheating partner rebuild your trust?

Reality Check

How things are:

How I would like things to be:

Red Flag(s):

Deal Breaker(s):

One action I can take:

Chapter 7

Communication

I've always heard that one should never go to bed angry… So, I slept on the couch.

Communication is the foundation of every relationship; each partner must feel heard and acknowledged. Each of us has our own fairy tale relationship in mind, but often reality bites us in the ass! We watch family shows and movies depicting how a partner treats his other half, and we expect our loved one to do the same with us. If our partner does not communicate with us in a way we understand, we could misinterpret their intentions. Again, getting to know our partner and communicating our thoughts and feelings is essential. When we do not communicate effectively, misunderstandings arise, trust diminishes, and distance grows between us. This breakdown in communication often leads to couples drifting apart and left unchecked, eventually breaking up.

The Language of Love

Love Language refers to how we prefer to give and receive love, affection, and care from others. People have unique needs and preferences when expressing and experiencing love. These preferences significantly affect the quality and sustainability of our relationships.

In *The Five Love Languages: The Secret to Love that Lasts* (2015), Dr. Gary Chapman explores how men and women express their love differently through five distinct love languages:

1. **Words of Affirmation Love Language** refers to verbal expressions of love such as compliments, encouragement, and kind words.
2. **Acts of Service Love Language** involves doing things for our partner that make their life easier, such as cooking a meal, cleaning the house, or running errands.
3. **Receiving Gifts Love Language** includes giving and receiving tangible gifts to express love and affection.
4. **Quality Time Love Language** means spending time together and giving undivided attention to our partner.
5. **Physical Touch Love Language** refers to physical touch and closeness, such as holding hands, hugging, and kissing.

Expressing our love language shows our partner how much we care in ways they will automatically understand. But we each do this differently. Our love language may involve a homemade dinner cooked for us while our partner expresses their love by taking us out to eat. Kelly loves cooking for her spouse as an expression of love, and he likes to take her out for dinner. So it works well that when she doesn't feel like cooking, they go out to eat!

Understanding each other's Love Language is key to building and maintaining a healthy relationship. When we express love that is meaningful to our partner, it strengthens the bond between us and helps us feel more connected and loved. What a surprise when Laurie bought her partner the same Valentine's Day card as he got for her! That is when you know your love language speaks volumes!

Relationships break down because of poor or non-existent communication, including:

- Avoiding expressing needs, wants, and feelings.
- Expecting our partner to read our mind.
- Slamming doors or throwing things; rather than verbally expressing unhappiness, applying passive-aggressive actions.
- Expressing frustration and belittling someone with passive-aggressive behaviour.
- Blaming, gaslighting, controlling, ignoring, and manipulating.
- Shutting down your partner's feelings, throwing gas on the fire of anger and fuelling resentment.

Grievances

Complaining and nagging are two of the most common killers of effective communication. They usually stem from petty grievances or trivial things that have built up. Let's explore the differences and how to combat these two demons through effective communication.

Complaining

We all have them—complaints, which are typically un-communicated requests. These range from icy sidewalks and cold drafts to particular behaviours that drive us crazy. It could be something we're putting off or putting up with. Usually, a complaint is something we tolerate from ourselves or another person.

When we complain, we express an unmet need that usually results from a fear of being unable to meet that need. For example, it's too cold in the bedroom. Either the window is open, or the heater is turned down. We may not have enough blankets on the bed. How can we have our needs met? Think back to wants versus needs (See Chapter 2). I want the window closed, but my partner wants it open. I *need* the window closed because I am shivering or have a cold.

My complaining won't change having my needs met, while a workable compromise can. Let's look at how I can fix the situation: I can put on an extra layer of clothing or another blanket, turn up the heat, shut the window, or close it part-way. There is a fix. And we can meet halfway to have both our needs met.

EXERCISE A: List your Complaints

Yes, you read that right: Complain (about the cap off the toothpaste tube, wet towels on the floor)!

1. Write a list of your top complaints in your relationship. Focus on three to five priority items.
2. Review your list and create a written request to address each complaint. Target your request to your partner.
3. For each complaint, write a fix you'd like to see. What can you do to resolve the complaint to meet your needs? What might you need from your partner? Work to remedy as many complaints as you can.

Nagging

Saying something over and over sounds exactly like the word nagging, and it's not pretty! We need only state our feelings once—twice as a reminder. After that, it becomes nagging. No one enjoys hearing the same thing repeatedly. After a while, our partner stops listening; they tune us out! It's not as if they have no clue what bothers us. When we repeat our complaint, the other person learns to ignore it, especially if they can't or won't change the situation.

Sometimes, the issues are not petty grievances, and identify a red flag—or even a deal breaker. Instead of respecting ourselves and communicating our needs based on our core values, we nag. Are we trying to fix the unfixable? Or is there a middle ground where we can work on building consensus? Keep reading because the following communication concepts apply as you make sense of complaining and nagging.

You should always feel you can talk to your partner and vice versa. And talking is just one half of communication—active listening is the other half, so each of you feels heard. People communicate differently, and sometimes communication styles vary between partners. Understanding diverse communication styles leads to effective self-expression and better understanding from your partner.

Four Communication Styles

We each communicate in our unique way. According to the book *Law of Attraction* by Michael J. Losier (2009), there are four communication styles:

- ❖ Visual: "Show me the whole enchilada."
- ❖ Auditory: "I hear you loud and clear."
- ❖ Kinesthetic: "It feels right to me."

❖ Digital: "Make sense of it."

For example, Laurie uses car analogies to get her points across to her partner because he knows the workings of a car inside and out. She has learned to explain that he needs to eat fibre—comparing it to his car needing an oil change. And he gets it!

Applying Active Listening

We were born with two ears and one mouth for a reason. Active listening is a crucial skill and a prerequisite for any relationship. Just ask the person who laments: *You never listen to me!*

Active listening techniques:

1. Stop talking.
2. Listen up: for feelings, for body language (non-verbal cues).
3. Be quiet (still).
4. Apply:

    ❖ Paraphrasing: Rephrase what you heard in your own words. Example: *If I hear you correctly, what you are saying is …* Summarize their words. Do not parrot. That's a tip-off you're trying too hard. Repeat in your own words what your partner has said.
    ❖ Reflecting their feelings: Feed their feelings back to them. *Example: You're angry.* Or *I can see how upset you are.*

5. Remain quiet.
6. Listen and observe.
7. By now, you should clearly understand how your partner feels. And you didn't have to say a thing!

Note: It isn't an agreement you are trying to reach but simply a listening exercise where you try to understand what your partner is saying and feeling. Engaging wholeheartedly in listening to your partner makes them more willing to listen to you. It's always better if you take turns to ensure equal talk time and understanding.

Indigenous cultures (ICT, 2015) use a talking stick to maintain respect during meetings. The person holding the stick—and only that person—may speak. All others must listen quietly and respectfully. When facilitating groups, Kelly and Laurie use talking sticks to promote active listening during group discussions. This practice ensures that everyone who wishes to say something can speak and be heard.

If a stick does not represent you, choose another item you resonate with, such as a ball, key, pencil, or stone, or simply hold hands. If you listen actively to your partner, you can ask meaningful questions, signalling you are paying attention. When your partner feels heard, they feel loved, respected, and safe.

Conflict Management

Healthy relationships depend on open communication, understanding diverse communication styles, and fair conflict resolution. Everyone gets angry occasionally; sometimes, we even say terrible things we don't mean. The deal breaker arises when people are nasty during every argument.

The following behaviours are not conducive to managing conflict:

- ❖ Belittling you and calling you rude or degrading names
- ❖ Gaslighting you, which makes you feel crazy
- ❖ Rehashing past mistakes to incite guilt
- ❖ Giving you the silent treatment (e.g., ignores you, leaves the environment, or ghosts you)

We sometimes negatively express our feelings instead of communicating directly, which translates to passive-aggressive behaviour. For example, our spouse agrees to do household chores but repeatedly procrastinates or performs them inefficiently, leading to tension and frustration in the household. When approached about their behaviour, they respond with excuses or dismissive remarks, avoiding direct confrontation or responsibility for their actions. Instead of openly discussing their feelings or concerns, they may use subtle digs or sarcasm to express dissatisfaction, causing confusion and resentment in the relationship.

An argument should end with a resolution. If it is not possible to resolve the issue, step away, take time to process, and revisit your concern later or the following day. Feeling worse after an argument or when one of you feels obliged to agree, especially when afraid to speak up, means no resolution. Think of the reasons you may hesitate to express your feelings. Sometimes, a lack of communication is a red flag of manipulative, mean, or abusive behaviour. If so, review Abuse in Chapter 4.

You know you are in a healthy relationship when you can raise concerns to your partner, they listen, and offer to help you to problem-solve. Even if you disagree wholeheartedly with the decision, you feel heard and supported. You think before expressing your honest opinion to avoid offending each other. While couples may avoid arguments like the plague, when you manage conflict respectfully, this develops a deep trust that brings you closer.

EXERCISE B: My Communication Style

1. What are your communication styles? How are they different or similar?
2. Is there anything on which you might improve?
3. Do you or your partner use unfair fighting practices during arguments/disagreements? Please check all that apply:

    ❖ Brings up past arguments
    ❖ Insults, belittles, or calls you degrading names
    ❖ Gaslights you, so you think you are crazy
    ❖ Attacks your character instead of voicing the issue
    ❖ Gives you the silent treatment, leaves, or ghosts you

4. On a scale of one to ten, how drained do you feel afterward?
5. If it takes two to argue, what part do you jointly play in resolving the issue?

A healthy conflict management approach in relationships looks like this:

❖ Lovingly voicing your honest opinion using effective communication and listening skills
❖ Wanting the best for each other
❖ Problem-solving together by making concessions (as opposed to one person getting their way)
❖ Understanding there is no right or wrong, simply what is suitable for your couple
❖ Detaching with love

Anger

Anger tells you that someone has crossed your boundary, so it is normal to feel rising emotion—like your blood is boiling. What matters is how you manage your powerful emotions. Before spewing angry words or lashing out (that you might later regret), you must walk away—take a time out and calm down, so you can process your feelings and work toward a resolution. Taking your anger out on someone else is never acceptable. Negative expressions towards your partner can harm trust and safety, damaging the relationship. To deal with anger, assert yourself and address the triggering behaviour.

Assertiveness

Asserting yourself involves stating your feelings in a calm, non-blaming way. Knowing your boundaries will support you when you need to assert yourself (See more about boundaries in Chapter 3). You know when someone has crossed the line, and if you continue to allow that, you risk becoming resentful. And that resentment festers and becomes a poison, slowly choking the life out of your relationship.

Back to assertiveness. The best way to tell someone how you feel—positive or negative—is to apply the four-part assertion or "I"-message:

1. When X happens (State the observable behaviour that crosses a boundary).
2. I feel X (Insert emotion here).
3. Because X (Label the consequences of your partner's actions).
4. I need X (State what you need).

For example: "When you raise your voice at me, I feel nervous because intense anger scares me. I need you to speak calmly."

You can then apply a natural consequence such as "Next time you yell at me, I will walk away."

> **REFLECTION**
>
> Check all that apply:
>
> ☐ I have a handle on my anger and so does my partner.
> ☐ My partner has an anger management issue.
> ☐ My partner angers me so much that I want to explode (or commit X).
> ☐ The body is already buried! (Note: This is a red flag.)

Loving Detachment

There will be times when, no matter what you do, say, or how you feel, you reach an impasse with your partner. Your partner may engage in a behaviour that bothers you, and all efforts (and pleading) for change lead nowhere. You may feel exasperated and throw your hands in the air. This is when you can practice loving detachment, where you choose to maintain a sense of love and compassion while simultaneously letting go of outcomes and expectations.

You can love your partner and feel compassion for their frustration, but you need not take it on. Let's say your partner frequently misplaces items such as their cell phone, keys, or wallet. Loving detachment means that, while you empathize, you avoid searching for these lost items. If you search while they sit and watch, you are enabling their behaviour. While it may frustrate you when your partner asks you to help them do something they can and should do for themselves, loving detachment lets you carry on with your life while they live the consequences of their behaviour. The above example is simple, and we must navigate the more serious ones in the same way.

It's paradoxical because on the one hand you love your partner and have a genuine concern for their happiness, yet you let go of the emotional dependency that has you clinging to a particular outcome. Instead of letting their behaviour eat away at you, causing resentment and stress, you let your partner navigate their challenge without feeling overly affected by it. This lets you maintain your healthy boundaries while finding inner peace.

Jealousy and Possessiveness

Jealousy is a complex emotion that arises when someone feels insecure or perceives a threat to their relationship. Possessiveness refers to the desire to control or dominate one's partner, often out of fear of losing them. Possessive behaviour includes excessive monitoring, control, or unreasonable demands. It can also involve guilt or manipulation to maintain control over the relationship. Be aware of how alienating jealousy and possessiveness can be in your relationship, especially when your partner aims to isolate you from your support system.

Jealousy and possessiveness can destroy trust, create tension, and cause conflict in a relationship. The debate over jealousy is often contentious. Some people view jealousy as a negative emotion leading to unhealthy behaviours and destructive outcomes. Others contend that a certain level of jealousy is a natural response and can be an indicator of how much one cares for their partner. Excessive jealousy can lead to anxiety, insecurity, anger, and suspicion, causing relationship problems.

> **REFLECTION**
>
> How would you feel if your partner:
>
> ❖ Acts jealous of you
> ❖ Maintains friendships with their exes
> ❖ Has opposite-sex friendships
> ❖ Does not have any friends
> ❖ Meets secretly with a friend

Causes of Jealousy

Common causes of jealousy include:

❖ Feeling insecure about our appearance, achievements, or self-worth can make us feel inadequate and easily threatened by others.
❖ Experiencing negative events, like cheating or childhood traumas.
❖ Lacking trust in our partner's loyalty and commitment to the relationship.
❖ Communicating poorly or not at all within the couple may lead to misunderstandings and assumptions.
❖ Continuously comparing yourself to others, particularly in terms of looks, achievements, or social status.

If you must audit everything your partner does without a valid reason for distrust, it's a red flag and points to something more concerning. A healthy relationship never involves one or both partners trying to control the other.

Effects of Jealousy

Jealousy strains trust. Excessive jealousy can erode trust between partners and create a toxic atmosphere of suspicion. It can lead to controlling actions, such as monitoring one's partner's activities or isolating them from friends and family. This results in emotional distress and anxiety, which causes emotional instability and mood swings. When not effectively addressed, jealousy can hinder open, honest communication between partners.

Managing and Overcoming Jealousy

Handling jealousy differs for every couple. People must recognize their feelings and be honest and open with their partner regarding jealousy and their source. Consider the following to manage your jealousy:

- ❖ Notice your insecurities and triggers and work to develop your self-confidence and self-esteem.
- ❖ Talk to your partner about jealousy and encourage them to share their perspective. Honest and respectful communication is critical to addressing any underlying issues.
- ❖ Create clear boundaries with your partner to minimize jealousy triggers.
- ❖ Focus on building trust in the relationship by being dependable, honest, and supportive.
- ❖ Seek professional help to address underlying issues and the problems jealousy is causing in the relationship.

For example, discuss what may trigger your partner's need to check your phone and state your clear boundaries. Also, share how uncomfortable you feel when your partner regularly spends time with their ex-partner. It boils down to trusting your partner and yourself.

Sometimes, our mistrust of others reflects a lack of trust in ourselves. Distrust can come from doubts sparked in our mind over fear we are not good enough, may lose the other person, and will never find happiness.

Finding the right balance between respecting your partner's feelings and maintaining independence and trust is crucial in a relationship. Working as a couple to understand and manage jealousy can lead to a more vital and fulfilling partnership. Where there is trust, jealousy is not an issue, since you share the same values.

> **REFLECTION**
>
> 1. Does your partner get jealous and isolate you from loved ones? (See Red Flags and Deal Breakers in Chapter 4).
> 2. Does your partner ask you to re-tell your conversations with friends or family verbatim?
> 3. Does your partner insist you portray them as outstanding when talking to your friends?

Solving Common Problems

Solving everyday problems involves listening to each other and communicating our wants and needs. Couples need to work together to solve problems, whether they're minor tasks or life-changing issues. Working through issues together brings us closer and builds trust.

A Collaborative Problem-Solving Approach

This approach aims for a result that is good for both because it allows you and your partner to build consensus as you collaborate to resolve an issue. It involves the following steps:

1. Identifying the problem
2. Defining how the problem affects you
3. Brainstorming workable solutions, which requires listening and keeping an open mind
4. Choosing one or a combination of solutions together
5. Implementing the solution(s) and committing to following through
6. Evaluating the outcome(s), which may involve revisiting the issue to see how the resolution worked

You may need to return to the drawing board to brainstorm repeatedly. Return to step three if the problem is still unresolved and stay open to all possibilities. Solving problems requires active listening and respectfully communicating our wants and needs. It also requires a huge dose of patience because change takes time.

Fighting Fair

Only our partner has the power to ignite our deepest passion and cause us to feel so passionately angry—to the point of seeing red (and we don't mean red flag). Arguing, bickering, and outright fighting is a reality we will face as a couple. Don't feel guilty when people tell you they never fight with their partner—perhaps they have simply mastered the art of fighting fairly.

Anger arises when we feel someone has crossed our boundary (See

Types of Boundaries in Chapter 3). Our partner may have said or done something that feels disrespectful or tests our limits. Or we react to a perceived slight by our partner. Sometimes our partner has no clue what they even did to make us feel pissed. So, how do we deal when we share a space and bed with our partner? We've all heard the expression "Never go to bed angry." Well, newsflash…you will!

It's not always easy to overcome powerful emotions that cause ire and displeasure. But what we do with those potent feelings is key. Consider these ideas:

- Time out is not only for little kids; Go to another room or go out. Remove yourself from the intense energy of the fight.
- Think before you lash out. Count to ten and take a deep breath. Your anger is about you. You may feel justified in your anger, but you cannot take back nasty remarks made in the heat of the moment.
- Keep your voice level. The tendency when we are angry is to shout. This feels menacing and only strains our vocal cords.
- Avoid dragging every other issue or argument you've ever had into your current beef.
- Do not lay blame, because this is counterproductive to resolving the issue. It takes two to tango!
- Do not ignore your partner for a prolonged period. This is torment. Try to work through your feelings while remaining civil.
- If you must go to bed angry, let your partner know you are still dealing with your powerful emotions and will feel better equipped to speak after a good (most likely a bad) night's sleep.

If you have anger management issues, seriously consider professional help to deal with these because your partner is not your punching bag, and your relationship is not the fighting ring!

Couple Therapy

Occasionally, partners in a relationship hit a bump in the road that causes more than a disagreement. Most relationship breakdowns occur because of a lack of communication. Consider consulting a therapist or counsellor if you cannot resolve your conflict. In seeking outside help, you gain tools that will last much longer than the sessions you attend. Learning to argue effectively to benefit your relationship will turn you into a power couple.

> **REFLECTION**
>
> 1. How initiative-taking are you when resolving conflict?
> 2. If you could not resolve issues, would you consider seeking professional help?
> 3. What would you do if your partner refused to see a counsellor?
> 4. If you showed your partner the mountain, and he/she refused to climb it, would you carry him/her up, anyway?

Decisions, Decisions

People make thousands of decisions daily, usually subconsciously. Decisions are part of a couple's life, from navigating the simple what-to-eat for dinner to expensive purchases and having children. The challenge is to make decisions that benefit the relationship while honouring one another's needs. To help your decision-making, revisit the collaborative problem-solving formula above and follow the steps. You should make important decisions together to ensure they benefit both of you. Again, keep both parties' needs in mind and respect one another's choices.

Consider that you feel cramped in your small condominium and want to save for a home. However, your partner is happy in your apartment and would prefer to spend money on travel. After brainstorming, you propose two options: either travel for two more years or stay put and save for a home. If you both agree to one option, awesome! But if you find yourselves at an impasse, apply the collaborative problem-solving approach above. Your aim is to strive for a resolution or combination of solutions that satisfy both of you.

Deciding together regarding expectations, needs, and wants requires a baseline of honesty, and putting all cards on the table. You cannot hold back because if you do not take part jointly, you risk resentment and regret, which can erode a relationship like water to a rock. Sometimes it will be you deciding, and other times it will be your partner. It's not ideal for one person to make all the decisions unless the other person cannot do so because of medical or intellectual reasons. You are a team, and the goal is to build consensus, even if you do not always agree—in which case, you seek the middle ground.

As you approach the problem-solving process, have confidence that both of you will be pleased with the outcome. Otherwise, while sitting in your new home leafing through travel magazines, your partner may resent you, thinking, "If only we had done X, Y, or Z...." Remember, we often regret the things we didn't do.

REFLECTION

1. Is there one person in your relationship who makes all the decisions?
2. Why is it that person?
3. Are both partners' feelings considered, and have you communicated your wants and needs honestly?
4. If your wants and needs are unmet, what do you believe is the reason for this?
5. How might you resolve your problems as a couple?

Reality Check

How things are:

How I would like things to be:

Red Flag(s):

Deal Breaker(s):

One action I can take:

Chapter 8

Becoming Mr. & Mrs. (or any combo)

There's no free milk when you buy the cow!

Preparing for Marriage

This involves exciting steps, from getting engaged to planning the wedding. Every culture has its unique way of preparing for marriage, and there are too many to discuss in this book. In certain cultures, people seek guidance from their spiritual leader, community, parents, or grandparents to create a happy union.

Some couples opt for a marriage preparation course, which covers topics such as spiritual growth, raising children with shared beliefs, and using faith to resolve conflict. Guidance from a relationship coach before marriage can help you identify your needs, wants, and goals and enhance communication as a couple. Consulting a lawyer or other legal advisor in your local region can help you deal with the legal realities that every relationship will face.

The book combines real-life experiences and topics often covered in marriage preparation courses. Use this book to work through the exercises with your partner and supplement any marriage preparation—faith-based or other—you choose to do. You can never over-prepare; we encourage you to research marriage preparation in any way you feel comfortable and respected.

Lifestyle and Living Arrangements

When we cohabit or marry, we merge our diverse lifestyles and families. We may be happy to share accommodations that focus only on what we like and have in common, but we must also integrate one another's differing preferences. And it's these differences that can become sticking points as we search for and adapt to sharing a home.

When embarking on a life together, one of the primary questions is: "Where will we live?" There are many configurations of living and lifestyle arrangements, starting with renting versus buying a home. Whether you rent or own, you must decide if you will move into a new home that you choose together or into one of your existing homes. You must be clear about who will pay for what. The key is to ensure that the partner investing in the other's home will not lose any money.

Other factors to consider include living arrangements and personal space, which we'll discuss later.

Living with Family or a Roommate

When additional people become a part of your living space on a long-term basis, it can have a significant effect on both your physical and emotional well-being as a couple. It is crucial to have a conversation if you choose to move in with one or both of your parents/in-laws. There are diverse aspects to negotiate and agree upon.

Gone are the days when you can freely parade around naked or clean the house in your French maid outfit. Living with others requires setting clear boundaries and expectations. For instance, you may find that your mother-in-law involves herself in your arguments, often siding with her own child. This can be challenging to navigate without clear boundaries in place.

Similarly, if you decide to take on a roommate to minimize expenses, you must weigh the monetary considerations against your couple's overall happiness. Clearly communicate your goals, expectations, and boundaries to ensure that everyone involved agrees with the terms you set for your successful living arrangement. Whether it is moving in with parents or taking on a roommate, having open and honest conversations about your needs and boundaries is essential. By doing so, you can create a harmonious living environment and maintain a healthy dynamic within your couple.

Property

What is yours is yours. What is theirs is theirs. And you divide what you acquire together equally. What you earn, inherit, or win is yours. MOSTLY. Learn about the legalities of joint property in marriage and cohabitation by researching state or provincial laws. Become informed of how your government or state defines common-law and marital properties.

If your name does not appear on the lease or deed and your partner puts you out of your shared home, you may have no legal right to enter the premises. Kelly lived this painful reality. Because the deed was in her common-law partner's name, she had to ask the police for help when he unreasonably locked her out of their home.

If you are married, you can declare your home as the family

residence, which means your partner cannot sell or evict you without your consent. Again, please check your provincial or state regulations.

Should you decide to cohabitate and do not want to put your partner on the lease, they have no obligation to pay rent if things go south. Be prepared because you may be stuck bearing a hefty housing cost alone.

The point underscored here is that when things are good, they are great. Should the tides turn, discord can make us unreasonable. When scorned, we are not looking to make the other person's life comfortable. Being hurt by our former partner can make it hard for us to think clearly, especially after we had feelings and dreams for a future together.

Personal Space Versus Shared Space

Personal space refers to a person's boundary within their environment, and no one else but you define what that is. Sometimes people are clueless, and you must physically take one step backwards when someone invades your 'bubble' (measured by two arm's length between you).

However, when you decide to forge a life with someone else, considering your shared space versus your need for personal space is critical. As real estate gets smaller and more expensive, it's challenging to have a dedicated space just for yourself. A separate room, corner, or spending alone time in another part of the shared home is not a luxury but a necessity. Even when you are together in a tiny space, you must respect one another's need for retreat.

If you work from home and need a home office, studio, or workshop, you might also want a separate area for rest, meditation/prayer, or creative pursuits. If one of you wants to meditate in silence while the other is watching television, you must have a plan for respecting your interests and needs. You also need assurances that your belongings, such as a journal or other sensitive documents, can be in your shared space and your partner will not touch them.

Personal space also refers to space for emotional growth and development. For example, you need help to express your feelings, and your partner supports you by saying it's okay—they are there for you while you're working on yourself. Not talking to or interrupting your partner while they are engaged in another activity is an example of respecting personal space. We must consider the importance of privacy and focus while being in a shared space, even if it's usually understood without words.

Sleeping Arrangements

One of you prefers separate sleeping arrangements—either separate beds, rooms, or sleep schedules. Here is where you cry: *Oh, but we must sleep together!* Not so fast! While warm, cuddly, and convenient, co-sleeping is not for everyone. Sleeping apart is more common than you may think. Some couples opt to sleep separately or have their own bedrooms, a tradition linked to the wealthy and aristocrats.

Instances where sleeping solo might be preferable:

- ❖ You or your partner have sleep-related issues like tossing and turning, snoring, sleep apnea, restless leg syndrome, or sleep violence (Yes, it's a real thing).
- ❖ One of you has a chronic illness or disability that makes sharing a bed challenging.
- ❖ You sleep better alone.
- ❖ You would rather sleep with your iguana!
- ❖ You wake up to *buzzard breath*!

Hence the question: One bed or separate beds? Sometimes, sleeping apart begins innocuously. Your partner has the flu, and you don't want to catch it. You move to the guest room, but after the second night, you realize your sleep was much better than when you slept together! The same goes for the people who snore—and it sounds like you're sleeping with an eighteen-wheeler revving its engine.

There is a rare and little-known phenomenon called sleep violence. It is where you awaken to your partner pummelling you while they are still sleeping. This is an actual condition that, according to Dr. Michael J. Breus (2018), is a sleep disorder linked with parasomnia such as sleepwalking and talking in your sleep and is more dangerous. The perpetrator rarely knows of their violent behaviour as they are not awake. But for their partner, the assault is confusing and anger-invoking because it's downright confronting to awaken to being assailed!

As we age, a good night's sleep becomes more sought-after because we know we won't function well without our Zs. We risk becoming irritable with our partner if we've not had enough or quality sleep, so the prospect of separate beds, and even separate rooms, can be a workaround for couples with sleep issues.

When deciding to sleep separately, instead of walking away in a huff, clutching your pillow, hold a conversation about your needs. Avoid blaming your partner. Tell them how you sleep better when X, Y, or Z happens. Instead of "You hog the blankets," say: "I get cold and need more blankets in the middle of the night." Collaborate to find a sleep solution that meets both your needs.

Consider how you'll maintain intimacy without snuggling in bed. While cuddling in bed creates a connection, so does snuggling on the couch before bed or having a little goodnight chat over hot cocoa. You may decide to start out in one bed or have sex in either of your beds like a date and move to the other bed or room afterward. You, as a couple, decide what intimacy means for you and how to maintain it.

As with any couple's decision, discuss and choose, knowing you can always revisit and re-evaluate.

> **REFLECTION**
>
> 1. How do you express your need for time alone, and does your partner give you your personal space?
> 2. How critical is having a designated space (corner, studio, office) when living with someone?
> 3. Can you afford a large enough house (or apartment) for each person to have their own area?
> 4. How can you feel content if your home has limited square footage?

Living Together or Apart

Yes, you read that right! As if the idea of separate beds or rooms is not shocking enough, imagine being committed but living in entirely different digs! Living apart together (LAT) refers to a romantic relationship in which two people are a committed couple but choose to live in separate homes. This option is becoming more popular among older adults and those with past marriages or cohabitation experience.

Being in a LAT relationship means having both commitment and independence. While unconventional, this type of relationship offers a unique sense of independence and privacy. Someone shared with Kelly how she opted not to live with her significant other, the father of their now-grown children. Though they often spend time together, they own their own homes to avoid the stress of sharing a common space. While this is a novel arrangement, it can work for some couples. You may think: *Why bother being in a relationship?*

With the cost of accommodation rising, living apart may be counterintuitive. However, if you can afford it and know you would be happier if you lived this way, you may opt for this living arrangement for the sake of your relationship. Living with someone's quirks can be challenging for you. One may be messy, while the other is fanatically neat and organised. One couple (Tiny House Expedition, online), live in His & Hers tiny homes parked side by side and share a common outdoor space. Having married later in life and being fiercely independent, they cite their reasons for LAT and their different tastes in decor.

People may suggest your partnership is in trouble if you don't share the same roof. It's one thing if your children ask questions, but it's another if your nosey neighbour queries you. It's nobody's business but yours as you decide what makes you happy. Living apart and still being a (power) couple makes sense for assorted reasons. There are pros and cons to living apart.

The positives are:

- **Autonomy and independence:** Living apart allows each partner to maintain a sense of independence and autonomy. They can pursue their interests and activities without compromising their partner's schedule or preferences.
- **Reduced conflict:** Living apart can limit the amount of conflict in a relationship. Couples may find that they argue less when they have space and time for themselves.
- **Greater appreciation:** Being apart can lead to a greater appreciation for the time spent together. It can also help couples avoid taking one another for granted.
- **Flexibility:** Living apart can allow for more flexibility in a relationship. Couples can easily adapt their living arrangements to fit their work or family's needs.
- **Financial benefits:** Living apart can offer financial benefits. Couples may save on rent or other living expenses by living in separate homes.
- **Cleanliness:** You don't have to pick up after anyone else.
- **Social activities:** You have someone with whom to take part in activities and still maintain a personal space for quiet time.

Besides, the TV remote is yours—you can watch whatever you want on television, and you don't have to stare at their iguana every day! Potential drawbacks of living apart are:

- ❖ **Limited time together:** One of the biggest challenges of a LAT relationship is that you may need more physical time together. This can make building intimacy, trust, and emotional connection challenging.
- ❖ **Social stigma:** People may disapprove of the LAT arrangement because of its unconventional nature, which can create family or social pressures.
- ❖ **Finances:** Maintaining two households can be costly and limit your ability to save.
- ❖ **Connection:** Being in separate places makes it challenging to share activities and goals with your partner. This can lead to disconnection and isolation, which can affect the relationship's longevity because it is harder to build and sustain intimacy.
- ❖ **Support:** Living apart can also mean lacking support during tough times, such as illness, stress, or other life challenges. You might feel alone in facing these challenges without your partner's support.
- ❖ **Commitment:** Being apart may lead to infidelity since there are more possibilities to engage in secret relationships.

As with all decisions, it comes back to your 'why.' If you agree, then explore how a relationship can work while living apart. You can always revisit your options if you change your mind (or if the iguana dies). The success of a LAT relationship depends on the individuals and their circumstances. Partners in a healthy relationship—whether living together or apart—must have open discussions about their boundaries, expectations, and needs.

> **REFLECTION**
>
> 1. What is your motivation for living apart as a couple?
> 2. If you don't sleep (or live) together, what are your options for maintaining intimacy?
> 3. How will you manage the social stigma of living apart?
> 4. If you choose LAT, how will you maintain your commitment to each other?

The Wedding

It was a fairy-tale wedding—until we got the bill! Weddings come in all shapes and sizes. The wedding industry features heavily in popular media, influencing (mostly) women to desire extravagant bridal magazine-spread weddings.

First, the Prenup

You may subscribe to: *What's mine is mine, what's yours is mine, and what's ours is mine,* but the prenup (prenuptial agreement) can help you establish how you would handle assets, debts, and other financial matters if you divorce, separate, or one of you dies. A lawyer can assist you in creating a prenuptial agreement that benefits both partners. Consider:

- Why have a prenup?
- What must it include? (I get the dog and you can keep the frog!)
- You cheat, and the prenup is void!

Prenuptial agreements provide clarity and certainty about financial matters, potentially reducing conflicts and disputes during a divorce. It allows the couple to discuss and agree on financial issues while they are on good terms because we all know how bad blood and bitter arguments potentially erupt when the couple breaks up.

The main reason for a prenup is to protect the assets each partner brings into the marriage, such as property, businesses, investments, and more. Without a prenup, these assets may be divided according to the laws of your province or state. A prenup is critical for protecting one spouse from assuming the other's debts if they divorce by outlining debts incurred before and during the marriage. And it ensures the fair distribution of jointly gained assets.

While the idea of a prenup may feel unromantic, there are distinct reasons it makes sense for couples to choose to have one. If one or both spouses own a business, a prenup can specify how to handle the business if a divorce occurs. If you come into the marriage with significant family wealth or stand to inherit the family fortune, having a prenup can ensure these assets remain within the family in case of a divorce. A prenup can also set the terms for spousal support, which can provide financial security or limit financial obligations. Last, individuals who have been through a divorce (and entering a second marriage) may use a prenup to protect the monetary interests of children from a previous marriage.

Prenuptial agreements can be valuable in certain situations, but they may not be appropriate for every couple. Laws regarding prenuptial agreements vary by district, so it's best to consult with legal professionals to ensure that any agreement is valid and enforceable. Open communication and mutual understanding are crucial when discussing the terms of a prenup to avoid misunderstandings and potential conflicts.

Writing your Wedding Vows

A beautiful and personal way to express your love and commitment to your partner is to write personalised marriage vows. Couples may incorporate stories and heartfelt sentiments. There are no prescribed wordings, and you can find a plethora of examples online. The officiant will always need to integrate the standard blah blah into their spiel to make your marriage legally binding. Consider the length of your vows to keep your guests engaged and awake. And avoid mentioning embarrassing incidents, like getting drunk or peeing on your partner. Otherwise,

- ❖ Be sincere and speak from the heart. It's okay to show vulnerability, and those genuine emotions can make the moment even more special.
- ❖ Note the special moments, challenges you've overcome, and qualities you love about your partner.
- ❖ Share specific qualities, actions, or gestures that you appreciate and cherish about your partner.
- ❖ Include specific examples that highlight your feelings and experiences. This could be a funny anecdote, a touching moment, or a shared memory that symbolizes your love.
- ❖ You may choose to exchange your vows with your partner before the wedding day, ensuring the tone and length of your vows complement each other.

Remember, your wedding vows are a personal expression of your love and commitment. Be true to yourselves as a couple. It is your wedding, but remember that your family will watch, take photos, and video-record your special day!

Size Matters—The Wedding Guests

Who will you invite, and how far back into the family will you go? He wants to invite his boisterous drinking uncle, who makes off-colour jokes. She wants to invite her brother's mother-in-law's stepsister. You can't agree. You try to keep the guest list manageable because it's overwhelming and expensive to host so many people. The list can quickly become long and include loads of relatives and friends you rarely see, causing tension and making you want to elope.

Whether you ask for it, family members will always have (and offer!) an opinion. Often, the parents of the bride/groom will want to impress their community of friends by holding an extravagant wedding. While many of the three hundred guests your parents have invited are not your friends, you do not want to offend them. How do you navigate this delicate situation when your parents insist on paying for an extravagant wedding?

Know your limits and cut-offs if you pay for your wedding using your savings. Consider who you might invite and whether they will be in your life in the future. And remember, this is your special day—you get to create the wedding you exactly want!

Non-Traditional Weddings

Sometimes we want to distance ourselves from the idea of that fairy tale wedding, so we opt for something unconventional and keep the guests to a minimum. We either invite the entire gang or we keep it small because who can afford to fly to Saint-Tropez, anyway? Here are common options and considerations:

- ❖ **Eloping:** There's a little white chapel in Las Vegas, Nevada, where you can be in, married, and out before you're sober!

There are other fun options, including Elvis impersonators (Elvis did indeed leave the building!) as officiants and drive-through chapels. It's fast and economical (travel notwithstanding) and is genuinely about you, witnessed by two people (you may have pulled off the Strip).

- ❖ **Destination Wedding:** Planning a wedding on a beach (Hold the bikini) in a tropical paradise or other location can be stunning, but you must consider the costs. What is your responsibility to your guests who have travelled to celebrate with you? Some guests may not afford travel and other expenses. Stating clear and concise financial responsibilities avoids making people resentful at having to schlep all the way down south to watch you get married. Couples may hold a brunch the day after the wedding for out-of-town guests without the expectation of entertaining them further.
- ❖ **Justice of the Peace:** You go to your local City Hall with your besties and tie the knot in private. And you share a celebratory meal at a cosy restaurant afterward (not a drive-through).
- ❖ **Backyard or Home:** You can organize your own pop-up outdoor home wedding with tents, chairs, and decorations, inviting a rabbi, priest, minister, or your friend who is credentialed to marry you, and away you go!

These are only a few examples of unconventional options for getting hitched. Your imagination only limits you—let it run wild to create your memorable wedding!

The Honeymoon

This one has a double meaning, but we are not only talking about the gooey-eyed honeymoon phase that starts with dating (although you may still experience that if you are tying the knot within weeks of first meeting). The honeymoon period is the time immediately following your wedding. Often reserved for a trip to celebrate your nuptials, this can involve spending your wedding weekend at a hotel or taking a multiple-week vacation. This joyful time reminds you of the beginning of your relationship, except your partner is still leaving the cap off the toothpaste!

> **REFLECTION**
>
> 1. Do you dream of a small or large wedding?
> 2. Can you afford to have the wedding of your dreams, and who will pay for it?
> 3. Do you feel obliged to have a culturally specific or traditional wedding?
> 4. Would you consider a non-traditional wedding?
> 5. How would you like to celebrate your honeymoon?

The Aftermath

The wedding was so beautiful that even the cake was in tiers! The wedding is over, the gifts unwrapped, and the guests have all departed, wishing you well (at least to your face). Now you can move forward as a married couple and return to your life and work. Planning and holding a wedding are exhilarating, but the aftermath can be anti-climatic as you face the wedding bills (not bells), settle in together, and sit on a cold porcelain bowl because your partner left the seat up. Again.

Cohabiting Instead of Marrying

You've been dating for a while, paying two rents, and feel it's time to take your relationship to the next level, but not marry. Perhaps you stayed the night and never left, or he said: "We're paying two rents; why not move in together?" So, you decide to share a home and merge your lives and take the leap to shack up. Also called common-law or de facto union, you choose to cohabit instead of legally marry.

Your friends have helped you move, leaving you with a bazillion boxes to unpack. (*Now, where did I pack my vibrator?*) They've polished off the pizza and beer. You arrange your belongings and discuss where to put the ceramic frog statue his aunt gifted you.

Some people feel the only genuine commitment is marriage; they view cohabiting as a lack of commitment. Traditionally, people considered it sinful to live together without a legal or church-sanctioned marriage covenant. Living together is only problematic when it goes against your values or if you cannot protect yourself with a cohabitation agreement. Why choose to cohabitate if you would instead marry? You must be able to discuss and answer this question with your partner before moving one stick of furniture into the same space.

The Cohabitation Agreement

You move in together. And you believe you are protected because you share a home and pay the bills jointly. The government taxing you as de facto spouses compounds this false sense of security. If you don't have a will, the government won't consider you a spouse, so you won't get spousal support, alimony, or pension benefits if you separate or die.

Regulations regarding common-law unions vary from province, state, and country, so you must do your research and due diligence. The cohabitation agreement is a legal contract that you make with a lawyer to outline what happens if your relationship ends. This document is protection instead of a legal marriage. Once you agree to be a common-law couple, you must have a cohabitation agreement, especially when you bring children into your union. Define verbally and on paper what you are giving up and receiving. You can have a notary or lawyer prepare a document that specifies what will happen in case of a breakup or death, especially if you share assets. However, a cohabitation agreement does not replace a legal will. Inform yourself to avoid pitfalls (See Money and Spending in Chapter 10).

Labels Matter

How do you refer to the person with whom you cohabit or are married? When referring to their common-law partner, people may prefer distinct labels, such as partner, boyfriend/girlfriend, or fiancé instead of spouse/husband/wife. Others avoid the label and refer to their partner by name or say 'My partner' or 'My significant other' when speaking with people. Married people may opt to call each other 'spouses' or 'partners' instead of the traditional 'husband/wife' combo. Precise labels may be important to you and your partner or may not matter, depending on your values. And there is always the beautiful label: 'My better half!'

It may not be appropriate to call our brother's partner his girlfriend or our common-law partner's father our father-in-law. Believing in marriage before living together doesn't excuse us from not referring to our brother's girlfriend as our "sister-in-law." Kelly had this very experience as she was introducing her brother's common-law partner to another family member and hesitated before saying: "And this is my sister-in-law." The misstep was awkward and made her brother's partner uncomfortable. It is always best to ask someone what they prefer before assuming how you think you should address them. P.S.: Married people do not appreciate being referred to as 'The-old-ball-and-chain'!

Discuss honestly and openly with your partner to decide which labels you are both comfortable with. For example, Kelly cohabited and had a child with her then-partner for over two decades, but she wanted to be married. It was difficult for her to refer to him when talking to unfamiliar people. When they referred to one another as spouses over the years, that didn't sit right with her, either. She felt fraudulent because she was going against her values, using a label that did not reflect their status and commitment. When they separated after twenty-four years, she started calling him 'my child's father,' (as opposed to 'my ex'), which reflects the reality and feels more comfortable to her now.

Laurie and her partner have been together for fourteen years (as of 2024). Though they did not have a legal marriage ceremony, she refers to him as her husband. They are equally happy with their commitment. Before moving in, she discussed being protected if a breakup or death occurs. They solidified their commitment by seeing a lawyer, making wills, and legalising all paperwork. They discussed how their 'What if' scenarios would reflect their legal wills—same office, same room with the legal team, so no secrets. Despite both partners trusting one another, legal documents must be created under professional advice to provide peace of mind should anything go horribly wrong.

REFLECTION

1. Does one of you want marriage while the other prefers to cohabit? (Is one of you settling?)
2. Are you moving in together intending to marry or to test the waters?
3. Are there valid reasons you're putting off marrying?
4. What level of support do you have from family and friends around your decision?
5. Does your family consider your partner an outsider because you are not legally married?

Reality Check

How things are:

How I would like things to be:

Red Flag(s):

Deal Breaker(s):

One action I can take:

Chapter 9

Work, Career, and Learning

I got a job at a paperless office, and everything was great until I used the bathroom!

Unless we are independently wealthy, we must work to live, and we start careers to create meaningful working lives. Continued learning is what we do along the way for personal and professional development. But let's face it: while we spend a significant part of our day working, it can be soul-sucking as we find ourselves mired in earning a living instead of living while we earn.

Work Versus Career

We work to make money to support ourselves. A career is how we derive meaning from our work. We may be a career homemaker or doctor who enjoys our contribution to our family and society. We can be judges, politicians, or artists earning a great living but still frustrated in our efforts and see no way to improve our career enjoyment. So, work and career are interchangeable and only sometimes lead to job satisfaction. Alongside the necessity of earning a living to support our family, there are various other factors that contribute to our overall enjoyment and the levels of stress we experience in our work life.

Entrepreneurship

Are you an entrepreneur whose business operates with no fixed or guaranteed income? Entrepreneurship can create snags in your relationship, especially if your partner has a nine-to-five job. Your partner may need to understand the challenges of being a business owner with the hours required to start up and maintain. If you have a team managing your business operations, you can achieve balance, but it means having to manage employees. For most entrepreneurs, their businesses are their babies. And we all know that a baby requires copious amounts of attention!

Your partner, who has a nine-to-five job, may need help to grasp why you, as an entrepreneur, answer your phone at all hours. Addressing expectations and boundaries is necessary to prevent chaos in emotions and finances. And if you work for your partner's business, it is imperative that you have a contractual agreement that protects you in the event of divorce or death. Kelly tutored a student in a Transition to Work program who had spent her career employed in her spouse's business. When the student divorced, she felt she needed to start all over again and return to studies, despite her rich transferable skills!

Communication remains key when one partner becomes—or is presently—an entrepreneur. Set your expectations with each other for how you will manage family life and business responsibilities, your expected level of involvement, and what will happen if your partner's business succeeds or fails.

> **REFLECTION**
>
> 1. If either of you are an entrepreneur, how much time does the business realistically consume?
> 2. If your partner approached you wanting to become a full-time entrepreneur, how would you react? Would you support your partner through the start-up of their business and vice versa?
> 3. How would you pay for your living expenses?
> 4. If you separate in the future, do you have legal rights to monies and copyrights?
> 5. If one partner hires the other, what provisions will you make for income and insurance (in case of divorce or death)?

Parental Leave

Ah yes, that magical time of diaper changing, midnight feedings, and puke! Regarding parental leave, do you have a plan for who will stay home with the baby? Traditional roles suggest mothers stay home. However, these conventions are slowly moving towards a more equalised trend, especially now that same-sex couples can raise children and provide an equally nurturing environment. Considerations for parental leave include:

- ❖ Deciding which parent takes time off when the baby is born, knowing which partner is in a better financial position to take parental leave (if only one person can).
- ❖ Calculating how much income you may lose while on parental leave (preferably before you create the baby).
- ❖ Meeting your financial obligations with a (temporarily) lower family income.

Employment and government subsidies, such as paid parental leave, family allowance payouts, and childcare benefits, may play a role in your decision about who takes how much time off with the new baby. These subsidies help ease the financial burden of taking time off work and may influence how parental leave is distributed between partners. Consider these factors in your calculations before embarking on *And Baby Makes Three*.

Taking a Sabbatical

Why did the teacher take a sabbatical? Because she needed a break from all the *class*-ic stress! A sabbatical, sometimes called a 'sabbatical leave' or a 'sabbatical year,' is an extended break from work or study. It's a period where employees or students can engage in other activities for personal growth or career development. Sabbatical lengths differ depending on individual needs and policies. Some sabbaticals may last several months, while others may be as long as a year or more. Professionals, academics, and researchers take sabbaticals to pursue other projects. Sabbaticals can also allow people to recharge and gain new perspectives, which can benefit their work or studies when they return.

Sabbaticals are traditionally associated with institutions of higher learning, and they come with the opportunity for prestige as they piggyback on research funded by your employer. Or there may be a payback scheme whereby your employer pays a percentage of your salary while you are off or work half-time, so long as you return and commit to X number of years of employment. If that is your case, wonderful! Otherwise, you must save enough to afford that much-desired sabbatical year off work. If you are contemplating a sabbatical, ask your employer's Human Resources Department what programs exist to realise your dream. And don't forget to speak with your partner! You are not asking for permission, but you both must be aware (and in agreement), because a sabbatical can affect your relationship.

Continuing Education

Learning is lifelong and life-wide—from the cradle to the grave! You may have always dreamed of getting a degree or advancing your career through continuous learning. Or it may be time to do those higher-level studies because you have hit a glass ceiling in your job. There are myriad considerations involving energy, time, finances, and stress when you decide to continue your studies.

During an orientation for the Master of Business Administration studies, a professor mentioned that half of married students may divorce during the two-year program, a statistic reported by Gardiner in the *Financial Times* (2004). Juggling family and education can lead to stress and relationship problems for couples with children. It is realistic to expect that a program of study adds pressure to your relationship. It takes time away from your couple and family, and although it may be for a fixed period, while you are studying, it may feel like forever. Know there will be trade-offs. You are not home evenings as you attend classes, and you must miss your child's basketball match to study for an exam. These are the trade-offs of returning to school for your betterment, which can yield a more lucrative career with a higher salary. It depends on how willing you are to sacrifice to achieve your goals.

> **REFLECTION**
>
> 1. Do you desire to continue your education, and would you have your partner's support (financial and moral)?
> 2. Would you return to school part time or full time?
> 3. Would you feel resentful of the missed opportunity if you did not continue your education?

Life Balance and Blend

We juggle work, family, social life, and personal time. Everyone is striving to attain a work-life balance. Having balance means we manage our time to be available for all the parts of our lives, and no one part dominates. It's how we can feel whole and in control of the moving pieces that overwhelm us. Sometimes, we need to consider it a work-life blend because we may need to blend our diverse priorities, as they will only sometimes balance.

Life blend means integrating various aspects of your life in a balanced and harmonious way. This may involve managing work and personal life, being social and pursuing hobbies, and taking care of yourself. Achieving *life blend* can help you feel more fulfilled because it reduces stress and burnout. It can also help you build stronger relationships and connections with others and improve your overall well-being.

Children, especially when they are young, demand a massive amount of our time. We often hear how parents put their children first. While this is a selfless thought, putting *ourselves* first ensures we replenish energy stores to care for our children properly. If we give until it hurts, we risk playing the martyr. Those precious mini-mes will take everything they can, so we must establish well-defined boundaries to have a balanced relationship with our children.

As life becomes more hectic, our couple often takes a significant hit. We may feel like ships passing in the night. Spending time as a couple taking part in activities will nurture a healthy relationship. Your couple's intimacy can suffer if you do not consciously try to connect.

One of you works less than the other, who is constantly working. This imbalance can lead to problems in the relationship, such as financial burdens and frustration for the partner with more free time and potential resentment by the partner working to provide. And this can affect closeness.

The choice to not work often differs for the sexes. Women are biological child-bearers, and this fundamental role typically (and evolutionally) casts females as the best nurturers of children (See Stereotypes in Chapter 11). While, as a couple, you may opt for the woman to stay home and care for the children, commonly, we see stay-at-home parent men who assume the caring and nurturing roles. Couples may decide that the higher earner will provide for the family while the other manages home and children.

Discuss with each other before deciding whether one partner takes a hiatus from working. For example, if one of you loses their job and does not want to return to work or is not recovering easily yet can work, this can strain the relationship (See Job Loss in Chapter 15). Be mindful that job loss can affect your life balance and blend because it disrupts your financial stability, daily routine, social connections, and emotional well-being.

Each partner's idea of a life blend is shaped by their values, priorities, and circumstances. It is crucial to find a balance that brings happiness and fulfillment in your couple and family life. Your career aspirations, financial stability, and personal responsibilities also influence the balance you strive for. Life transitions are inevitable, so you must stay flexible and adaptable. Discuss with your partner how these changes will affect your home and work responsibilities. Regularly revisit, reassess, and realign your priorities to ensure that your chosen life balance remains fulfilling for both partners.

REFLECTION

1. Are you working full time, part time, or not at all?
2. Do you and your partner make time for activities as a couple?
3. If one of you will be a stay-at-home parent, how will it affect your finances?
4. What decisions will you make to foster life balance in your relationship?
5. If you had an accident and could not work, how would this affect you economically?

Reality Check

How things are:

How I would like things to be:

Red Flag(s):

Deal Breaker(s):

One action I can take:

Chapter 10

Money and Spending

Be generous with your heart and wise with your money.

Money and spending are enormous topics for most couples that they deserve an entire chapter. Every person has a unique view of money and how to spend, save, invest, and allocate it. According to Ramit Sethi in *How to Get Rich* (2023), we all come with our money psychology. Holding different views on money is a significant issue. Many couples find it challenging to overcome the strain of finances. Working together towards an end goal is easier when you have similar financial goals.

Managing Money as a Couple

It takes finesse and a dose of realism to manage your money together. For example, the wife makes sixty thousand a year, and the husband makes thirty thousand. Since the wife earns more, she takes on more household expenses than her partner. Decide what works for you both—no need to keep up with the Joneses here. As a couple, you can create rules that reflect your values.

On one end of the spectrum, there is a partner who is overly generous with resources, sometimes to a fault. On the other end, there is a partner who is very protective of their money and reluctant to spend it. If your partner is a spendthrift, they may over-commit resources that run low and cause a financial burden.

Conversely, if you notice your partner is consistently cheap and refuses to help others despite having the means, this is a huge red flag! This type of person cannot acknowledge the value of others and may look for someone to help share their rent instead of their life. Knowing your partner's money values is vital before merging your finances.

Saving and Investing

Managing your money involves using a strategy for living on what you need and saving the rest for contingencies and your future. Couples may opt to live on one salary and save the other. Investing is a complex endeavour and involves planning for a rainy day, your future, and your retirement. Planned savings like tax-free accounts, and retirement and educational funds are critical discussion points as you decide how to allot, save, and grow your money together. It's always best to engage the services of a financial planner who can help you decide how much and where to invest. Start as young as possible with whatever you can afford.

> ### REFLECTION
>
> 1. Are you both working, and, if so, how do you manage your expenses?
> 2. Does one of you pay the mortgage, and the other pays all the amenities?
> 3. Do you use one income to pay all the bills and stash the other for all other purchases?
> 4. Is there a vast difference between your incomes that you have taken a percentage of income and put it towards living expenses?
> 5. What are both of your values regarding generosity and frugality?

> ### EXERCISE: Couple Finances
>
> How will you manage your finances as a couple? Check any that apply:
>
> - ☐ Separately
> - ☐ Bank one salary and live on the other
> - ☐ Based on the percentage earned
> - ☐ Another formula (Which one?)

Separate as to Property

What you enter the relationship with is yours, and anything you inherit is yours. What you earn throughout your relationship is also yours, notwithstanding family patrimony. When one person enters a marriage with a significant amount of wealth, having a prenuptial agreement can protect that wealth in case of a breakup. Become familiar with your province's or state's laws and the parameters of any cohabitation or prenuptial contracts you sign.

The Laws of Entitlement

Become informed about common-law unions because the laws governing these in case of a break-up are clear. Depending on your location, you may not have any entitlements when your de facto relationship ends. When she ended her long-term common-law relationship, friends told Kelly she should get a settlement. But provincial law stated that she was not eligible to claim anything because she did not have a cohabitation agreement.

Remember, when you decide to live with each other, the practicalities must precede your feelings. And cohabitating becomes more complex when you bring children into the mix! Avoid guesswork and heartache by consulting a lawyer for a cohabitation agreement. You might say: "But that is why we are living together; we don't want all that legal wrangling." It may surprise you to learn you have no legal right to the home, despite financially contributing to it through the years.

To Rent or Own

Nowadays, it's increasingly challenging for young couples to afford real estate—even if both partners work full-time. With the rising cost of construction materials, housing, and interest rates, individuals and even couples find buying a home out of reach. Rents have skyrocketed because of rising costs of building materials and services property owners must pay. We must not take affordable housing for granted. The issue becomes how to save to buy a home while paying a hefty rent. We must sacrifice to own a home and be willing to live on less.

Joint or Separate Accounts

A joint bank account for shared household expenses, such as rent or mortgage, insurance, utilities, and food, is practical. However, ideally, you also both have your own bank accounts. Separate banking maintains your financial autonomy—keeping a credit score that can serve you in the future if you ever apply for a loan in your name only.

Separate bank accounts also allow for individual financial goals and personal spending. It enables each partner to budget, save, and spend money according to their individual priorities and preferences. Having your own bank accounts promotes transparency and accountability in managing personal finances. Each of you can track your expenses and understand your financial situation. This can help prevent conflicts or misunderstandings regarding money matters within your shared household.

Having separate accounts can provide a sense of independence and security. It ensures each partner has access to their own funds in case of emergencies or unforeseen circumstances. It also allows for personal financial growth and the freedom to make financial decisions without relying solely on the joint account.

While a joint bank account for shared household expenses is practical and convenient, maintaining separate bank accounts is also essential for preserving financial autonomy, building individual credit scores, and achieving personal financial goals. It creates that middle ground, allowing for shared responsibilities while also promoting individual financial independence within the household.

One Car or Two

Owning and operating a car can cost approximately nine thousand (Canadian) dollars a year. And if you own a luxury car or SUV, this amount climbs. Multiply that by two, and an enormous chunk of your income pours into your transportation. Two cars mean double maintenance, insurance, and gas. Ideally, you can share a car. It all depends on the accessibility of public transport where you live and your commuting needs. Remote working, ever more popular since the Pandemic, cuts transportation costs.

The Cost of Children

Experts estimate that raising a child to age eighteen costs over two hundred thousand dollars. Multiply that by the number of children you would like to have. Also, consider the costs of college and university and the possibility that you may need to support them again if they boomerang home.

Investment Properties

You may envision buying a vacation property on a lake or in the countryside for a weekend and holiday getaway. Or you are putting money aside to buy an investment property or live in a multi-unit home to defray the costs of your mortgage. (This is how you might afford a mortgage.) Living in a multiplex means sharing your house, dealing with noise, maintenance, and rent.

REFLECTION

1. How are you and your partner compatible with finances?
2. How do you envision working toward common financial goals as a couple?
3. If you are not working towards shared financial goals, what will you need to feel financially secure moving forward?
4. If you are not working towards shared financial goals, what will make you feel financially secure moving forward?
5. What happens if one of you changes your goals?

Reality Check

How things are:

How I would like things to be:

Red Flag(s):

Deal Breaker(s):

One action I can take:

Chapter 11

Sharing the Load

I'll share the load, but you're on your own if it gets too heavy!

It takes time and energy to maintain our physical environment—from daily cleaning to home repairs and yard work; there is always something to do around the house to keep a clean, organised, safe space to live joyfully.

Stereotypes

We have ingrained assumed beliefs about who does what chores within a relationship. These stereotypes are generalizations and do not apply to every couple or individual. People have different preferences, beliefs, and circumstances that shape their approach to sharing responsibilities.

As children, the beliefs we learn about traditional roles shape us. Often, these beliefs are westernised (and colonised) they stem from deeply entrenched family values depicting inculcated stereotypes. For example, the man as breadwinner and woman as homemaker stereotypes suggest men are more career-oriented and primarily focus on providing financial support and women are more naturally inclined to care for children and the home. Today's reality requires two incomes to support a household and family, so both partners must assume the roles of provider and equally manage the home. For instance, we see women in non-traditional occupations (engineering, car mechanics) and stay-at-home dads—proof that these archaic roles are changing!

Categories of Household Chores

We constantly juggle family responsibilities with work around the home. There is no shortage of home maintenance to do based on a running list. Then there is the normal wear and tear that causes items to break and need replacement or repair, along with the many emergency situations that arise. Below are the broad categories of load to consider regarding sharing tasks.

Housework

We must do daily chores like dishes, laundry, vacuuming, and dusting to maintain a clean and comfortable environment. We must also plan for seasonal cleaning, such as spring cleaning, which involves a deeper cleaning of our home. While we may feel time-crunched, one way to approach housework is to clean as you go. This way, we do not face the overwhelming task of tackling an entire cleaning routine that takes hours to execute and typically feels punishing. Learn to pick up a room by taking items with it as you leave that room. For example, you're watching a movie with your honey. As the credits roll and your eyes feel heavy, pick up that popcorn bowl and empty drink glass to deposit into the kitchen sink on your way to bed. If you do this by putting items back in their rightful spots, the house stays cleaner and easier to maintain. Statistics show that "…women do 50% more unpaid housework than men…" (Labbé, 2022).

Yard Work

Taking care of our yard, including mowing the lawn, gardening, and clearing debris, helps us avoid citations and keeps it tidy so we can enjoy the added outdoor space—especially when the weather is beautiful, and we can eat on our patio. Adopt a goat instead of an iguana! The same holds true about yard work as housework. Avoid letting your yard go because an overgrown lawn and garden becomes more overwhelming to clear.

Food Shopping and Preparation

Purchasing groceries, meal planning, and cooking can be a huge time drain if you don't like preparing food. For people who could live in the kitchen, cooking is a creative outlet, and they make beautiful meals with love! Others prefer buying pre-made meals or engaging a delivery service that curates a menu for you to follow. Since healthy eating is vital, cooking is a life skill. Consider planning a fun experience by taking a cooking class with your partner.

Car Maintenance

What happens when Froggie's car breaks down? It gets *toad*! Keeping your car(s) in good running order, such as regular oil changes, servicing, and washing, requires diligence and time. Is one of you a tinkerer who likes to work under the hood? If so, you may opt to do your own car mechanics, tire, and oil changes! This is extremely economical if you have the time for it.

Childcare

One of the most exciting decisions is to have children, but it entails additional responsibilities and challenges. One of the most important decisions we will make is how to manage childcare. Caring for your children involves supervision, maintaining daily routines, education, and homework, as well as being available to bond. You must plan for which parent stays home on sick days and who takes the child to doctor and dentist appointments. If your child has a chronic illness or debilitating condition, the burdens on your couple and the care are even more significant.

Equal partnership means sharing the load, with both parents actively taking part in all aspects of childcare. Open communication is key regarding expectations, concerns, and any issues that arise. Be flexible and adaptable when facing changing circumstances. And of course, have a support system, such as family, friends, and paid caregivers, for those times when you need additional help. Commit to working together to provide the best possible care and upbringing for your child to ensure a loving and nurturing environment where they can thrive.

Home Maintenance and Renovation

When renting an apartment, you may need to do small things, but overall, your maintenance and renovations fall to the owner. If you own your home, house maintenance, repairs, and renovations are constant.

Take initiative in dealing with minor issues, so they don't become significant repairs, resulting in costly renovations. A leak left unchecked can become water damage that may require replacing entire walls and tiles. As a couple, you must decide who will do these repairs. If one of you is handy, you can save mega dollars, provided the quality of the work is equivalent to that of a pro. Otherwise, be prepared to enlist the services of a builder, which requires research (Always ask for three quotes) and costs more money.

Home Organisation

According to Laurie Johnson in *Be the Ringmaster of Your Circus: Daredevil Tricks for Organizing your Life*, "When you feel in control of all the little things in your life—it helps calm you mentally." (2012, p. 4). To keep your home a peaceful and navigable environment, it's important to create systems for filing, tidying, purging, and reorganising. Every person has a way of organising (or NOT). Do a keyword search using "decluttering" and "home organising." The point is to maintain consistency. We do those tasks we like and procrastinate doing what we don't like. Stay mindful that we all organize differently and are comfortable with our unique approaches to maintaining order.

In certain countries, organising takes on a seasonal shift from summer to winter and vice versa. This includes clothes, tools, grills, patio furniture, shelters, plants, decorations, and even tires (For example, in Quebec, winter tires must be installed by December 1st).

Material things occupy space and real estate, often occupying mental real estate that bogs us down. External clutter and disorganisation may reflect an internal struggle. A red flag when dating is if your partner hangs onto everything, refusing to purge unused or old items. If you set up a house with someone who hoards possessions, you risk feeling overwhelmed by stuff that invades your living space, making the home unmanageable and hazardous. Often, hoarding behaviour requires professional intervention. You may require the help of a home organiser, coach, or psychologist who specializes in hoarding.

As your family expands, you'll gather possessions that will naturally become outdated and useless. Create a schedule of regular clean-up and reorganising with the family. Go through toys, electronics, clothes, and any other items that you haven't used in a while. The golden rule in this is if you haven't used it in a year, then out it goes! And don't forget to donate items that can be repurposed. If you have beautiful toys, games, or clothes that could help someone else, why not pass along the joy?

> **REFLECTION**
>
> Reflect on the following when purging an item:
>
> ❖ What feelings are attached to the item?
> ❖ Have I used this in the past year?
> ❖ Do I need this to be happy?
> ❖ Would I repurchase this item again (right now)?

Organising can feel overwhelming if you are looking around and don't know where to begin. You may not start at all. Using the above questions, apply the two-minute rule to purge your space and home. Break down tasks that seem overwhelming into smaller tasks. For example, if you feel cleaning your garage would take four hours, break it up into one-hour sessions over four days. Do not overthink it, and rather, prioritise it—do it first thing—and as Brian Tracy (2017) says: "Eat that frog!"

> **EXERCISE A: Remove Ten Items**
>
> Starting with one room in your home, remove ten items. Choose easy items. It could be a piece of junk mail or something you no longer use or want. Do not overthink this. Merely go through and subtract ten items you no longer use, need, or love. Do this every day or whenever you have a free moment. Notice how your space breathes.

Social Organisation

Couples and families engage in activities and social outings, from kids' playdates to celebrations. Who organises these? Arranging playdates, organising events and dinners, and bringing the family together for special traditions and celebrations is a massive load of work! If you are the person tasked with playing host, it is unlikely you can fully enjoy the festivities during the gathering. This is the reason potlucks are lucky!

Talk with your partner in advance concerning hosting responsibilities. Establish roles and responsibilities such as:

- Shopping for favours, gifts, and food
- Preparing the home (decorating and cleaning, setting the table)
- Cooking the meal
- Welcoming and serving guests
- Cleaning up post-event

We may fall into the trap of overdoing it and feeling frustrated, especially when hosting dinners, family holiday celebrations, and vacation planning. Part of this comes from thinking our way is the only or best way. Remember, we are all different and have lots going on in our heads, so we must communicate clearly what we expect and what tasks we will take on.

Even if you hold the event elsewhere, it still requires preparation. Decide who will prepare the dish, buy the gift, pack the car, and drive to the event. If you do not ask for help, you risk arriving at the event already tired and irritable, and resenting your partner for not doing enough. Discuss responsibilities beforehand, rather than taking the entire job on and then playing the martyr when you feel exhausted from doing all the work. Learn to delegate—giving others the opportunity to step up so you do not burn out taking on the entire load. Nobody appreciates martyrs and their guilt trips.

Reminding yourself how you are making cherished memories can help you stay focused on what is most important. Gatherings and celebrations fill the air with love, so what's a few pots and pans to clean afterwards? Alternatively, you can ask your guests to prolong the joy of their stay by helping to clear away the dishes. Personally, we've had some great conversations over clean-up!

Family Caregiving

There may come a day when you must care for a parent or family member. It could be your aging parents, a sibling with mental or physical health issues, your child, or your partner's family. Caregiving includes assisting with personal care, shopping, handling finances, and promoting social engagement. It involves the executive functions we typically do for ourselves and may need to do for a family member who is physically or mentally inept. Discuss caregiving as it pertains to yourself and your partner. Everyone ages, and accidents happen—have a plan for contingencies (See more in Chapter 15).

Young Carers

The plight of young carers is another topic that is rarely considered and deserves to be highlighted. Children under twenty-five who care for sick or disabled family members are an underserved, forgotten group. Family circumstances where one or both parents become infirm also thrust the child into the role of a caregiver. The Young Caregivers Association (online, n.d.) defines young caregivers as those who care for a family member with chronic illness, disability, mental health problems, substance misuse, or socioeconomic difficulties.

The care involves medical help, personal grooming, sibling care, financial aid, and emotional support. Practical care includes household chores such as doing laundry, washing dishes, and making meals and school lunches. Physical care includes giving medicine, assisting with movement, bathing, grooming, and translating languages. Emotional care involves listening, giving advice, worrying, and helping a family member through their day.

We see this in situations involving an addicted parent. Also, the standard is when a parent experiences a significant illness or accident. Kelly was a young carer because her mother had a chronic life-altering disease that made her weak and dependent and involved frequent hospital stays. Although they had a babysitter, the oldest, Kelly took on cooking and light housework and cared for their mother. This burdened her as a child, forcing her to grow up quickly. Dealing with a sick parent can rob a child of their childhood, creating a pattern of dysfunction that can affect them for life.

There are many organisations available for carers. Look for local groups, charities, and other types of support so you can get the respite care you need.

> **REFLECTION**
>
> If you or your partner were to become ill:
>
> 1. What provisions would you want to implement for your minor children?
> 2. Do you have a family member or friend to whom you would entrust the care of your child if you cannot care for yourself and your child?

Negotiating Roles

Despite the advancements of the twenty-first century and the huge milestones made in society, there are remnants of those archaic ideals. The burden of household chores, home management, and caregiving responsibilities still falls disproportionately to women, who are expected to work full time while contributing financially to the household.

Couples must have honest discussions about their strengths, preferences, and availability. Negotiate and assign tasks based on these factors, aiming for a mutually agreed-upon distribution of labour. The focus of this approach is on teamwork, flexibility, and acknowledging the individual strengths of both partners.

Remember that stereotypes alone should not dictate how a couple divides labour. Couples must consider their circumstances, preferences, and values when deciding who will take on which responsibilities. The question becomes: *How will you share the load with your partner?*

Splitting Chores

By dividing household tasks equally or according to personal preferences and strengths, couples strive to maintain a harmonious balance in their domestic responsibilities. This approach ensures that the workload is distributed fairly, taking into consideration factors such as availability, skills, and individual preferences. Whether it's taking turns in cooking, cleaning, doing laundry, or any other chores, this method aims to create a system where both partners contribute equally and efficiently to the smooth running of their household.

> **EXERCISE B: Household Task Inventory**
>
> Create an inventory of all household tasks:
>
> 1. Are there specific tasks you would like to do? Circle those items using a coloured pen or highlighter.
> 2. Are there specific tasks that your partner would like to do? Circle these in another colour.
> 3. What is leftover, and how will you choose who does what? If cleaning the bathroom every week is not your cup of tea, you can always share this task so that you only need to do it every two weeks.
> 4. Which task may be easier for one partner? If one of you cannot lift heavy things, your partner may be strong and easily take on the heavier chores. You may put yourself in charge of preparing meals more often than your partner if you possess better kitchen skills.

If a paper inventory list feels boring and overwhelming, install a fun erasable 'Honey-Do' board in the high-traffic area of your home. Then show specific tasks chosen by family members and write it down. This visual reminder keeps jobs up to date and everyone accountable and hopefully reduces the need to nag. Add avatars or visuals to your 'honey-do' boards. Making chores fun is the motivation to get them done!

Outsourcing

During the process of negotiating roles, couples may opt to outsource specific tasks by hiring professionals or using services—a fairer arrangement. This can include hiring a cleaner or gardener or using delivery services for groceries or meals. By outsourcing these tasks, couples can free up valuable time they can spend on their careers, hobbies, or simply enjoying quality time together. For example, hiring a cleaner relieves couples of the stress and burden of their cleaning chores. Using delivery services for groceries or meals saves time on grocery shopping and meal preparation. Having their groceries or meals conveniently delivered to their doorstep also reduces the mental load associated with planning and cooking meals.

Outsourcing also contributes to a healthier work-life balance for couples. By delegating these responsibilities to professionals or services, couples can prioritise their physical and mental well-being, allowing them to focus on what truly matters, whether it's advancing their careers, nurturing their relationship, or simply enjoying life's pleasures.

Reality Check

How things are:

How I would like things to be:

Red Flag(s):

Deal Breaker(s):

One action I can take:

Chapter 12

Expanding Your Family

And a pet makes three! Go forth and have a litter! (How soon can the nanny or dog sitter start?)

So, as a couple, you adopt a pet before deciding to have children. Adopting a fur-baby will test your relationship because a pet requires commitment and long-term care. Who walks the dog at six a.m. or who feeds the iguana live flies? Those daily routines and responsibilities reveal what your partner is made of. Sometimes it is so heartwarming to see your partner snuggled up with the cat (or iguana) that you decide he/she would be an amazing parent.

But not so fast....

Pets: I don't wanna your iguana!

He wants a dog, and you are a cat person. Or one of you has allergies to dogs or cats. Your partner owns an exotic pet, and you feel an iguana belongs on a rock in sunny Jamaica. Or you are terrified of snakes, and your partner owns a python (Deal breaker). Suddenly, the pot-bellied pig no longer fits in your downtown four-and-half apartment.

Animals are cute and cuddly when tiny, but they grow into more enormous dependent responsibilities that are not so cute. It's not like a pet can care for itself (aside from cats grooming themselves). Dogs can live ten to fifteen years, with some living to eighteen. Cats can live thirteen to seventeen years and even into their twenties. The record is thirty-eight years for a cat named Creme Puff! And all cats come with their personalities, quirks, behaviours, and behavioural issues.

If your partner already has a pet (cat, dog, or frog), consider that the pet may not take to you or vice versa. Some people believe a pet can sense if your partner is a good person. Perhaps the pet is being protective, or it perceives your new flame as a threat. Your animal may react out of fear or anxiety as they pick up on your emotions, or they may have a natural response to someone unknown to them. Also, if your pet has had a negative experience with a particular person or certain type of individual, they may react differently when encountering someone similar. It's best to pay attention to your pet's behaviour and your partner's actions and notice observable cues and avoid jumping to conclusions based solely on your pet's reaction.

We learn a lot about our partner by how they interact with animals. Watching our beloved care for something besides themselves is telling. Helen Anne Travis (PetMD online, 2017) explains how pets teach us about love and bonding—all important traits to notice in a romantic partner. Another vital thing to watch for in partners is the fickleness of giving up a beloved pet for a partner. Once you have a pet, it's a lifelong commitment and they become like your child. Your partner's willingness to part with something they cherish may suggest that you are also replaceable.

Are you committed to your pet for the long haul? People abandon their pets every year when they move houses because property owners stipulate no pets in their leases. At other times, when a pet no longer feels convenient, people re-home their beloved companions. Consider the Easter cuddly bunnies and cute chicks that grow into feces-producing rabbits and chickens. The novelty wears off, and the poor animal is homeless. Consider dog-sitting for a friend for the weekend to gauge how your home would feel with the added responsibility of a pet. Sometimes that's all it takes to realise you are ready or that you don't want the added work of caring for a completely dependent animal.

If you decide to get a puppy together, know that your pet will disrupt your life. Your pet is acclimating to your home and routine and vital pet care, such as vet visits, play and walk time, and feeding and caring tasks, will consume you. Discuss and clarify responsibilities with your partner as you consider who will:

- Walk the dog
- Play/interact with the pet
- Change the cat litter, clean the fish tank or hamster cage/backyard
- Feed the pet
- Book and pay for veterinary care
- Care for your pet when you are out of town
- Polish Froggie's crown

Consider the costs associated with pet ownership. According to the Ontario Veterinary Medical Association (online, n.d.), the average cost of owning a dog in Canada in 2021 was $3,724 annually. The American Society for the Prevention of Cruelty to Animals (ASPCA) pegs the cost of cat or dog ownership at $700 to $1000 and more per year (online, n.d.), which rises when your pet has a health issue. If you plan to own an exotic animal or multiple pets, multiply your costs. Contemplate long-term pet ownership, such as lifespan and needs, before taking the plunge, and save yourself and the animal the heartache.

> **EXERCISE A: Pet Ownership**
>
> 1. What are your thoughts about owning a pet?
> 2. Regarding caring for pets, what are your most significant disagreements?
> 3. Does your partner embrace any existing pet(s) you bring into your living arrangement?
> 4. If your relationship ends, who will get custody of the pet?
> 5. Have either of you noted this in your prenup or cohabitation agreement?

Deciding to have Children

Okay, so you've navigated the responsibilities of owning a pet, and you're ready to add another bundle of joy! But before deciding on expanding on your family in the biggest way possible, get clear with your spouse (or partner) about your motivation for wanting children.

> **REFLECTION**
>
> Check all that apply:
> - ☐ I want a mini-me.
> - ☐ I want a mini-you.
> - ☐ I want someone to love me unconditionally.
> - ☐ My parents are begging to be grandparents.
> - ☐ I have *so* much to give a child.
> - ☐ We want to raise a family together.
> - ☐ I must continue the family name.
> - ☐ I want someone who can care for me in my old age.
> - ☐ What? Do you mean I can't give the child back?
> - ☐ I do not want children (They are mind-boggling, time-sucking, fridge-emptying parasites)!

In the honeymoon phase, people experience utter euphoria, so the thought of having found a brilliant match might be a blind spot. You may never have wanted kids, but because of this euphoria, you talk yourself into wanting a baseball team of children to please your partner. Once the honeymoon phase ends, you decide there is no way in hell you want to give birth to anything.

Babies, children, and teenagers are a tremendous responsibility, and require extraordinary amounts of time and energy. These adorable, helpless beings need your care twenty-four/seven until they reach legal age. And even then, sometimes your legal-age children need your emotional and financial support. Your adult children may stay longer or boomerang back after leaving the nest (See Boomerangers later in this chapter).

As they mature, adolescent children want all the privileges of adulthood, yet they still depend on you for their lifestyle and well-being. They live under your roof and often expect to be in charge. Establish clear limits with your children as they grow into adulthood. It's important you maintain your status as the head of your household, and not accept any sort of abusive behaviour from your child.

Parents often want to make it comfortable for their children. Every parent wants to pamper and spoil their child, but we must be mindful of going overboard. Kelly knows a couple who decided to 'de-feather the nest,' which involved not remodelling the family playroom with modern furniture and electronics. The couple wanted to avoid making it too comfortable for their adult children and instead encouraged them to take wing and leave.

Children can bring so much joy into your life! Raising a child to adulthood is time-consuming and costly. The values you instil will go a long way towards ensuring you grow a happy, adjusted child who matures into a productive adult who can take care of themselves. This is what we all hope for in our children.

REFLECTION

Review the checklist above and answer the following questions:

1. Do you like children (enough to have them)?
2. Why do you want to have children?
3. When is your milestone to start a family, and how many children do you want?
4. What type of parent do you think you would be?
5. In which ways would your partner make a good co-parent with you?
6. What would you do if your partner agreed to have children at the beginning of your relationship and later changed their mind, or vice versa?
7. How do you foresee managing those hard ages and stages (the terrible twos and hormonal teenagers)?
8. How will you distribute the financial and childcare responsibilities?

EXERCISE B: Couple Motivations for Having Children

Discuss your list with your partner.

1. Do you see any similarities and differences in your motivations to have and raise children together?
2. If you have conflicting ideas, how do you want to proceed?

Delaying Having Children

Couples may be clear they want children, but choose to postpone having them until later for a variety of reasons:

- ❖ Establishing their careers
- ❖ Finishing studies
- ❖ Wanting more couple time
- ❖ Desiring time to travel and enjoy their twenties and early thirties
- ❖ Lack of readiness
- ❖ Financial reasons
- ❖ Indecisiveness about having children

There are risks involved in late maternal and paternal age when conceiving:

- ❖ Difficulty conceiving
- ❖ Cost of fertility treatments
- ❖ Children with disabilities
- ❖ Health issues caused by advanced maternal age
- ❖ Lack of energy/patience as an older parent
- ❖ There is a more significant generational gap between you and your child

Balancing personal time and couple time becomes difficult after having children. Be a couple first, and once you have forged a strong bond, go forth and copulate (and have fun doing it)!

The Importance of Planning

Sometimes a couple has an oopsie—they conceive a baby before they are ready. If you decide to delay having children, have a conversation about birth control so you are both on the same page (of the fairy tale picture book).

It is each partner's responsibility to use birth control if you do not want children. If you are ready to have sex, then you must be ready to take the precautions. Speaking with your doctor will help you both find an option that works for you and your couple. The 'withdrawal method' is only useful in your bank and doesn't work to avoid pregnancy. And the rhythm method is notorious for creating families—BIG ones!

Many methods of birth control exist to ensure no mistakes happen. Do your research with a trusted health professional (instead of online). Using condoms, medications, and surgical procedures are all possibilities—or you can always abstain completely! Your doctor will consider your health and family history to determine which method of birth control is safe for you.

Having a baby before either of you is ready takes precious time away from having special time as a couple and may cause resentment in the relationship. Laurie knows of one couple where the husband threw it in his wife's face every time they fought: "I only married you because you were pregnant!" He wouldn't acknowledge that he was equally responsible!

Birth control should always be a topic of discussion for couples in committed relationships. Consider each partner's personal preferences, health considerations, and future aspirations when deciding about the most suitable contraceptive method.

> **REFLECTION**
>
> 1. Are you ready to conceive a child?
> 2. Who will be the person to take birth control measures?
> 3. Have you consulted with your doctor?
> 4. What is your method of birth control?
> 5. What would you do if you accidentally got pregnant?

Genetics

We bring our gene pool to the procreation equation. Our unique genes determine our child's physical and biological characteristics, determining various traits including eye colour, hair type, height, and susceptibility to disease. Knowing our genetic and family medical backgrounds can help us identify the potential health risks for our children and take preventive actions to protect the well-being of future generations. When we are aware of our genetic predispositions, we can be proactive about any inherited diseases or conditions (certain types of cancer, heart disease, genetic disorders, or disabilities) that may be passed down to our children.

When we are aware of our genetics, we can work closely with our healthcare providers to create individualised healthcare plans, take preventative measures, and make informed reproductive decisions. Ultimately, having knowledge of our genetic and family medical backgrounds empowers us to take initiative in safeguarding the health of our children and secure a healthier and more promising future for them.

> **REFLECTION**
>
> 1. Are you aware of any genetic conditions that may reproduce in your offspring?
> 2. If yes, what conversation must you have with your partner?
> 3. How will this affect your joint decision to have children?

Reproductive Options

You've been together for X number of years and the questions from curious people start: "When is a little junior coming?" The query not only catches you off-guard, but it also makes you feel uncomfortable because you don't want to justify your reproductive choices to other people. You may decide to delay having children, have difficulty or cannot conceive, or simply choose not to bring a mini-me into the world. You owe no explanations to anyone and may need to craft a ready response that feels right. Try these:

- ✓ *My crystal ball is currently in the shop, but I'll let you know as soon as the stars align and the stork files its flight plan.*
- ✓ *We're still working on the perfect recipe. Apparently, baby-making is a bit more complicated than baking cookies. Once we get the ingredients just right, we'll let you know!*
- ✓ *We're amid a home improvement project. You know, creating the perfect nest for our future little DIY project. As soon as the construction dust settles, we'll get to work on the tiny details.*
- ✓ *Ah, the million-dollar question! We're currently waiting for our baby stocks to mature and our investment in sleep futures to pay off. As soon as our financial forecast looks promising, we'll consider expanding our portfolio.*

Or you can simply say: "That's an interesting question. Why do you ask?" And let your interrogator justify themselves to you.

A Woman's Choice

One assumption members of the fairy tale society may make is that to have the quintessential white picket fence life, a couple must procreate and have children. There are valid reasons a woman (or man) may choose not to have children. Alternatively, a woman who wants to have a child may opt to undergo fertility treatments and insemination without being in an intimate relationship. A woman may opt not to have children at all, choosing instead to focus on career or creative pursuits. There are so many combinations and permutations of family today that we must accept people's choices and mind our own damn business!

Laurie always adored children, and in her younger years wanted to have a child of her own. She never found a partner with whom she could envision a life, never mind adding a child to the equation. As the years passed, she met her Person Charming, but menopause had taken over her body, making any chances of having a baby impossible.

Kelly knows of someone who, in her thirties, her fertility window is closing, and she wants to experience motherhood and have a child despite not being in an intimate relationship. She is currently undergoing fertility treatments with the goal of achieving a pregnancy via donor sperm. It is truly remarkable and inspiring to see this young woman asserting her autonomy and taking control of her fertility and family planning decisions.

Fertility

Planning for and having a baby when you want is challenging, even when you are emotionally and financially ready. Picture the additional challenges of an unplanned pregnancy, miscarriage, abortion, or fertility struggles. These are all profound changes and choices that test you as a couple.

A woman's fertility diminishes with age. Women have a finite number of eggs, and these deteriorate as she gets older. So, as a woman gets older, she has fewer and lower quality eggs that can be fertilised. It has become a common trend among women to postpone having children until they have achieved certain milestones, such as feeling settled, completing their studies, travelling, living independently, or purely out of choice. Infertility is a huge issue for couples who expected "And baby makes three."

Kelly waited to conceive a second child and learned she had secondary infertility. She had consulted a fertility specialist and went through various procedures, including insemination, all to no avail. Her body refused to bear more children, and she suffered multiple miscarriages. Reality hit her the day she donated her maternity wear, baby clothing, furniture, and supplies from her first pregnancy. She remembers experiencing a profound loss as she watched her partner fill the car with all these items and drive away with her dream of having another child.

Miscarriage

Miscarriage is a massive trial for a couple. You pin all your hopes and dreams on the life you've conceived, only to learn it is not viable or healthy, or it spontaneously aborts from your body. Or worse, you carry the baby to term, and it is stillborn or dies of sudden infant death syndrome within the months following birth. You have all the pregnancy hormones coursing through your body, leading to emotional upheaval.

Your partner will also feel an intense loss. Losing a baby through miscarriage or sudden death is unfathomable, unexpected, and grievous. You must mourn the loss in whichever way you need to, in as much time as you need. Keeping communication open between yourselves is vital. And we highly recommend seeking professional help. The goal is not to forget, but to honour your child.

Abortion

Abortion is a choice, regardless of its legality in certain regions of the world. The ultimate decision about whether to proceed with her pregnancy, considering the risks of childbirth and the economics and duties of parenting, rests with the woman. People have distinct reasons for choosing abortion, such as pregnancy complications, rape, health issues, financial difficulties, and not being mature enough or emotionally ready to raise a child.

Surrogacy

Some couples choose surrogacy, where another woman (the surrogate) carries the couple's baby (comprising either their own eggs and sperm or a donor's eggs/sperm). This arrangement typically occurs when the intended parents cannot conceive or carry a pregnancy themselves. In surrogacy, the surrogate mother undergoes in vitro fertilisation (IVF) using either the intended parents' genetic material or donated eggs and sperm. Then, the surrogate mother carries the pregnancy to term and gives birth to a child who is genetically related to the intended parents. Surrogacy can be a complex and emotionally charged process, involving legal agreements, medical procedures, and ethical considerations.

Adoption

If they cannot conceive on their own, a couple may choose to adopt a child (which requires more effort than adopting a pet). Most people prefer babies, so there is a worldwide surplus of older children seeking their forever homes. The sad reality is these children end up in foster care and age out of the system, finding themselves alone at eighteen with no family support.

Adopting another person's child brings a myriad of responsibilities, including:

- ❖ Qualifying to adopt
- ❖ Waiting for a child (especially a baby because they are in high demand)
- ❖ International adoption, which is costly and involves many steps involving travel and legal wrangling between countries
- ❖ Dealing with the birth parent(s)
- ❖ Accepting there may be unknown genetic and health issues
- ❖ Disclosing their true origin to your adopted child
- ❖ Dealing with open adoption where the adopted child will know their birth parents
- ❖ Cultural differences and racial discrimination

An adopted child may sense something different regarding the circumstances of their birth. What to tell them, at what age, and how much technical detail they can manage are all issues with which you must deal.

Multiple Births

Fertility plunges after age twenty-seven in women, while men can procreate with viable sperm into their senior years. The jury is still out on the quality of the older man's sperm regarding health risks in the fetus. To deal with declining fertility, you may consider costly treatments such as hormones, insemination, or in-vitro fertilization. These treatments may cause multiple pregnancies, especially today as couples delay getting pregnant until their thirties and forties. You grow from zero to two or more children, and significant costs in time, energy, and financial resources grow exponentially. You have no clue how you might cope with multiple babies simultaneously and the higher risks associated with carrying them to term.

No matter what option you consider for starting and raising a family, there is a bounty of information from credible sources (in print and online). You must do your research because information is power. Get informed and have serious conversations to prepare for unexpected situations and minimize stress.

> **REFLECTION**
>
> 1. If you have difficulty conceiving, what options will you consider for having children?
> 2. Would you consider fertility treatments or adoption if you have problems conceiving a child? Are you aware of the emotional and financial costs and how these may affect your relationship?
> 3. Why would you adopt or use a surrogate over having children of your own?
> 4. Under what circumstances would you consider an abortion?
> 5. What are your feelings about the possibility of having multiples (Are there any twins/multiples in your family)?

Raising Children

Deciding to have children is MEGA life-changing because of the time, resources, and money required for their care. The fantasy of your own babe in arms sounds lovely until you miss sleep at two in the morning and find a chunk of your disposable income going into disposable diapers!

Another critical consideration is who will be your child's primary caregiver—initially and then when both spouses return to work full time. With new laws granting parental leave to either parent, couples may opt to split the early caregiving. Discuss who should stay home, when, and how long before you decide to get pregnant. Winging it is one option, and while doable, it will be challenging with the unexpected realities of life. If you can bring a child into the world together, you can also decide on the parameters of its care.

It can be challenging for a parent, especially a mother, to leave her child with someone else while she goes to work (or school). Child development experts say that young children experience separation anxiety, which is a normal part of their growth. It usually starts around six to seven months and reaches its peak between fourteen and eighteen months. It can be heart-wrenching for a parent to drop their clinging baby off with a caregiver or leave home when the nanny arrives. This stresses new parents, making them question their rationale for returning to work.

If you have the luxury of staying home full time, even leaving your child with a babysitter on date nights can be stressful. They always want Mom or Dad. Grandma and Grandpa are often excellent stand-ins, and so is extended family, a preference for parents who struggle emotionally with leaving their child behind. Proper planning and open communication with your partner can ease the guilt of going back to work. As for date night, you'll often spend it thinking, worrying, and talking about your offspring. But don't give up—it gets easier!

Those delicious weekends when your child goes to grandma's, a camp, or a sleepover at a friend's home will allow you to lounge in bed. Eventually, your date nights will focus less on your kids and more on your connection with your partner!

> **REFLECTION**
>
> 1. Who will stay home according to their job/income opportunities?
> 2. Will you opt for home daycare, a live-in nanny, a family member as a caregiver, or daycare?

Parenting Style and Discipline

Parenting styles refer to the overall approach parents apply to raise their children. Scholars have suggested different models to categorize parenting styles based on various behaviours. Scholar Diana Baumrind (1966) developed a parenting model with three styles: authoritative, authoritarian, and permissive (online). Later, Maccoby and Martin expanded this model to include a fourth style called uninvolved/neglectful (Zeltser, 2021). Here's an overview of each:

1. **Authoritative Parenting:** Authoritative parents are demanding, but also nurturing and responsive. They set clear expectations and rules for their children and involve their children in decision-making. The outcomes of this style are high self-esteem, social competence, and academic success.
2. **Authoritarian Parenting:** Authoritarian parents are highly demanding and less responsive. They enforce strict rules and use punishment (such as spanking) instead of reasoning for disobedience. Children of strict parents may have lower self-esteem, weaker social skills, and a higher chance of rebelling or being aggressive.
3. **Permissive Parenting:** Permissive parents are lenient, setting few demands or controls. They are more responsive than demanding and may avoid confrontation, treating their children

like friends. Children in relaxed environments may struggle with self-control and fitting in socially or academically.
4. **Uninvolved/Neglectful Parenting:** Uninvolved parents are neither demanding nor responsive. They provide the necessities but are uninvolved in their child's life and lack emotional responsiveness. Neglected children may face emotional and behavioural issues and struggle with forming healthy relationships.

These styles are conceptual frameworks, and parents exhibit a combination of these traits. Parenting effectiveness is influenced by cultural norms, the child's temperament, and the environment. More recent research has explored additional dimensions and variations in parenting styles, such as free-range parenting, which means choosing activities the child can do independently to build confidence. There are also helicopter parents who hover over their child's every move. Some universities have banned over-involved parents from attending frosh week!

Attachment Parenting

Attachment parenting means taking cues from your child about their needs. It promotes a close bond between parent and child through caring activities outlined in the following eight principles by Attachment Parenting International (API):

1. Preparing for pregnancy, birth, and parenting.
2. Feeding with love and respect (including breastfeeding).
3. Responding with sensitivity.
4. Using a nurturing touch.
5. Ensuring safe sleep—physically and emotionally.
6. Providing consistent and loving care.
7. Practicing positive discipline.

8. Striving for balance in your personal and family life.

Some expressions of attachment parenting include: co-sleeping (or the family bed where your child sleeps in bed with you), breastfeeding on demand and for as long as the baby/child wants to (even into toddlerhood and preschool age), disciplining with love and applying natural consequences instead of punishing and spanking, getting down on your child's level to speak with them, and doing so in neutral, soft tones, and homeschooling your child.

All parents should strive to create the closest bond possible with the child because what is the alternative? Detachment parenting? Also, with authoritarian discipline, parents focus more on their own anger than on teaching their child how to behave. We are our children's first teachers. If we want our children to be responsible adults, we should help them develop self-management skills. As API writes, the above eight principles are foundational: we must seek to "nurture our children for a more compassionate world" (n.d., online).

REFLECTION

1. What is your parenting style?
2. What are your beliefs about setting limits and consequences for your child, and are they the same as your partner's?
3. What elements of attachment parenting would you like to implement?
4. Will you breastfeed your child (and for how long)?
5. What will you do if your child wants to sleep in your bed?

> **EXERCISE C: Parenting Together**
>
> Once you're clear on your why and ready to embark upon getting pregnant, discuss these questions with your partner:
>
> 1. How will you prepare together for pregnancy and childbirth?
> 2. What parenting style will you adopt?
> 3. Do you plan to breastfeed? How long?
> 4. Will you insist your child sleep in their own bed as a baby (Until what age)?
> 5. Who will discipline, and how will you discipline your child?
> 6. What childcare arrangements will you make—extended family, in-home nanny, or institutional daycare?

Your preferences and answers to these questions stem from your values. Nowhere do our values show than when we raise children. We are our children's first teachers, so we impart these values naturally.

Monetary Responsibilities

Children are priceless, yet extremely expensive. Money doesn't grow on trees (or in your backyard, it does). Before deciding to have children, research and discuss the financial responsibilities involved. It may shock you that your income is much less than expected, and the last thing you will need as new parents is money stress. Crunch the numbers as you consider having children. Every country's provincial/state or government can provide accurate information about:

❖ **Parental leave:** Who would take parental leave, whether you

would split it, and how much income do you need during that time?
- ❖ **IVF treatments or adoption costs**: If you cannot have children naturally, you may opt for IVF treatments or explore adoption. Depending on your personal circumstances, this can be financially and mentally draining (Not to mention what to do with unused embryos if your marriage ends).
- ❖ **Raising dependent children:** Know what it costs to feed, clothe, educate, and care for a child from birth to legal age. And if you separate, consider that you must legally determine the fiscal responsibilities for raising children. Confirm the state/provincial laws governing the age of majority legal age when you are no longer responsible for your child.
- ❖ **Special needs:** If your child has special needs, what category do they fall under and what financial help does the government provide for their care?

Giving Your Child an Allowance

A weekly allowance can be an excellent way to empower your child to deal with money. In one of the author's homes, her child received his weekly allowance according to his age. One day, he said: "Hey, Mom, when I'm ten, I'll get ten dollars a week, and eleven dollars when I am eleven?" And on he went, his little mind correlating his advancing age with the increasing amounts—until he hit eighteen. His mother stopped him. "I think by then you'll have a job, and there will be no more allowance."

Certain banks can assist parents in teaching their children about money management. We won't suggest specific programs, but you can check your local banks and decide which plan would work for you and your child(ren). When her son was ten years old, Kelly brought him to the bank because he wanted to open his first savings account. He felt confident as he walked up to the teller, who asked him what he was there for, and replied: "What kinds of accounts do you offer?"

Educating your child on money and values is paramount. Is your child clear on the purpose of their allowance and how it fosters independence and self-respect? You may pay them to do chores expected to be done as part of a family unit. For instance, paying your child to do dishes may give them the wrong impression that they're only meant to help the family unit if they get paid. This shows children we expect them to take part in the regular running of the household because it's their home too.

Some parents believe in paying their children for school achievements or household chores, while others don't. A parent's job is to create a functional, social, happy, and self-supporting human being. This involves showing your kids that helping others is emotionally rich instead of monetarily rewarding. Taking accountability for their chores will grow your child's self-confidence and sense of independence.

Entitlement

Sometimes, the culture to which we expose our children influences their feelings of entitlement. We live in a fast-paced society that increasingly promotes instant gratification and materialistic values, which our children may internalize and thus believe they deserve expensive possessions without understanding the importance of working diligently and taking responsibility.

When we or caregivers overindulge our children, giving them everything they want without having to earn or appreciate it, we may cultivate their belief that they are entitled to those things. Pandering to your child's sense of entitlement can hinder their personal and social development and their ability to function effectively in the world.

That sense of deservingness and expectation of special treatment or privileges in a child without genuine effort or merit is the bane of the parent who never says "no," tries to make up for parental guilt, or simply sets no healthy boundaries. Entitled children lack resilience and perseverance and expect things to be handed to them rather than setting and working towards goals. They may struggle with feeling empathy and appreciation for others as they focus on their own needs and desires.

Our role as parents is to instil the value of working for what we want, delaying gratification, and cultivating empathy toward others so our children grow into mature, responsible adults capable of contributing and being accountable for their actions and behaviour.

Education

Together, you must discuss plans for educating your children and who will mange the costs. One parent may want private schooling, while the other parent is content with sending their child to the public school system. Or you believe the way to go is homeschooling, which entails an opportunity loss for the parent who stays home or works part time.

Kelly home-educated her child from birth to adult, working part-time as a teacher and education consultant and often from home. Fortunately, grandparents helped significantly, and her partner pitched in because he had a flexible job. It was a hugely rewarding experience.

Initially, Kelly and her child's father disagreed about homeschooling, but Kelly was adamant that it was the best approach for their child. Naysaying friends doubted her choice to educate her child at home. It worked out beautifully because Kelly's homeschooled child is an independent, self-supporting, adult, and a top earner for a major company.

Home education is a beautiful gift for your child, healthy for family dynamics, and instills core values. We recognize that not all parents are ready and willing to take this step. What is key is that you stay involved in your child's education. Parent may think school is the child's principal educator, sending the kid off and expecting teachers and the system to do the rest. Instead, you, the parents, are your child's primary educators. And your children sponge up lessons you don't realize you are imparting!

It is not merely instructing your child to tie their shoes or ride a bike; education is modelling your core values, showing an interest in your child, and being present as they experience life and school. Instilling strong values is vital because of the enormous negative effects of social media on adolescents. How you show up for your own child has more influence on their values than public or private education—whose role is to impart knowledge, not teach values.

> **REFLECTION**
>
> 1. What are your individual goals for your child's education?
> 2. If your goals differ, how will you decide how and where they will learn?
> 3. Private or public school, and why or why not?
> 4. Homeschooling—which parent would take on the educator role?

Higher Education

What are your hopes and expectations for your children regarding higher education? Attending college or university costs can vary depending on where you live. Your young adult may attend trade school instead, and you will need to discuss the charges. Determine the funds for education by exploring savings plans, loans, and bursaries. Your young adult may also decide to move back home to focus on studies, find a part-time job and pay for their books and clothes. Mapping out a plan can help with navigating these challenges. Although it is a plan on paper, you can (and should) continually re-evaluate and update it as needed.

Special Needs Children

What if you have a special needs child, one with disabilities, which presents unique challenges? Consider how long your child will live with you, how much care your child will need (depending upon the diagnosis), and how much it will cost. These factors will affect your couple and family relationships. And if you are a single parent or your partner is not willing to help raise a special needs child, the complexities of care become amplified.

Considerations if you have a special needs child:

- Educating yourself about your child's disability and how to advocate for them
- Requiring medical support and specialised treatment and services
- Living expenses and government funding
- Modifying your home (elevator, ramps, special equipment)
- Establishing a daily routine for stability and security
- Placing your adult special needs child in a dedicated residence
- Enrolling your child in special education - availability and cost
- Having a dedicated support network for both you and your child
- Engaging respite care so you can take a break from caregiving and better care for your child
- Assigning guardianship in case you cannot parent because of illness or death

❖ Entrusting and allocating your assets for your disabled child when you die

Raising a special needs child can be an incredibly rewarding and challenging experience. It requires patience, reliance, and a (lifelong) commitment to their well-being. If you embrace the journey with an open heart and mind, learn from others, and cherish your child's uniqueness, you can create a quality life for your family while providing your special needs child with the tools they need to live a fulfilling and independent (as possible) life. It is crucial for couples to support each other during these tough times and seek the resources and help to navigate the complexities of raising a child with special needs.

Empty Nest

The empty nest syndrome refers to a psychological phenomenon parents often experience when their children leave home for the first time. You and your partner are now alone. Empty nest syndrome may include a deep sense of loss, causing sadness and grief, a shift in identity for parents. The family home (a three-bedroom, four-bathroom sprawling dwelling) now feels like an empty mansion, and feelings of loneliness and isolation might set in. When children leave, parents may struggle with their purpose. The relationship dynamic changes, so the focus is no longer on nurturing and parenting. Couples may need to rediscover and redefine their relationship—with themselves and each other.

Not all is grim, though. On the positive side, your active parenting duties have diminished! Parents can shift the focus to their couple, their personal interests and goals, or any neglected area of life because there is more free time. While parents may experience an increase in pride in their child's accomplishments as they watch their little birds fly, which feels so fulfilling, this duality creates a mixed complex experience as an empty-nester.

Coping strategies for parents may involve staying connected with the children through communication, fostering new interests and hobbies, or investing in your couple relationship (Think back to when you were dating). Seek support from friends or a therapist and balance your new family dynamic.

Boomers and Boomerangers

Nowadays, kids rarely leave home at eighteen to find a job and build a life. In today's norms, children attend college and university and often leave home much later. Another contributing factor to children boomeranging is the prohibitive cost of housing. Young adults increasingly find affordable housing out of reach, often having to take on a roommate or even defer home ownership altogether. Adult children commonly boomerang home when they lose jobs or find the cost of living alone impossible.

If you are aging, your reality may be that your offspring are more of a help than a hindrance, and having your child return to live with you is delightful. However, adult children can slip into the same dynamic of relying on parents to clean up after and care for them as though they had never left. Having your adult child move back in with you can be challenging and may cause changes in the family dynamics and household routines. (You had finally gotten used to a new dynamic after your child left home!)

Not all parents experience empty nest syndrome or react to it the same way. While some parents may embrace this newfound freedom and opportunities for personal growth, others may find it challenging to adjust. The intensity and duration of empty nest syndrome varies from person to person and may only be temporary when you factor in boomeranging. Form a united front with your partner and be clear about your boundaries so you can navigate this reality for the best interests of you, your couple, and family.

> **REFLECTION**
>
> 1. How will you enjoy your extra time as an empty-nester?
> 2. How do you see your relationship with your partner now that you are alone together?
> 3. Would you be happy to have your children move back with you?
> 4. Would your children contribute financially? If yes, how much?
> 5. How long are you willing to have your children live with you?

Reality Check

How things are:

How I would like things to be:

Red Flag(s):

Deal Breaker(s):

One action I can take:

Chapter 13

Blended and Extended Families

Contour brushes are not included!

There are two outcomes when blending families: either it's a gigantic mess, or it's a beautifully crafted masterpiece. Consider the diversity of social classes, cultures, races, religions, values, beliefs, and expectations. When partners have conflicting values, it may be impossible to merge their lives. It's unfair to exclude those dear to either of your lives. In time, understanding will deepen, and hopefully, as a couple, you will reconcile, define, and integrate your two worlds.

Exes and Uh-Ohs

A ghost haunts your home. Everywhere you turn, you confront this formidable presence. You cannot exorcise it because it's your ex! Didn't you intend to end their unreasonable demands when leaving your former partner? Unfortunately, you remain connected by a thread—no, a thick rope—that is your shared child! And surprise—your new husband also has an ex. Two exes or ghosts to deal with make your new relationship feel like a haunted house!

Your Ex

A love gone wrong will mark you, even if it happens years from now. It might affect your new relationship (positively) by helping you learn from mistakes and improve in the future. We all carry baggage from our pasts, but we should not let it disrupt the present. How will you merge your lives and begin a meaningful relationship if you have not gotten rid of the old baggage you lug around?

You and your ex may end amicably and harbour no ill feelings. You may even consider yourselves good friends. But your present beau tells you he feels uncomfortable with the close friendship you have with your ex. Your intimate relationship could deteriorate rapidly if boundaries are unclear, and your communication isn't honest.

Your Partner's Ex

There may be times when your partner's ex is more present in your life than you would like. When your partner cannot emotionally detach from their ex, trust issues may arise in your relationship. If your partner has children with their ex, this will directly affect your happiness as a couple. There will be a schedule for when the children come to stay. As with any plan, things could change on a dime. How you navigate those moments requires compromise and assertiveness.

Here's a true story to illustrate this: Imagine booking a surprise weekend getaway for you and your partner. It's his weekend without the kids and the family dog, who always goes wherever the kids are. You are looking forward to having quality time together! Your partner's ex-wife wants him to take the dog this weekend because she has plans with the kids. Oh, and he then informs you he has agreed. Although your partner didn't know about the surprise, he should have discussed it with you beforehand, since taking care of a dog involves more than providing a warm home.

Tell your partner that it would have been respectful to ask for your opinion instead of deciding for you. Also, ask him to call his ex and let her know he cannot take the dog. Prevent problems by clearly defining limits for shared time and discussing any plan changes ahead of time. Setting clear boundaries ensures respectful communication and prevents future arguments.

Both partners must take the time to heal from a past relationship. "Life will test you along the way to see if you've learned the lessons of your pain" (Howarth, 2020, p. 127). Otherwise, you risk carrying past baggage into your relationship. You must build a new house on something other than an old foundation. Kelly knows a woman who moved into her partner's home. The decor had not changed from the original paint colours and wallpaper selected by the ex. The new wife kept saying they needed to redecorate; years later, they were still living with the ex-wife's décor!

This is not how you rebuild your life to include a new partner. You may be comfortable with the old wallpaper, but that does not mean you shouldn't change it, especially when you invite someone new into your life. This is why some women cut their hair differently upon divorcing! Called the 'divorce cut,' it symbolizes a fresh start.

> **REFLECTION**
>
> 1. Is one of you NOT over your ex or experiencing unresolved issues?
> 2. Do either of you have children with your ex?
> 3. How is the relationship with you or your partner's ex?
> 4. Have you discussed extended-family boundaries with your present partner?
> 5. Is one of you hesitant or defensive about implementing boundaries with an ex?

Alimony and Palimony

You've met the person of your dreams and find out they have financial obligations to their former partner or spouse which could be child support, alimony, or division of assets in a divorce. Your partner's sense of responsibility towards fulfilling these commitments shows their integrity and willingness to honour their past commitments, which are qualities you value in a partner.

You may also feel uneasy and concerned about what these financial obligations mean. This outflow of cash to another household will affect your joint disposable income if you move in or marry. It is natural to question how they might affect your future together, particularly if they involve substantial amounts of money or long-term commitments.

Is it reasonable to ask your partner for details about their financial obligations? Hell, YES! These financial commitments may affect your joint financial goals, such as buying a house or starting a family. Before you commit to sharing your life and household, it is crucial to discuss any financial arrangements your partner may have with their former spouse to gain a clearer understanding of how much they pay, how often, and for how long. Ask to see clear, official paperwork, especially before marriage, because you may have to support your partner's children financially. Inform yourself about the laws of your province or state regarding your joint financial commitment to an ex who is the parent of your shared children.

Navigating a relationship where one partner has financial obligations to a former partner requires open communication, trust, and a willingness to adapt. Approach the situation with empathy and understanding while also prioritising your own financial well-being and future goals.

> **REFLECTION**
>
> 1. Is one or both of you still legally married to another person?
> 2. What financial obligations do either of you have to an ex-partner?
> 3. In which ways will your partner's financial responsibilities to their former spouse affect your relationship (and vice versa)?

Co-parenting

Deciding to leave your couple is huge, but parenting together in the best interests of your children is a massive undertaking. Co-parenting is not only an action—it is an attitude involving getting along for the sake of your shared children. The primary goal of co-parenting is to maintain a positive and supportive relationship for the well-being of the children. It focuses on shared responsibilities, communication, and collaboration between the parents to ensure the children have a stable and healthy upbringing.

When a couple's breakup is difficult and fraught with tension, it is challenging to co-parent. Children suffer when parents going through a bitter breakup cannot get along. Your child is not at fault in your break-up, so you must co-parent responsibly and avoid pitting your child against the other parent. Whatever has driven you apart as a couple should not impede your child's experience of their parent.

Your child is not your confidant. For example, if the other parent is unreliable and does not follow through on pre-arranged pickups, discuss directly with the other parent, keep your frustrations to yourself, or tell a friend. Blasting a parent because previous experiences trigger you is never helpful and only creates an inner conflict for your child. Your job is to provide comfort and support for your child, to reassure your child that you love them, and that any disagreements are not their fault.

Co-parenting involves discussing and agreeing on schedules, holidays, and support payments. This will depend on the legalities and other details of your separation or divorce. If you have joint custody and are amicable, you might decide to split the bills fifty-fifty. The court determines who takes care of the children and who pays alimony and child support. Respect legal agreements, stay flexible and adaptable, and keep the best interests of your child's well-being at the centre of your co-parenting.

Stepparenting

"I want a new Daddy!" You remember your oldest wailing in the mall parking lot when his father strapped him into his stroller instead of letting him run between the parked cars. Well, now this statement is coming back to haunt you!

A stepparent comes into a pre-existing family dynamic, and this creates all kinds of change and tension, which must be managed. The stepparent may entertain a fantasy of a perfect household with beautiful, perfect step-kids. Often, life doesn't manifest the way films and folklore (fairy tales) portray blended family life. Look at Cinderella for the wicked stepmother stereotype that appears embedded in our consciousness whenever we hear about women entering already established families. Kelly remembers her stepmother telling her she wished they had been babies when she'd come into their lives because she felt it would have been easier to mould them from a younger age.

It's common for a stepchild to resent the new partner, especially since this person will cause changes in the household that the child may not like. This also depends on whether you introduce them to potential partners prematurely or often. Don't be surprised if your children are more ready than you are!

Your kids may refuse to accept any new person you introduce, and this may show that your children refuse to share you with someone else. While there is a natural inclination to expect your child to like your new partner, avoid pushing the relationship. It will build on its own, and it's up to your children and new partner to navigate this with your help and understanding.

If you decide to live together (whether in your home or your partner's) the dynamics will change. Like dogs that show their teeth to defend their space, everyone marks their territory. When your child(ren) shows signs of dislike upon meeting your new sweetheart, you must openly discuss what your child(ren) does not like about your partner. Often, kids are fiercely protective of their parents and want them to reconcile. If your children have gotten to know this new person in your life, and still do not warm up to them, you must engage in an open dialogue where you listen to their concerns.

A new parental figure in the home is confusing, especially for the stepparent. You take part in the day-to-day chores for the children, but they are not yours and may constantly remind you of that! It's best to establish rules and boundaries to navigate the muddy waters of these challenges. Stepparents have their own sets of boundaries, which the children will test, but you should not adjust them just to gain favour. If your stepchildren dislike your limits, explaining why you created your boundaries will provide insight into who you are.

Children benefit when you model healthy boundaries; eventually, they will develop boundaries of their own and respect yours. If your stepchild tests your limits, discuss it privately with your partner (their parent) and decide on the consequences together. As a stepparent, you do not have the authority to discipline the child without the parent's agreement. Once you decide how to address the situation, hold a family meeting.

A stepparent should never speak ill of the child's parent in front of the child—no matter what. Part of the adult's job is to use good judgement, so the adage: "If you have nothing nice to say, say nothing." applies. Don't be the wicked stepparent by creating a barrier between yourself and your stepchildren.

Rules can be negotiable, but boundaries are not. For instance, the parent can adjust the rule of a ten o'clock curfew on weeknights if the child shows up on time and achieves excellent grades. Not accepting foul language is one example of a non-negotiable boundary.

The kids may want an evening with their parents (your partner), which is normal and should always be respected. Couples should prioritise spending time together, and one-on-one with their children, by planning distinct types of quality time. Integrating your new partner can be as simple as playing board games during family night, which brings laughter and builds connection. We learn about each other and bond through play, so consider fun activities you might do together instead of sitting in awkward silence.

Everyone in the home should meet regularly to discuss how things are going and whether anything needs to be tweaked. Kids are astute observers, so if you and your partner disagree with the rules, children can see this, and they may seek to divide and conquer. Ensure that you and your partner agree. If there are any big decisions, discuss them privately and arrange another meeting with the children present to announce your decision. Be open to questions or feedback.

Family meetings encourage honest and respectful communication, helping to address conflicts confidently. Everyone shares in an open exchange of feelings, boundaries, expectations, and how to resolve issues. When you show your children healthy examples, they will learn good habits for themselves and their future relationships. And this is the best gift parents can give their children.

Stepparents typically have no economic responsibility for their stepchildren. Whatever they choose to contribute to the child's care and well-being (education, extra-curricular activities, and clothes) regarding time and financial resources is considered 'gifting.' There must be a financial discussion concerning stepchildren and what economic role the stepparent plays. It is a huge red flag if your partner expects you to provide financial support for their dependent children.

If you are married and have legally adopted your partner's child, you may have taken on some of the economic responsibility for them. Consult a lawyer in your area for legal advice about financial responsibilities regarding adoption and custody matters.

EXERCISE: Hold an Open Conversation

If your children are having challenges relating to your new partner, pose the following questions:

1. Is the stepparent treating the child(ren) well?
2. What is the stepparent doing that may upset your children?
3. Is someone else influencing the child(ren)'s perspective of your partner?

Extended Family

Differentiating between blood-related families and close family friends has become challenging because of the variety of family structures. Divorce is commonplace, so the notion of family stretches far beyond the nuclear family of the 1950s and 60s. *Modern Family* (Lloyd et al., 2009-2020) is a hit show that humorously portrays the diverse family structures of today and how members navigate various situations.

The extended family includes grandparents, aunts, uncles, cousins, in-laws, and step relatives. Connected through blood or marriage, extended family members frequently interact and share significant life events, providing emotional and financial support to their members. They may also play critical roles in child-rearing and caregiving. The size and structure of extended families vary across cultures and regions, with certain ethnicities emphasising the extended family as a source of social and cultural identity.

Terms of Endearment

Referring to extended family members can be confusing. Sometimes we call close friends aunties or uncles. In certain cultures, everyone in the community is automatically called auntie or uncle—despite no relation. While it takes a village to raise a child, we must be comfortable with the terms, especially if we are attaching an importance or respect to the relationship in the eyes of our child, because that comes with responsibility.

If we force our children to call someone by a term of endearment, and that someone jeopardizes our child's safety or well-being, then the label can stop the child from feeling brave enough to tell us what is going on. Always be vigilant—around all friends and family members. Otherwise, open communication and permission are the way to go when asking an extended family member or friend how they want to be addressed.

Multi-Generational Living

A grandmother says to her newly married grandson: "Come live in my home, which I will sell to you well below market value. But there is one string attached: you will care for me as I age." Suddenly, the new couple's cardboard box under a train bridge looks welcoming!

It's common in certain families and cultures to live with multiple family members of different generations. Kelly knows of a multigenerational family based on a matriarchal structure where the grandmother, mother, daughter, and granddaughter shared a home and made it work.

If you decide to have your parents live with you, ensure you engage in multiple conversations and set healthy boundaries beforehand. Buying a home with a grandparent suite may be practical, especially when you have children, and your parents want to be hands on. But your parents will age, may require care, and eventually become your responsibility. Despite having other siblings—usually, the ones living closest take on the bulk of their parent's care.

Remember: Two is company, and three is a crowd. Before anyone comes to live with you, you must discuss expectations and ensure you agree, acting as a team. This other person could be a sister, child, stepchild, or uncle. Once you decide to take someone in to live with you, meet with that person as a couple. Discuss expectations, rules, possibilities, and finances. After having an honest, respectful conversation, you can go home and decide as a couple. No one should make significant life decisions without first consulting their partner. Talking about expectations beforehand can help find solutions everyone agrees on.

Laurie and her partner left the city to move to the countryside to be closer to his father, who would come live with them. They had honest conversations concerning each other's expectations about tasks and finances, and they arrived at a consensus, so everything worked out beautifully. Respect is vital, and all parties involved must agree when dividing household obligations.

Living with a relative means merging residences and adjusting lifestyles. What is your 'why'? Here are common motivations for moving in with a parent or relative:

- ❖ Cutting down on expenses to save money
- ❖ Losing a job
- ❖ Beginning studies or a new job
- ❖ Divorcing/Death of a spouse
- ❖ Experiencing a life (or midlife) crisis
- ❖ Undergoing health and well-being (physical or mental) issues
- ❖ Gaining or providing companionship
- ❖ Adhering to family and cultural traditions

Considerations when deciding to live with your parent(s)/relative(s) include:

- ❖ What is this person's age, and how autonomous are they?
- ❖ Which space will this person occupy? Will you designate communal areas? What are they, and how will you use them?
- ❖ Have you talked about what it means to live together, including noise, socialising, cooking, cleaning, and maintenance?
- ❖ How will you navigate personal time (afternoon sex) with your partner while sharing a home with someone else?
- ❖ What are the financial implications of having another person in your home?
- ❖ Who will contribute financially, and what amount?
- ❖ Are there clear rules and roles set for the household, and is everyone aware and agreeable?

❖ What will need to happen if the living arrangement does not work out? Are all parties aware and in agreement?

Although it's helpful to have someone contribute to living costs, the strain of sharing your space and personal life may outweigh the additional money. Splitting the bills can ease financial burdens because it distributes the costs of rent, utilities, and other expenses, making it easier for everyone involved. This can also free up your disposable income for other needs and desires.

However, living with someone means sacrificing a certain level of privacy and autonomy. It may involve compromising on personal preferences, habits, and routines. Conflicts over cleanliness, noise levels, and diverse habits and lifestyles can arise, leading to tensions and strained relationships.

The dynamics of the household can change significantly when someone new moves in. Consider the effects on existing relationships, whether they are family members, friends, or romantic partners. Changes in boundaries and dynamics can sometimes lead to conflicts and disagreements, potentially outweighing the financial benefits.

Have an honest and open conversation with everyone in the household. Weigh the pros and cons to ensure that everyone involved is comfortable with the arrangement before deciding. And keep communication lines open along the way because issues will arise that can make you question your 'why.'

Reality Check

How things are:

How I would like things to be:

Red Flag(s):

Deal Breaker(s):

One action I can take:

Chapter 14

Making Time Count

Nothing is set in stone except the words on your headstone.

Dating involves doing fun things together as you get to know someone. Whether it's an outing to the movies, seeing friends, or taking a trip, it's all fun and new. Who would think you will eventually need to make room for and plan your entertainment as a couple and alone? When children come into the picture, you must manage activities, playdates, travel, and visitors. The challenge eventually becomes one of finding the time to play and entertain.

Me Time

There is a balancing act to carve out enough time in a relationship for your couple, your children, and your extended family and friends, let alone for yourself. Taking time for ourselves allows us to recharge and rejuvenate. By prioritising alone time and self-care, we ensure we can show up fully in our relationships.

Open and honest communication is key to negotiating boundaries and finding a mutually beneficial arrangement. When we neglect our own needs, we may become resentful or burnt out, which can strain our connection with our partner. By nurturing ourselves, we not only enhance our well-being but also become more capable of providing support and care to our loved ones. It is crucial to respect and honour our needs and those of our partner, finding compromises that allow for both individual and shared time.

When we are in a good place mentally, emotionally, and physically, we are better equipped to show up as a loving and supportive partner and create a harmonious and fulfilling partnership where both feel valued and supported.

Couple Time

Couple time is not a luxury—it is necessary. It's too easy to get bogged down in life priorities to the point we neglect to make time only with our partner. Some couples create and stick to a date night. They take an evening or weekend to reconnect while having their children cared for by extended family or a trusted sitter. P.S.: It's easier said than done because parents think, worry, and discuss their child the entire time! Reflect on your reasons for planning 'couple time' and what you both need to keep the spark in your relationship. What a beautiful way to show your children how you prioritise each other. Kelly knows a young man who says his wife is his priority above his child because without her, he would have no child. The baby knows this because a common comment from outsiders is how happy this baby is!

Activities and Hobbies

Engaging in activities and hobbies makes our lives interesting and makes us dynamic as individuals. So, there are two aspects to having activities and hobbies. First, we must have our own interests that do not involve our partner. This gives us something to call our own, as we do not need to share everything we do with our partner. Second, we must find activities to do as a couple or family.

We only need a little money to create special memories with our partner. Packing a simple picnic basket with goodies and games and exploring a new park can be just as fun! Holding a lie-in or breakfast in bed on Sunday can also be a treat! The goal is to find playful activities that nourish your inner child, together and apart, and watch how you connect on a deeper level.

Activities are as crucial for developing your intimacy as honouring your independence is. Just because your partner enjoys golf doesn't mean you have to partake. This provides the opportunity for you to engage in separate outings with friends.

Vacation and Travel

Who doesn't love time off and time away? Vacation and travelling can be a wonderful experience or a dreadful one. It all depends on the pleasure you derive from exploring and, more often, with whom you are exploring!

Your partner has pinned all the places they plan to visit on a large world map. You just want to go anywhere that you don't have to do the dishes! Discussing vacation and travel at the beginning is vital because it can make or break a relationship—but it doesn't have to! For example, if you love camping and the other does not, you can go with friends while the other has a quiet weekend alone. Or you may tag along and meet people with common interests. Perhaps you have always dreamed of camping in the Amazon jungle, but your partner is a five-star vacationer. By remaining open-minded, you can make some fantastic discoveries. There are no rules that say that you must do everything as a couple.

It boils down to what is comfortable for you in your relationship and how you respect one another's needs. Just like getting all your shots before visiting certain countries is critical, so is how you envision your vacation time (together or apart). Anticipate disagreements during planning and prioritise communication, respect, and what is best for your relationship.

At the beginning of a relationship, you and your partner may put aside your desires to make the other happy. But as the honeymoon stage slows down, you will become less accommodating. After being together for a long time, couples may opt to go on vacations with friends instead of alone.

There are diverse considerations when travelling with a partner, so discuss your expectations before deciding where you will go and what you wish to do. Expectations are silent killers of joy because, usually, we do not communicate these until someone is upset.

Consider what type of vacation you desire with your partner:

- What is your ideal climate (A menopausal woman may not want to vacation in the South)?
- Camping, glamping, or five-star (i.e., indoor plumbing versus squatting in the woods)?
- How do you feel about driving vacations (Hit the road, Jack)?
- Do either of you have eating considerations and dietary restrictions (i.e., diabetic, gluten-free, vegan, keto)?
- Will you include other family members or friends in your travel plans and how (Three's a crowd)?

- ❖ Do you have mobility issues (i.e., You cannot walk for prolonged periods or need wheelchair access)?
- ❖ What are your must-haves (Are you open to compromising)?

Remember, it can be stressful sharing close quarters, such as a hotel room, tent, or camper. And if you are visiting family or friends, anticipate that you'll be gaining a glimpse into how they live—and it isn't always pretty! Plan for alone time so you don't need a vacation from your vacation!

Family Time

Families must make time and be available to play together. We're not talking about the arguments over homework or rushed conversations during car rides to activities. Think family game night, pizza night, exploratory nature walks or sharing a hobby where you close all electronic devices and enjoy fun, enriching activities with your children. These times promote bonding, build trust, and go a long way toward instilling those family values you wish to transmit to your kids. Like in dating, we learn through playing together.

REFLECTION

1. What is your need for alone time? (How often, how much?)
2. What is your need for time with your partner, family, and friends?
3. What are your partner's needs?
4. How do you envision spending family time?

Extended Family and Friendships

Maintaining individual connections with our extended family and friends is vital for our well-being. During challenging times, friends are there to connect with and provide a shoulder to lean on. We do activities with our friends that do not include our partners. Our outside relationships and friendships help us connect and understand each other's experiences.

The best advice can come from our friends because they know us well and can recognize our blind spots in dating. One of Laurie's friends had warned her of becoming serious with a particular person, but she ignored the advice. She suffered the consequences of her ignorance with unpaid bills from stores where her ex-boyfriend had shopped under her good name.

Perhaps you've had an opposite-sex friend since childhood. Chatting with an opposite-sex friend can provide insight and perspective. Respecting the boundaries of your relationship plays a role here; ensure your partner is okay with you sharing personal information. If either of you sneaks into secret meetings with friends, it may mean that your partner disapproves of that person or that you are having an emotional affair.

Sharing with friends and family intending to help your relationship is one thing. Sneaking off to complain about your relationship to someone new you met on social media is like seeking a hero to step in and save you from your couple. Be careful, as there is always a fine line between sharing with a stranger for the sake of having another point of view and emotional infidelity.

Sometimes, our friends can be jealous and cause issues with our relationships. It can go either way, so it's vital to listen to your gut as you take other people's advice with a grain of salt. A genuine friend is someone with whom you can talk but who does not interfere in your relationship.

Kelly experienced the challenge of being disliked and not trusted by one of her partner's friends because of a false rumour spread by someone else. She notices a weird vibe from the person when she is in their presence. It's awkward and feels uncomfortable, but she sees it as that person's problem. In the meantime, she flushed the gossiper from all her social media platforms.

We have no control over any untruths people choose to believe. Let's face it: Some people like tea, and others like coffee! Perhaps minimising contact is best—because who wants to be around people who dislike them? We can withstand not being liked by everyone in our social circle. Still, we do not need to put ourselves in situations or around people who make us uncomfortable.

Confidants and Confidentiality

We sometimes need a listening ear when we hit a bump in our relationship as a couple. Confiding with a friend helps us sort our emotions and feel less alone with our pain. If we confide in a friend an issue we face with our partner, we need to trust our friend will keep it confidential. If our friend shares this sensitive information, this can damage our friendship.

Confidants and confidentiality relate to trust, communication, and protecting sensitive information. Confidants are individuals you trust with your private thoughts, feelings, and secrets. Typically, these people are close friends, family members, or professionals like therapists. They provide emotional support, empathy, and a listening ear. Confidants play a crucial role in mental and emotional well-being by offering a safe space for us to express ourselves.

Confidentiality ensures that sensitive information shared with professionals or organisations remains protected. Breaching confidentiality can have severe consequences, eroding trust, and damaging relationships.

Sometimes, we need to share sensitive information with our

partners, trusting them to handle it responsibly. Actions speak louder than words. If your partner has proven that they are trustworthy, this value is worth millions! If your partner screws up and breaks your trust, you must discuss which actions they would need for you to give them your trust again.

Couple Friendships

Having close friendships with other couples can be enriching. Doing so can bring us immense joy and fulfillment as we share experiences with like-minded people who are important to us. Whether it's a weekly game night, a monthly dinner date, or an occasional weekend getaway, scheduling time together is wonderful! This can help us build a strong bond, spending consistent, quality time.

Building friendships with other couples can also serve as a gauge for the health of our relationship and highlight areas upon which we can improve. Imagine having dinner with another couple you are both remarkably close to. You open the subject of the toilet seat up versus leaving it down. You mention your partner does not put the toilet seat up, which causes you to fall into the toilet. (That's never happened to you, right?)

The other wife says that she has learned to check before sitting down, and that it doesn't bother her anymore. The difference in perspective highlights that you are as equally responsible as your husband for your ass not falling into the toilet!

Listening to other couple's stories and being supportive is a wonderful way to show that we value our friends and their friendship. Opening and being vulnerable with our friends can also be beneficial, allowing for a deeper connection and emotional growth. Through respect, we can create an environment where our friendships can thrive and benefit our relationship.

> **REFLECTION**
>
> 1. Do you and your partner have mutual friends?
> 2. What social groups do you belong to?
> 3. How do these connections enrich your relationship?

Visitors

What we love more than having visitors is when they finally leave! Hosting people in our home is work, especially when they stay more than one night. Visitors affect the rhythm and routine of our household. Whether family or friends, they influence preparation, grocery shopping, cooking, and housecleaning. We may lose our alone time to accommodate house guests. If one of us is an introvert who needs solitude to refuel, hosting visitors can be draining. If we are extroverted, we may feel enthusiastic about the extended opportunity to cater and socialize.

While it's wonderful to receive and welcome others, your partner may have family members or friends you may not like. And vice versa. You have options for managing this:

- ❖ Lie and say that you can't wait to see _____ again!
- ❖ Accommodate because you know it will make your partner happy, but secretly fantasize about them not showing up.
- ❖ Be honest and gently tell your partner you dislike that family member or friend, but agree to host them, anyway.
- ❖ Offer your out-of-town guests a list of nearby hotels.

It is essential to respect each other's boundaries when someone asks about visiting, especially for an extended period.

Reality Check

How things are:

How I would like things to be:

Red Flag(s):

Deal Breaker(s):

One action I can take:

Chapter 15

Life Transitions

Make lemonade from lemons and add a bucket of GIN!

Life is all about change. Significant transitions require that we adapt. Change is an inevitable part of life that can be challenging, exciting, or both. As you transition from one stage to another, you will experience assorted challenges—each with its inherent joys and frustrations. You will experience death and non-death losses, which means you must grieve no matter how positive the transition. You let go of one thing in favour of something else, adapting to a new reality, which means grieving the loss.

When does a life transition present a red flag versus a deal breaker? Changes in lifestyle, such as chronic unemployment, perpetual student status, continuous desire for children, and leading a double life, can have a negative impact on relationships. It's one thing if these are common goals, but if one partner has a hidden agenda that impedes your couple and family life, this can cause problems with anger and resentment. It can be abusive when you expect your partner to follow your whims and compulsions. At the outset, communicating your wishes and needs lets you be clear and live according to your values while honouring your couple.

Life is full of challenges, and being able to count on someone to catch you when you fall is vital. We are stronger as a committed couple. The key word is commitment. You don't only sign up for the good stuff. Being a couple entails pinch-hitting for the other and riding the waves of pleasure and disappointment together.

Transitions as Stressors

Holmes and Rahe (Stress.org, 2019) developed an inventory of everyday life events. This rating scale helps us understand how stress affects our well-being. Sometimes, we forget how critical life events affect us and are not so gentle and patient with ourselves or our partner. Review this inventory periodically to understand your stress levels and how they affect you.

> **EXERCISE A: Stress Inventory**
>
> Review the *Holmes-Rahe Life Stress Inventory* (See Bibliography):
>
> 1. How would you and your partner rate your overall stress?
> 2. Does stress affect your relationship, and in what way(s)?
> 3. During unexpected life events, what actions do you take to show you care?
> 4. Were there any surprises in your approaches to navigating life transitions?

Life changes entail loss and require grieving—yes, even positive changes. Moving on to something new can bring feelings of losing the old and familiar, even if we are uncomfortable in our comfort zone. For example, we leave a job we did not enjoy but felt comfortable doing because we knew the people and the work. Although we have a new position, we can still miss parts of our old job, so we must grieve the loss.

These types of losses are called non-death losses and often carry the same hallmarks of grieving, involving the five stages proposed by Dr. Elizabeth Kübler-Ross (2014) in her pivotal research on death and dying: denial, bargaining, depression/sadness, anger, and acceptance. David Kessler (2019), her co-author, has since added a sixth stage to Kübler-Ross's grief model. The following are the combined stages:

1. **Denial** is the initial stage where individuals struggle to accept the loss.
2. **Bargaining** involves attempting to negotiate or make deals to undo or mitigate the loss.
3. **Depression/sadness** encompasses feelings of deep sorrow and emptiness.
4. **Anger** may arise as individuals grapple with the unfairness or injustice of the loss.
5. **Acceptance** involves coming to terms with the loss and finding a way to move forward.
6. **Finding Meaning** is transcending and transforming the loss, making sense of it.

These stages, which we do not always follow linearly, are how we deal with change and protect ourselves as we adapt to our new reality.

Transition and trauma are inevitable, especially if you live long enough to experience the distinct phases and changes life will bring. As a couple, you may undergo changes and adaptations resulting from the following momentous events and life transitions:

Buying a House

It's exciting and fun to buy a new home, and while you both have the same visions and dreams of your dream home, differences can cause major head-butting. Purchasing a home together is both an emotionally and legally significant transition. First, you must both agree on a house that meets your desires for location and meets your family's needs as you imagine the possibilities. Then you can decide what you will bring to your new house, such as furniture, décor, and other items. Decorating is a fun way to personalize your house and make it feel like home. And you may not always agree. There is constant negotiation, give and take, and lots of compromise.

You face the dreaded task of packing, and it can be overwhelming and tedious, but it is a necessary step in the emotional transition of changing homes. Finding a realtor to sell your present house or find you a new one is the first step in reconciling your dreams and visions with legal realities. You must first agree on a fair price and consider whether the new house will gain value. Review the paperwork carefully to understand and account for all legal implications. Hiring a home inspector and making wills are valuable for property assessment and investment security. Taking the time to consider all these steps can help ensure that your real estate venture is successful.

Moving

First, you pack. Then, you physically move. Then you unpack! Organising your move at the outset by adequately packing and labelling boxes is critical to ensure a smooth transition. The stress of not finding your gadget when you thought it was in the box labelled 'Kitchen' can be stressful and time-consuming. Ensure that your creature comforts are in place first so you can resume and enjoy your everyday living routine.

You need to adjust to your unfamiliar environment, learn the neighbourhood, find local services, and more. Kelly experienced incredible frustration when she moved from the suburbs to the city and could not locate her postal box during her first week living in her new neighbourhood! The mailbox was a metaphor for the transition that uprooted the author as she grieved the loss of her familiar life.

Home Renovations

Renovating your home can be a significant step and a massive life transition. Whether you're starting a family, downsizing, or updating your space, the renovation process can help you achieve a fresh start and a new outlook on life. And it can make you reconsider your relationship!

Undertaking home renovations is one of the most significant sources of stress a couple will face. Imagine living in your space during renovations, dealing with dust, noise, and workers arriving early in the morning. Consider the myriad decisions you will butt heads over and negotiate, such as paint colours for the living room. You may be without a functioning kitchen and bathroom, and while the white bucket can resolve many dilemmas, it's still a *bucket*! If you renovate your shared home, you will experience tension, discord, and frustration, and your relationship will be tested! Kelly experienced three separate instances of contractors putting a foot through the tresses and Gyproc while renovating her upstairs bathroom, piercing the dining room ceiling.

Renovating your home can help you shake old memories and embrace new beginnings. Specific zones or elements of your property may hold negative associations and memories you wish to move past. A home renovation allows you to change your physical environment to support your emotional and psychological growth. The renovation process can help you establish a new identity by creating a space that reflects your current needs, values, and lifestyle. Your home renovation may coincide with personal changes, like a new job or a move, adding to the mix of stress.

A home renovation can catalyze personal growth. As you plan and undertake this project, you will discover new talents and skills you never knew you had. Collaborating with contractors and facing unexpected obstacles can teach you patience, adaptability, and critical thinking skills. This can help you build your confidence and resilience, aiding you in other aspects of your life. Renovating your home can be a transformative experience that marks a fresh start in your life. Whether renovating completely or making small upgrades, it's important to embrace the chance for growth and renewal.

Becoming a Parent

Becoming a parent is a transformative journey that teaches us about ourselves and our place in the world. We produce the next generation! It's a time of momentous change and growth but also love, joy, and deep connection. Parenting brings immense rewards and profoundly affects our life. This transition involves physical, emotional, and psychological changes that can sometimes be overwhelming. It marks the end of one chapter of your life and the beginning of a new and exciting adventure.

Pushing a ten-pound anything out of a vagina is physically but mentally life-altering, too (Stick with ping-pong and charge an admission fee)! Women are more connected to their bodies and to the world. Once you become parents, their focus is on raising and nurturing and protecting your child. It's both exciting and challenging. Your tiny being demands cuddling, feeding, and diaper changing—while you try to sleep (because that is all you want to do)! If you choose to breastfeed your baby, this places additional physical and emotional demands on you. And your social circle will have tons of suggestions about raising your child(ren).

While navigating this transition, you may feel a range of emotions, from excitement and joy to fear and uncertainty. You may question your ability to be wonderful parents or worry about the health and well-being of your child. First-time parents must adjust to a new identity and way of life.

As all transitions are instigators of personal growth and development, they provide opportunities for new parents to let go of old ways and embrace a new set of priorities and values. We must learn patience, compassion, and resiliency as we face parenting challenges—with each other and with ourselves.

Career Change

Work consumes a considerable chunk of our lives. We typically work eight hours daily, representing approximately 2,688 hours a year. Because we must work to provide for ourselves and our families, we may define ourselves by our job title. The career we choose reflects our values and what we find meaningful.

Working at a job we dislike can cause unhappiness, directly affecting our relationships. We may become bitter and more stressed than ever, and our partner will undoubtedly notice our personality change. If you find yourself in this situation, it may be time for a career change. Career change is a significant transition we make for diverse reasons, such as:

- ❖ Finding more fulfillment in a different occupation
- ❖ Pursuing a passion
- ❖ Seeking a higher status or income
- ❖ Gaining more work-life balance

It means learning new skills and adjusting to different working conditions, which might involve starting at a lower level to gain experience and progress in the new field. Our idea of the quality of life may depend on our income, so if there is a sudden change to title, status, or income, it will force us to reassess, recalibrate, and redefine who we are again.

Job Loss

Job loss can be a horrible experience that can happen unexpectedly or because of economic factors. Losing a job induces a range of emotions, from anxiety and fear to relief or even excitement for new opportunities. Once the initial emotional shock is over, the transition involves:

- ❖ Reflecting on one's career goals
- ❖ Evaluating skill sets and experience
- ❖ Seeking new job opportunities or retraining to pivot to a different industry

A job loss can profoundly affect and require resilience, planning, and our willingness to adapt. The difference between losing one's job and choosing to leave one's job may have the same effects on our psyche, finances, and well-being. Managing these difficulties and changes individually and as a couple is challenging, but necessary. We must see ourselves as a team because we are stronger together than alone. If our partner loses their job, our understanding and support can help them face their emotions and feel confident enough to get back out there and find a new job.

Returning to Studies

Deciding to go back to school after a break in education can be a significant life transition. Whether advancing our existing career or pursuing an alternative path, returning to school requires considerable time, money, and effort.

It can invoke fear and uncertainty. Leaving the security of a job with an income to pursue studies will challenge most people. Then there is the slog of studying for and writing exams that brings us back to our high school years and can invoke insecurity and fear of failure.

Juggling learning, work, and personal responsibilities is a challenge. And if we have family responsibilities, the stress multiplies.

However, going back to school comes with significant accomplishment and personal growth. It's an opportunity to rediscover ourselves and explore new passions or interests, providing a chance to take control of our future by improving ourselves and our job prospects.

In addition, returning to studies can positively affect our mental and emotional well-being because it offers a sense of purpose, accomplishment, and confidence. With the right mindset and support system, we can successfully transition back to education and thrive in our chosen field.

Retirement

Retiring from our job or career is a significant life transition that brings a sense of freedom, excitement, uncertainty, and loss. It marks the end of one's career and the beginning of a new chapter in life. Retirees must adjust to a new pattern of life, fill their time with extra activities, and find ways of socialising and staying active. Retirement planning is critical to ensure financial stability and continued growth after leaving the workforce.

Retirement is a huge transition you and your partner will face someday. If either of you enjoyed a long-standing career and title (doctor, CEO, teacher, plumber, salesperson, entrepreneur), retirement might leave you feeling lost and questioning your identity. Compounding that common life transition are:

- Heavy financial responsibilities
- Emotional and mood swings
- Physical or health changes
- Downsizing or moving house
- An empty nest
- A nest that fills up again as your adult children boomerang home
- Caregiving for grandchildren or aging parents

On the note of caregiving, you may feel sandwiched between the needs of your aging/ailing parents and your children, especially if you had your children later in life, which makes you part of The Sandwich Generation. And if you are simultaneously caring for your parents and your grandchildren, you may experience The Club Sandwich Generation, a common phenomenon as our life expectancy increases.

Planned or forced retirement is a new and unknown chapter because it marks the end of an era. It can cause issues in your relationship if you are not emotionally or financially prepared. A common concern about retiring as a couple means being together twenty-four/seven—quite the departure from when you were dating and could not get enough of each other! Emotional and physical changes occur as we age, so you must prepare for these. When you suddenly share living space for long stretches, the reality isn't quite like the dream. (Oh, to go back to when we were dating and could not spend enough time together!)

Sometimes, we retire from a lengthy career only to realize that we still want to earn money, contribute, and make a difference in the world. Welcome to the second career! This occurs when we change course, work fewer hours, and with greater flexibility, but in another field or endeavour. The second career provides an opportunity to explore without the financial burden of earning a considerable income. The teacher-turned-life coach is one example.

Retirement Conundrums

It's time to retire! Yay! Yippee! Yahoo! But not so fast. We stop to think about money versus time because now we may have the money AND the time. Or, we have all this time, but limited money. Retirement comes with conundrums because we are not used to the financial and time freedom—if we are fortunate to have both. And we must adapt to not having to answer to anyone but ourselves. As we contemplate retiring from our job or career, we may question whether we feel ready, have enough money, and want to spend our days.

Here are common considerations regarding retirement:

- ❖ Am I ready, or when will I be ready/know I am ready to retire?
- ❖ Geographical - where will I live?
- ❖ Financial - how much money will I have?
- ❖ Empty nesters - how will I live alone?
- ❖ Relationship/Community/Friends - who will I have for support?
- ❖ Travel - do I want to travel (where, how far, for how long at a time?)
- ❖ How will I manage spending so much time with my partner?
- ❖ What if I retire and no one in my circle is there, or my partner is still working?
- ❖ What if I retire and must be a family caregiver? (See The Sandwich Generation later in this chapter).

Here are ways people choose to spend retirement:

- Volunteering
- Playing sports
- Engaging in leisure and social activities
- Travelling
- Taking classes or pursuing that degree you always wanted
- Engaging in hobbies
- Caring for grandchildren
- Making a second career/consulting (as many hours and as flexible as you choose)
- Dating (as a couple again)
- Waking up with no plan and doing whatever you like

You and your partner must have a financial plan for your economic well-being in case of unforeseen circumstances and especially for retirement. The general rule is to ensure that you are financially independent by having an income and enough money for yourself. You must negotiate with your partner what you set aside for any expenses you incur together.

Your newly retired partner may want to spend money travelling across the country in a campervan, but you want to be frugal, take long walks, and picnic by the lake. However, what happens if one of you becomes less mobile and cannot do the things you used to enjoy, requiring assisted care from a professional? You must factor life changes into your costs. Health can deteriorate at the drop of a hat, and simply because you feel great now does not mean you will be so lucky in the future. Retiring to the country and needing transport may be costly, so you may rethink retiring to your chalet in the middle of nowhere.

Perhaps you and your partner will retire at different ages, which can affect your relationship if you are still working while the other is at home all day. Your partner may be happier with a lower income, while you might work to put more money aside. Consider all the intricate details of retirement at least ten and five years before either of you plan to retire.

If one or more of your children boomerang back and move in with you, this can affect your life emotionally and financially. While you may love the idea of having your 'babies' return home, consider the cost of carrying the financial weight of your children into your retirement. Contemplate how this would affect your partner, especially if they have children from a previous marriage who may also boomerang home.

Regardless of your civil status, discuss your common goals regarding financial, emotional, physical, location, and extended family—as they relate to how you want to spend that glorious chapter of your life. You may need to revisit and revise these. Remember that you are not retiring from your job and role, and instead, to a new adventure.

> **EXERCISE B: Retiring From or Retiring To?**
>
> Consider how you envision retirement and your independent and shared goals for spending your retirement:
>
> 1. Where do we want to live when we retire?
> 2. What lifestyle plans do we have for retirement, and will our finances support those plans?
> 3. Do we both enjoy travelling or prefer to putter at home or watch birds?
> 4. How do we plan to include family/extended family in our retirement plans?
> 5. How can we reconcile differing retirement expectations?
> 6. What hobbies do we want to pursue when we retire?
> 7. Do we have personal and couple bucket lists—things we'd like to accomplish?

Health Changes

Our health changes constantly—from simple infections and common colds to more serious chronic and acute health crises. Simple daily self-care tasks can become more difficult to manage. A surprise illness may provide us with a wake-up call, forcing us to make a major lifestyle change as we take our health in hand and strive to improve our well-being. Inevitably, this causes a life transition.

These changes in our health can also lead to other life transitions, which can further complicate our physical and emotional well-being. It is common for us to take our own health, as well as the health of our loved ones, for granted. So, we must recognize and address these challenges to maintain a decent quality of life.

Intimate Care

Personal care between humans, especially partners, is not unlike monkeys. Monkeys groom one another to stay healthy by picking bugs and other matter out of their fur and eating them. Grooming is how primates reinforce social structures and bonds.

In humans, touching provides comfort and closeness and reinforces the bond. A back scratch, foot rub, or massage helps us feel loved and cared for. This act of intimacy becomes more critical as we age (because sex may not be possible) as human touch is vital for our well-being.

When in a committed relationship, we should be ready for our partner's unforeseen physical and emotional difficulties. Compassion, tenderness, and understanding are crucial elements of any relationship; your partner must still choose to love you for who you are and treat you with dignity, respect, and kindness, no matter your life stage. Pay attention to how your partner treats their aging parents or other ill family members. If your partner lacks compassion towards their loved ones, they will treat you the same way should you ever become ill.

While drafting this book, Kelly experienced an acute, life-threatening illness that required her partner to care for her around the clock for a month. He brought her to medical appointments and made multiple daily trips to the pharmacy for medicines and supplies and to the grocery store for special foods—while also caring for his ailing mother. He was a sandwiched caregiver! She knew her partner had her back through it all and would do what it took because he loved her.

If your partner can cope with all kinds of spew while you are ill and still kiss you on the lips and say, "I love you," you've got a keeper! This is the wedding vow's intention of the phrase: "In sickness and health," and it speaks volumes regarding relationship integrity (See Values and Compatibility in Chapter 2).

REFLECTION

1. What intimate care acts are present in your relationship?
2. Would you be comfortable giving personal care to a partner if they become disabled or ill?
3. How will you care for each other and what support will you need (emotionally, financially, or otherwise)?
4. Do you both have a care plan in case of disability or illness?

Mid-life Changes

The operative word in all sexes' midlife change is 'pause,' which tells us it's time to take a step back and take stock or pause. It's the perfect opportunity for us to ask ourselves key questions about where we have been versus where we want to go in this next phase of our life.

As we age, our bodies, emotions, and moods may also change. The shit is hitting the fan everywhere! We are taking stock of where we are versus where we thought we would be and want to be. We may call into question our entire existence when our lives are in full-swing with jobs, children, family obligations, and crises. While focused on the many internal conflicts, so much is happening externally. It's crucial to do the introspection necessary for smoothly navigating midlife change.

Menopause

Otherwise known as hell, menopause can wreak havoc in your life. There are three stages to menopause: perimenopause, menopause, and post-menopause. "… Most women experience menopause between ages 40 and 58. The average age is 51…" (The North American Menopause Society, n.d.). It may start naturally or result from health complications such as a hysterectomy, endometriosis, or other gynecological issues.

Basically, your estrogen goes missing-in-action (MIA). These physical changes will cause loads of frustration; your body is not the way it was before, and you may wonder why suddenly your trousers don't fit the way they used to, and everything is annoying. This is such a vulnerable phase for a woman to go through, and with feelings multiplied, it feels like a second puberty!

Symptoms include weight gain, dry skin, hot flashes, night sweats, crankiness, depression, loss of interest in sex, and more (a LOT more)! The lack of female hormones can even ruin your relationship! A usually calm woman may lash out at her partner for no apparent reason. Laurie experienced menopause so intensely that she considered living alone until it was over.

If you think you are perimenopausal or menopausal, the first thing you should do is consult with your physician and have bloodwork done. This will show where your estrogen levels are, confirming the diagnosis. If your primary physician refuses to do these tests, you need to seek a second opinion (and keep doing so until someone listens). During menopause, you may feel lonely enough, so it's unacceptable to feel dismissed by a healthcare provider. And not every woman's experience will be the same, which adds to the challenge of obtaining a diagnosis and treatment. The right physician will listen to you, order the appropriate tests, and offer you assorted options to manage your symptoms.

The second thing a woman must do is find a trusted person to share her feelings, either through a menopause group, life coach, therapist, or friend. Gathering female forces can help a woman feel empowered and not alone (or even crazy). This can save you and your relationship!

Andropause

If you have ever heard the line that men buying sports cars must be having a mid-life crisis, this is where it originates. Andropause describes age-related changes in male hormone levels of testosterone. The folk tale is that men in andropause are desperate to hold on to their youth and manliness, and this may occur when their hormone levels drop.

Unlike menopause in women, testosterone decline in men starts in middle age, around the late forties to early fifties. In andropause, men may experience symptoms such as fatigue, depression, irritability, reduced libido, and erectile dysfunction, often attributed to the gradual decline in testosterone levels. Not all men will experience andropause, and the symptoms can vary, affected by lifestyle factors such as diet, exercise, and stress management.

It is widely acknowledged that andropause, often referred to as male menopause, "…is now considered a pivotal event in a man's life," according to The Canadian Andropause Society (1999). During mid-life changes, there is more that unites us than divides us. It's vital to share our feelings and support each other. If both partners are open to consulting with a therapist, this can help deepen our respective understanding and bring us closer as a couple.

Traumatic Events

Falling victim to an accident, crime, or other terrifying event can be incredibly difficult and traumatic to experience. A traumatic event can leave a lasting imprint on someone's life long after the incident. You might feel fear, guilt, sadness, anger, difficulty sleeping, trouble focusing, and have flashbacks.

Trauma can also lead to physical symptoms like nausea, headaches, and chest pain. It can cause an anxiety disorder called post-traumatic stress disorder (PTSD). Common amongst soldiers, crime victims, rape survivors, and those betrayed, trauma can alter who a person is and how they live.

It is usually necessary to seek the help and support of professionals, such as doctors, mental health therapists, and counselors for support and guidance to help victims move forward. In addition, victims of crime or trauma may find comfort and understanding from family, friends, and support groups. Compassion and patience are crucial when dealing with a partner suffering from trauma. If you experience a traumatic event together, this can bring you closer based on your shared experience. However, your different methods of processing feelings can also cause you to drift apart.

No one should have to go through the experience of being a victim of crime or trauma alone. Victims can heal and move forward healthily and productively with proper guidance and support. Review Baggage in Chapter 3 as you consider the effects of trauma on your intimate relationship.

Disability and Illness

If you have dated someone with or have a disability or illness, you may understand what to expect regarding future care. They (or you) may already have specialised equipment and a support system. Entering a commitment fully aware of the situation, you can have a plan to a certain extent of how your relationship will progress.

But imagine a year into your marriage, you (or your partner) receive a life-changing health diagnosis. Loss of mobility or mental capacity can ignite major emotional upheaval. When your partner becomes severely incapacitated, you may find it challenging to navigate the complexities of intimacy.

During this challenging time, the other partner may seek intimacy elsewhere to satisfy their needs. This could mean having sex with someone else to satisfy physical needs or sharing emotions with someone else regularly. Engaging in an intimate relationship with someone (physically or emotionally) without your partner's consent is still cheating.

If we get sick, having a supportive partner is important for our recovery, while an unsupportive partner can make it harder for us to get better. A partner who lacks compassion is more likely to dis-serve you poorly if you develop health issues. An abusive partner will become more belligerent and mean as their frustrations rise while blaming *your* ill health for their bad mood.

A critical characteristic is the loss of autonomy and freedom—ranging from being able to drive a vehicle to living independently. Kelly had a father-in-law with Alzheimer's disease whose wife wanted him to continue driving as she never learned to drive. She would yell at him for going through stop signs and red lights. She was impatient and belligerent with him because she could not understand why he could not perform everyday tasks.

When one partner can't fully take part in intimacy, it's crucial to have a plan for disabilities or illnesses. While facing the prospect of incapacity is never easy, having a supportive and caring partner can make a world of difference during this challenging time. No matter how sensitive this topic is, you must discuss what you want for your relationship should you become incapacitated. Get to know your partner's future happiness without you and communicate their desires to you.

Discuss what permissions you are granting your partner regarding:

- ❖ Deciding on your behalf, accessing medical records, knowing your end-of-life care preferences, and communicating with doctors and healthcare providers.
- ❖ Accessing available emotional support and resources to navigate this challenging time, (including counselling or support groups, friends, and family who can offer emotional support and practical help with daily tasks).
- ❖ Feeling financially secure, accessing my assets and money to plan for my long-term care and other expenses.
- ❖ Knowing they are not alone and that you trust them to make the best decisions for both of you.
- ❖ Enjoying another intimate relationship if I am unfit (Not valid when your partner has the flu).

> **REFLECTION**
>
> Discuss your wishes in case of a long-term disability or a life-changing illness with your partner. Here are key talking points to help launch a hard conversation regarding your desires:
>
> 1. If you could not speak for yourself, what would be your wishes?
> 2. What other family members would you include?
> 3. Do you have signed legal documents (See Love and Legal Matters in Chapter 17)?

Moving forward in your relationship when you have an illness or disability requires open and honest communication about your expectations and boundaries. Establishing and prioritising trust and empathy can help you navigate challenging health issues. Developing a mutual understanding takes preparation, compassion, and a huge dose of communication.

> **EXERCISE C: What I Want for My Partner**
>
> If a significant illness leaves you physically and mentally compromised, would you be comfortable with your partner moving on?
>
> Take turns sharing, allowing one another to speak without interrupting. No questions—listen without immediately responding until your partner has finished talking:
>
> 1. If I were to become incapacitated, I would want ….
> 2. If I were to become incapacitated and could not participate fully in our couple, what I want for you is ….
> 3. If you were to become incapacitated, what I want for myself is ….

Aging Parents

Our parents age, becoming more vulnerable and requiring care and advocacy. Caring for aging and ailing family members usually falls on women's shoulders. Typically, we view eldercare as an extension of childcare. We assume distinct roles whereby society views men as providers and protectors and women as nurturers and, thus, caregivers. Unpaid (often unacknowledged) caregivers are the foundation on which the healthcare system relies for additional support that would otherwise cost millions. The balance is skewed, so you must communicate your feelings and know upfront how you would like to navigate caring for your couple.

Are you responsible for your partner's aging parents? The short answer is 'no.' However, you must know your boundaries and initiate a conversation with your partner to clarify family caregiving roles and set limits. Your partner must not assume that because you are a couple, you will automatically take on the role of caring for their aging parents (or vice versa). This is not only unfair, but it can cause resentment.

Kelly experienced this with her former partner, where she took on the caregiving of both his parents while raising their child, convincing herself that he needed the help because he was an only child. She often felt exhausted from doing wellness visits, coordinating care and doctor's appointments, shopping, and even moving her in-laws between care homes. And the more she undertook, the less their own son did for them. Kelly learned her lesson, and with her new husband, she stepped back from caregiving for his mother, choosing to help when she could but not as the primary carer.

When you are plunged into a caregiving crisis, it helps to know in advance what you will and will not take on. It must always be based on what is workable for you and your partner, and what you have discussed.

The Sandwich Generation

There may come a time when we feel sandwiched between the diverse needs of close family members. We may have to balance the care of our aging/ailing parents or relatives and our children, especially given the trend for couples to delay having children. And this may also occur when we retire from our career, thinking we'd have time to pursue our own interests. Add to the mix aging grandparents, and we experience

The Club Sandwich Generation, a common phenomenon as our life expectancy increases.

Health problems can make it hard for our relatives to move, think, stay safe, and take care of themselves, and this puts stress on an individual and couple. It also affects the family dynamic. For instance, let's say your partner has asked you to move into their home and has offered that you bring your mother to live with you. However, your mother has Alzheimer's disease and doesn't remember much, so you must repeat conversations, which can be draining. And imagine those nights when she wanders around. Your partner may become resentful, and eventually, this may affect your relationship.

The burdensome weight of caregiving can lead to overwhelm as we feel:

- Stretched and overextended
- Guilty about not doing enough
- Intense stress (Refer to *The Holmes-Rahe Life Stress Inventory* in the Bibliography)
- Chaos
- Confused
- Sad
- Angry
- Resentful
- Frustrated
- Burned out
- And more!

If either of you is unprepared for the time investment of caring for someone else, the burden of caregiving can strain your relationship. Inviting your aging, ailing parent to live with you may not be the right decision. And that is perfectly okay, too. Before getting involved in a situation you don't want, be honest with yourself and your partner.

You must decide whether to care for the family member in your home or in their environment. The latter means you will be absent from your house, family, work, and life as you navigate their daily routines, medical appointments, and overall care. There are also financial considerations concerning care needs and how to cover the costs. When caring for a loved one, you can choose between a care facility, hiring a caregiver, or seeking government subsidised in-home services. Consider all these diverse options because caregiving can put a strain on your relationship.

Complicating these matters is the quality of the relationship you and your partner have with your relatives. Even if you have a beautiful and loving relationship with your aging parent, relative, or in-law, like you, your parent/close relative has their values, goals, wants, and needs that drive their attitudes and behaviours. They are accustomed to doing things autonomously and their way (as you are). No wonder there are significant challenges broaching those tough conversations, especially in advance when things are going well. Rarely do people want to imagine a future where they may need help, care, and advocacy. You will need help to navigate this unfamiliar landscape when the time suddenly comes. It helps to understand what that involves.

You may feel challenged by issues with your aging/ailing parent or relative regarding:

- ❖ Starting that first difficult conversation about "What if?" or having those hard conversations.
- ❖ Talking about wills, power of attorney, and mandate in case of incapacity.
- ❖ Respecting their desire to feel autonomous.
- ❖ Preserving their privacy, dignity, and confidentiality.
- ❖ Dealing with their mood changes resulting from pain, reduced mobility, cognitive decline, depression, and more.
- ❖ Being thrust into what feels like the role of parent, a new

dynamic called "parentification" whereby the child must function as a parent to their parent.

If you wait until a crisis hits that requires moving your aging/ailing parent to a safer living environment, they will have a dual adjustment—first to the health issue (loss of mobility, cognition) and second, to a new living situation if they cannot return to their familiar environment. If your parent presently has dementia, you may find that reasoning with them will be your most significant challenge!

Levels of Care

The amount of care an aging parent requires varies according to their health. The Levels of Care Chart by NASSM (online, n.d.) outlines four distinct levels of care—from independent, to total assistance:

1. Minimum Assist - can respond in an emergency
2. Standby Assist - may need help in an emergency
3. Hands-on Assist - requires help during an emergency
4. Total Assist - needs help and supervision during an emergency

Everyone, including your other siblings, may disagree about caring for your aging parent. Those shouldering the most responsibility and care might opt for a residence, while others may balk at the idea. If the aging, ailing parent already lives with one sibling, the others may not know or appreciate the caregiving load. Add to the mix of emotions an inflated sense of duty, guilt, unresolved family dysfunction, fear of the unknown, and caregiving arrangements can become complicated.

If siblings live out of town (another province/state or country), the burden commonly falls on the one living closest to the parent. Resentment can build if the same family members take on all the caregiving while the others sit in the peanut gallery. There will always be a perception that one person is doing more. And if you are an only child, you will face the burden of all decisions and caregiving.

Problems occur when families don't talk about planning for their parents' later years until there's a crisis. When a health crisis hits that requires a move from the family home, it is doubly difficult. Not only is our aging, ailing parent dealing with the current health issue, but they must also cope with a move to unfamiliar surroundings—further compounding the change and adaptation.

Remember that certain personality traits may amplify in your aging relative over their later years. So, if your father was controlling and manipulative, this trait does not mellow as he ages. If he has dementia (cognitive decline), expect these negative traits to be more pronounced and prepare to meet with his belligerence when you try to find solutions for care.

There can be intense resistance to change, and if one or both of your parents have dementia, reasoning with them is impossible. Parents with cognitive decline lack the ability to advocate for themselves, as they can no longer decide or solve problems because they lack executive functioning. This puts the adult child in the problematic situation of 'parenting' their parents, a challenging role.

You must assess your aging parent before placing them into an appropriate living accommodation because it will depend on their needs. Social services can evaluate whether your parent needs independent, semi-independent, or full-time care.

Communication is critical, and having that difficult conversation is where you start. Advance Care Planning Canada (online, n.d.) provides helpful resources for initiating a crucial conversation with your parent/relative about their future needs and desires. See the Bibliography for the link to learn how to engage in tough conversations with family members.

> **REFLECTION**
>
> 1. If your relative currently requires care, what are their needs? (Review the Levels of Care items above)
> 2. What are your boundaries regarding caregiving or having your aging relative(s) live with you?
> 3. Which other family members or specific (respite care) services could help?

Be careful applying a laissez-faire approach because it's challenging to make informed caregiving decisions when you plunge into a crisis. If, despite your best efforts, your parent still refuses to discuss care planning, keep communication channels open, revisit as needed, and have a plan for how you will manage a crisis if it arises.

If you are thrust into caring for your parent or family member, consider consulting with your (or their) family doctor to find resources for caregivers. There may come a time when you can no longer shoulder the caregiving tasks, as your family member may require more medical interventions. While the guilt may overcome you, understand that you did the best you could given the circumstances and nature of your family member's health needs.

> **EXERCISE D: Caring for your Aging Relatives**
>
> Hold an honest conversation with your partner regarding your expectations about caregiving:
>
> 1. Do you and your partner feel confident approaching your respective parents on the sensitive topic of "What if?"
> 2. What level of care are you prepared to offer, and is there an agreement between everyone involved?
> 3. Is there a concrete plan in place and legal documentation supporting decisions for your parent(s)?
> 4. Are you in the space of taking a wait-and-see approach?
> 5. What structures can you implement to ensure a smooth transition when the time comes?

Loss

The years-long friendship that goes sour, a job or career change, leaving our familiar home, or losing a favourite item (and even unrequited love)—these represent the loss of something we value. We never expect to lose what we cherish; our hopes are dashed for what might have been, including the fantasy of what we thought we had. Any form of loss or damage always involves a life transition. We must adapt to a new reality as we grieve our former one.

Not only must we cope with the loss but also with the circumstances leading to and surrounding it. For example, Kelly left a job she loved because of the challenges of working with a bully manager. Although she doesn't regret walking away, Kelly misses the work and the gratification she enjoyed facilitating soft skills with groups of adult learners.

A loss can affect our self-esteem if we've had to deal with adverse conditions, sometimes resulting in our withdrawal from situations where we fear we may relive that experience. And often, our grief extends beyond the current loss because it encompasses other similar losses we have experienced (and may not have dealt with). We must recognize and address losses because they involve pain and grieving and have long-lasting effects.

Death

As you journey through life, you will inevitably experience the passing of significant people—be it family members, beloved pets, close friends, or colleagues. Each of these losses will affect you, stirring up intense emotions of bereavement for the person who is gone, forcing you to contemplate your own existence and mortality.

Of a Child

We believe that the death of a child is the toughest loss a parent can experience. This (we imagine) must be the ultimate heartbreak, because in the natural order of things, our children should outlive us. Neither Kelly nor Laurie has experienced the loss of a child, so we humbly suggest seeing a professional. Our hearts go out to anyone who has suffered this trauma.

Of our Partner/Spouse

If our beloved spouse dies, the loss can be overwhelming. We may feel completely lost and uncertain about how to move forward. This may be why we often see the surviving partner die within weeks or months of their deceased long-time partner.

Part of us is missing: our spouse was a significant part of our identity and daily life. They were the person we relied on for emotional support, decision-making, and sharing responsibilities. In a world that we navigated together, now we must make decisions without the comfort of our partner's input and guidance. We may have relied on their strengths to balance our weaknesses, and we are left to face those challenges alone.

We may feel a deep sense of loneliness as we have lost our confidant, cheerleader, and best friend. The void they leave behind is profound, and we may find it difficult to find solace in the company of others. While the pain of losing our spouse will never fully go away, we may find strength in knowing that our spouse would want us to continue living our lives to the fullest.

Through self-care, therapy, and the support of loved ones, we can learn to navigate this new world without their other half. Amid the grief, one can choose to honour their memory by embracing life, cherishing special moments together, and finding happiness again.

Of our Pet

Losing a beloved furry companion is an incredibly tough experience, leaving us with a profound sense of loss, as if someone has taken away a family member or our best friend. The bond we share with our pets goes beyond mere companionship; they become a source of comfort and connection in our lives. Their unwavering presence and unconditional love can bring immense joy and solace, making their departure more heart-wrenching.

The grieving process for a pet can be just as intense as mourning the loss of a human loved one. The emptiness they leave behind can be overwhelming, so give yourself time and space to heal. Lean on friends, family, or support groups who understand the depth of this loss. Cherish the memories and the special moments you shared with your furry friend. While the pain may never completely fade, over time, you will find solace and remember your pet with love and gratitude for their presence in your life.

Grieving

Death brings out the worst in all of us. While grieving, it's challenging to think clearly and function, let alone decide vital details, such as funeral arrangements. Someone you love has been ripped from your life. Be gentle with yourself and understanding of those around you. Recognize that we process grief uniquely, and there is no right or wrong way to mourn the departure of those who have touched our life.

There will be all the firsts to get through—that first birthday, special holidays, and other traditions where you made memories with your loved one. Then there will come the anniversary of the death, again reminding you of what you lost. Be compassionate toward yourself.

As we grieve, we must learn to adjust to a new normal (which feels abnormal). It is crucial not to isolate, but to seek support from friends, family, or support groups who can provide a listening ear and understanding. Allow yourself the time and space to process these emotions, as grieving is a necessary part of healing. It is through this process that you will find solace and eventually come to terms with the reality of your loss.

As described earlier in this chapter, Dr. Elizabeth Kübler-Ross (2014) developed the five stages of grief model (denial, anger, bargaining, depression, and acceptance). Kristen Rogers (*CNN*, 2023) explains these stages in full, which we suggest you read if you are grieving the loss of a loved one.

Complicated Grief

Our grief can be complicated if we had a hostile relationship with our deceased person. Unresolved adversity between partners leaves unfinished business. If our partner dies, we may feel angst, guilt, and resentment. This leads to complicated grief, which can last for months (or even years), cause significant stress, and interfere with daily life. This kind of grief calls for counselling to process our emotions and move toward healing and acceptance.

Adding to the complication is the death of someone without a will. When a person dies without a legal will, it is unclear who inherits the estate, who cares for their dependents, or other key decisions that pertain to settling their estate. This reality can be challenging if family members or friends are involved and can cause conflict over who gets what. Your partner's wishes may not be honoured, leading to disputes or confusion amongst surviving family members.

Navigating death shapes our understanding of mortality and the fragile nature of life. Though they may be challenging, these experiences help us learn to appreciate the preciousness of each moment and find meaning in loss. Cherish the memories and legacies left behind by those who died. Embrace the lessons they taught you, the love they shared, and how they affected your life. In this way, you honour and find strength in their memory.

Mourning someone (or something) is a huge life transition, with no set amount of time. It may help to seek grief counselling or other forms of support to process the emotions associated with grieving a death or non-death loss.

There are distinct types of grief tied to the circumstances of loss. Wendy Wisner (2023, online) discusses nine types of grief, which we recommend reviewing (See Bibliography) to understand more about bereavement and how it can affect our lives.

Reality Check

How things are:

How I would like things to be:

Red Flag(s):

Deal Breaker(s):

One action I can take:

Chapter 16

Growing Together or Growing Apart

The flames of desire or third-degree burns?

Growing as a couple is beautiful. It means you will spend time and effort building a robust and healthy relationship. It means you can communicate, compromise, and work through any issues. You become stronger as a couple when you grow together, and your love deepens. The key to growing as a couple is to work on your relationship. This means communicating openly and honestly and being willing to compromise or sacrifice for the sake of your relationship.

Growing apart as a couple can be a painful experience. You are drifting away from each other, feeling distant and disconnected, and are no longer in sync. This can happen because of a lack of communication, effort, or simply growing in different directions. If you are growing apart as a couple, explore and identify why. Relationships require constant effort and communication to thrive, and when couples notice signs of growing apart, it's essential to address them promptly.

If you're feeling disconnected in your relationship, seek counselling, make lifestyle changes, or have open discussions to resolve issues.

It takes time, effort, and dedication, but the rewards are well worth it. If you are growing apart as a couple, it's best to address issues before they become too large to overcome.

Deepening your Connection

Growing together requires maintaining connection. Intimacy is the clear pathway to deepening our connection with our partner. Spending quality time together deepens our connection with our partners. Active listening, loving touches, and other simple acts of care can promote intimacy.

In the daily hustle of juggling various personal and professional obligations, we can get lost in the tangle of stressors—both positive and negative. It's easy to forget why we became a couple in the first place. (*We wanted to spend the rest of our lives and grow old together, remember?*) In honouring our initial motivations, we must do the work to maintain our couple's momentum. So, it's time for a refresher!

Therapy Jeff (online) shares a series of questions, which we adapted to go deeper with your partner:

1. What specific moment made you realize you wanted to commit to me?
2. How has our relationship changed you for the better?
3. Is there anything you avoid sharing with me for fear of judgement?
4. Is there anything you want more of (besides sex)?
5. What is the best way to show you I care (besides sex)?
6. What insecurities arise from being in our relationship?
7. When did you realize you trust me?

8. How do you think I describe you to all my friends?
9. What is the most challenging part of our relationship for you?
10. What is your favourite memory of us?
11. What would you miss the most about me (and us) if our relationship ended (besides the SEX)?

> **EXERCISE A: Go Deeper Together**
>
> With your partner, take turns asking and answering the above questions. If your partner refuses to engage in this activity with you, do it alone. You will still get clear on your feelings and motivations. You may opt to share your answers with your partner.

Renewing your Vows

Time to do it all over again—get married! Some couples renew their vows after being married for a length of time. This is a meaningful and romantic way to celebrate and express your love for your partner. It can also be a beautiful way to celebrate a milestone in your relationship.

Sometimes, people want to renew their vows as a last effort to save a failing marriage. Kelly knew a couple experiencing challenges who renewed their vows and then divorced the following year! Again, know your 'why' when deciding to renew your marriage vows, as this is not an act to take lightly. If you choose to renew your wedding vows, consider these steps:

1. Discuss renewing your vows to ensure you are both on board with the idea and understand its significance.
2. Set a date, which may be on a significant anniversary of a meaningful date in your relationship.

3. Determine a budget based on how much you're willing to spend and plan your celebration accordingly.
4. Choose a venue that holds meaning for both of you. It could be where you first met, your favourite restaurant, a beautiful beach, or even your backyard.
5. Plan the ceremony, its style, whether it is a formal affair with invitations and guests or an intimate ceremony with just you.
6. Write your vows by taking this opportunity to express your love, gratitude, and commitment to one another in your own words.
7. Invite your guests by sending invitations well in advance, including all the details, such as the date, time, venue, and RSVP information.
8. Plan your renewal ceremony, its structure, which can be as traditional or as unique as you want. You can include readings, music, and meaningful rituals. Consider having a friend or family member officiate the ceremony or hire a professional officiant.
9. Celebrate and capture memories with your loved ones (guests) and enjoy the special day together. Hire a photographer or ask a talented friend to capture the moments so you have lasting memories of the day.
10. Hold a renewal reception afterward, which could be a formal dinner, a casual barbecue, or a fun party, depending on your preferences and budget.
11. Incorporate symbolic gestures like lighting a candle or doing a unity ritual.
12. Reflect and renew after the ceremony by thinking about the experience and what it means for your relationship. Use this renewed commitment as a foundation for your future together. Continue to communicate, appreciate the other, and work on your relationship.

Renewing your marriage vows can strengthen your bond and create lasting memories. It's a beautiful way to celebrate your love and honour your shared journey.

> **REFLECTION**
>
> So, you want to renew your marriage vows.
>
> 1. What are your motivations?
> 2. Is your partner on board?
> 3. How will you renew your vows (privately or in a ceremony with witnesses)?
> 4. How will renewing your vows affect or change your commitment to your partner?

Loss of Connection

Disconnecting with your partner often occurs slowly as minor annoyances become resentments and break down the walls of connection. Resentment is unhealthy for the person on the receiving end and the person resenting. Examine when your resentment started and what triggered it. Has it built up over time, or suddenly surfaced? The only way out is through, so have an open conversation with your partner about how you are feeling. Sometimes simply talking about things can lift a tremendous weight off your shoulders. Next, figure out together how you can work through this hiccup, and if you can't, perhaps you need time away from each other.

Complacency

We no longer cook their favourite meals, neglect dressing up, refrain from asking about their well-being, and even avoid kissing them in the morning, greeting them, or saying goodnight. We refrain from addressing shared goals, festering issues, and our future. We often underestimate the value of our partner and the minor acts of kindness they do for us, neglecting to show gratitude. The disease of complacency sets in. Being complacent in a romantic relationship means being fine with how things are and not putting in the effort to improve your relationship or address problems. There is a lack of motivation or investment in the relationship, and this may lead to stagnation, routine, or even neglecting the needs and aspirations of your partner.

Signs of complacency are:

- Lack of effort, such as not going on dates, planning surprises, or showing affection.
- Decreased communication where partners stop discussing their feelings, dreams, goals, or concerns.
- Ignoring or dismissing problems instead of addressing and resolving conflicts.
- Lack of emotional and physical intimacy (conversation, expressing feelings, sharing, affection, and touch).
- Taking each other for granted and stopping appreciating the little things you used to do for each other, expressing gratitude, or acknowledging efforts.
- Loss of shared goals whereby partners stop working together toward a common future.
- Seeking fulfillment outside the relationship by looking for attention from others, having emotional affairs, or pursuing individual hobbies and interests.

Being complacent can lead to a decline in intimacy, communication, and satisfaction in the relationship. But it doesn't always signal the end of the relationship. If you recognize any of these signs, it is vital to identify which areas need attention and start a conversation between you to rekindle your connection. Open and honest conversation, active effort, and a willingness to resolve issues can help overcome complacency and strengthen your couple relationship. Think back to your 'why,' date each other again, and reignite that spark.

Contempt

When we arrogantly disregard, dismiss, or denigrate our partner by making faces, eye-rolling, or responding with sarcasm, we eventually disengage from and feel negative about the relationship. Feelings of superiority, disrespect, and disdain characterize contempt, which Dr. John Gottman describes as '…a destructive emotion that can arise when one feels unappreciated and unrecognised in a romantic relationship….' (Lisitsa, online, n.d.).

Contempt is a significant factor in the decline of many long-term relationships, often resulting in a 'roommate marriage.' In such relationships, couples coexist under the same roof, leading separate lives and harbouring deep resentment towards each other. Stonewalling (intentionally avoiding conversation) and the silent treatment result in a refusal to communicate that harms the relationship. Dr. Gottman asserts that contempt is the most significant predictor of relationship failure (Rajendrakumar, online, 2024).

Overcoming this relationship-killer takes much work involving revisiting your 'why' and interacting positively. Remember when you loved your partner unconditionally? Go back to that place. Treat each other with kindness, dignity, and appreciation. (When was the last time you thanked your partner for something—anything?) Reopen communication channels by creating a safe and non-judgemental space for your partner to express feelings and concerns without the fear of retaliation. Practise forgiveness—of yourself and your partner—to let go of past hurts and resentments. Acknowledge your partner's feelings and be open to compromise.

This process requires commitment, patience, and consistent effort from both partners, and may involve couples' counselling. Commit to personal growth and take responsibility for your actions so you can be the best version of yourself in the relationship.

REFLECTION

1. What was the first moment you felt contempt for your partner?
2. In what ways have you contributed to the breakdown of the relationship?
3. What small step can you take towards rebuilding your relationship?

EXERCISE B: Gratitude Journal

Do this, not only for your couple, but for you. Using a dedicated notebook (purchased from your local Dollar Store), at the end of each day, write three to five things for which you are grateful. Include at least two items about your partner—something they did that made you happy or something positive they said. Preface your gratitude statement with: I feel grateful (blessed, thankful) for.... X, Y, or Z. Then write why.

Example: I feel thankful that my partner took the time to do an oil change in my car because it shows me he cares I am safe on the road.

You may also do this exercise using a whiteboard and place it where your partner can see it. (Positive incites positive.) When we cultivate a gratitude mindset, we create the conditions for abundance in our lives.

Separation and Divorce

Have you ever felt overwhelmed in your relationship and just wanted to escape to a beautiful island (especially after a driving vacation)? However, this differs from legally separating. Either the heart grows fonder or separating means out of sight, out of mind. Sometimes, a couple drags their feet instead of straight-up divorcing.

Canadian statistics place the divorce rate at forty percent of all marriages (Merchant Law Group, 2022). And that percentage rises for second (60%) and third (73%) marriages, especially during those vulnerable periods with a greater risk of breaking up, such as the one to two-year and seven to eight-year marks, according to Maria Indelicato (online, 2021). What we know in popular culture as the 'seven-year Itch' appears to bear out in the statistics surrounding when a marriage is most likely to end.

These statistics are concerning, suggesting that many couples cannot sustain their relationships. Divorce can affect individuals and families, leading to emotional and financial distress. The end of something once beautiful and consuming can cause grief, even for the partner who filed for divorce. It is a harsh slap of reality to accept, especially when your hopes, dreams, and life felt like a fairy tale.

Indelicato (2021) suggests the following common reasons marriages fail:

- ❖ Financial pressures caused by low income or debt (See Chapter 10).

- ❖ Different visions for the future (See Values and Goals in Chapter 2).
- ❖ Infidelity (See Chapter 6).
- ❖ Trouble with in-laws or other family members (See Chapter 4).
- ❖ Loss of connection, which can happen slowly over time and eat away at a relationship where petty annoyances become huge issues.

Other risk factors include:

- ❖ Early or childhood marriage because the risk of growing up and growing apart is greater when you marry too young.
- ❖ Early pregnancy, which can strain your couple's bond because you bring a child into the mix before establishing your relationship.
- ❖ Sexual problems when one partner's sexual needs remain unfulfilled, this can cause the loss of intimacy.
- ❖ Intimate partner violence (See Abuse in Chapter 4).
- ❖ Abusing substances or engaging in criminal behaviour.
- ❖ Experiencing your parents' divorce can shape how you deal with marital problems, often causing you to choose separation instead of trying to resolve conflicts.
- ❖ Any of the topics treated in the next chapter on Life Transitions.

There will always be upheaval when separating two entwined lives, and especially when you have children together. Although difficult, divorce is sometimes necessary to be happy because the alternative is living a miserable life fraught with discord—not healthy for either of your physical or mental well-being.

Getting an Annulment

It sounded like a great idea at the time: after too many cocktails you and your lover pulled up to a drive-thru (*Would you like fries with that?*) wedding chapel in Las Vegas—and we all know that what happens in Vegas stays in Vegas! NOT! Because it's the day after tying the knot, and you wake up as Mr. and Mrs. Oh no! That was sudden—we only met a month ago! Like the morning-after pill, there's a fix for THAT. You can have your marriage annulled.

Annulling your marriage is a complex legal process where you declare your marriage invalid, meaning it never legally existed. Common reasons for annulling a marriage include:

- ❖ Invalid unrecognised marriage ceremony which did not meet the legal requirements of the district, such as a lack of a valid officiant or the absence of a marriage license.
- ❖ Fraud or misrepresentation (where one spouse deceived the other into marriage, such as lying about their identity, criminal history, or concealing a significant fact such as substance abuse, sexually transmitted disease, infertility/impotence, and bigamy or polygamy).
- ❖ Lack of consent where one or both spouses could not give their genuine consent to the marriage (Underage marriage, or mental or physical capacity).
- ❖ Incestuous marriage where the spouses are blood-related (e.g., siblings, parent-child).
- ❖ Physical incapacity where one spouse is incapable or does not consummate the marriage and this was unknown to the other partner.

Also, in certain faiths, you must have an annulment before being allowed to marry again in the church. The annulment is a declaration that the marriage never existed (in the eyes of God) because of unmet conditions or other significant factors that rendered the union invalid. It gives people the opportunity to marry again within the confines of their faith.

Annulments typically require filing a petition with the court, providing supporting documentation, and attending court hearings. Because it affects property division, spousal support, and child custody arrangements, it is crucial to consult with a knowledgeable attorney who specializes in family law to guide you through this complex legal process. Each district has its own specific laws and regulations regarding annulment.

Break-up Sex or Make-up Sex

You've split from your partner or spouse but still go back for the goods. There are different motivations for having sex with your ex. Perhaps you are legally separated and are trying to re-establish your connection because you aren't convinced you want to end your marriage. Or you're simply horny and "better the devil you know," right?

Sex clouds your judgement and sends mixed signals to your partner. If you are taking a break to see whether you will reconcile or completely end your legal marriage or common-law partnership, having sex may only delay the healing process.

When Kelly was leaving her common-law partner, she immediately stopped all sexual intimacy so she could remain clear and focused on her motivations. She moved into the spare bedroom and did not waver from her commitment to herself, especially given the sudden circumstances that precipitated the split. Of course, her partner tried to convince her to have sex, and she refused.

If you have separated and are unsure whether you want to dissolve the relationship, abstain from sex (even if it is amazing), and go on dates instead. Pretend you are meeting for the first time again and see if the sparks are still there! Imagine that you are strangers meeting for the first time and get to know each other on a deeper level.

Divorce Care

Divorce is a major life transition and a loss. You feel emotionally wrought from your split and have no clue how to cope because you feel like the rug was pulled from under you—even if you saw it coming!

To navigate this emotionally distressing time, people may seek divorce care, a support group or program designed to help individuals who have recently gone through a divorce or separation. It provides a community where the participants can share their divorce or separation experiences in a safe and supportive environment.

The divorce care curriculum covers a range of topics related to the divorce and separation process, including:

- Dealing with the emotional aspects of the process
- Coping with the practical and financial changes
- Communicating with ex-spouses
- Co-parenting
- Finding healing and moving forward

Divorce care can help people feeling isolated or overwhelmed during this tough transition by offering understanding and support. If you are considering joining a group, research the specifics of the program to ensure it aligns with your values, goals, needs, and expectations. Sessions incorporate videos, discussions, and group activities to address these topics. They offer tools and insights to help participants navigate their new circumstances and support their affected children during this transition.

If you feel more comfortable, find a therapist or a certified coach that you can see one-on-one.

Collateral Damage

Divorce complicates and affects all our relationships (and sometimes in a good way). It is crucial to be aware of these changes and prepare to manage unkind or adverse reactions. When you divorce, people may take sides. People in your circle may not understand your decision and become distant or even hostile towards you. You may need to redefine new boundaries with people, such as what information is not okay to share with your ex and clarify your need for trust and support to feel safe in your other relationships.

The Children

Children never entertain the thought that their parents will split—it defies all logic to the child whose brain is still developing. Their childhood reality rests on the belief that Mom, Dad, and I are one unit. The consequences (trauma) of divorce vary according to circumstances, children's age, and how parents handle the break-up. It's no wonder parents think long and hard about remaining together for the sake of their children.

While you are going through a marital or cohabitation breakup, your emotions are all over the place. Having children together can make this time doubly stressful because you are thinking about your children as well as yourself while trying to juggle your life responsibilities and priorities.

Parents sometimes fear their children will hold a grudge against them for leaving the relationship. But staying together when you are unhappy is not helpful for your child. Witnessing their parents' unhappiness will create a toxic environment that can negatively affect the child's emotional well-being and even their view of marriage (See Laurie's perspective in Chapter 6).

Here are common ways divorce can affect the parent-child relationship:

- Children feel sad, angry, confused, and anxious, and these emotions can strain their relationship with both parents.
- A prominent level of conflict between parents can leave their children feeling caught in the middle. Witnessing conflicts can be distressing and negatively affect the parent-child relationship.
- Children may have less time with one or both parents after divorce, which can lead to spending less time together, and this can harm the parent-child bond.
- Financial strain for both parents can limit the resources available for the children, affecting their lifestyle and well-being.
- Parents dealing with the aftermath of divorce may find it hard to support and stabilize their children emotionally. This stress can affect the parent-child relationship.
- When parents start dating and then remarry, it can be difficult for children to adjust to new family dynamics. This can lead to tension and affect the relationship between parents and children.
- Research shows that children of divorced parents might struggle in their future relationships with trust issues, commitment, and intimacy.

Before announcing to your children that you plan to divorce, you must discuss what you envision your new family to look like. Have a family meeting with your child(ren) in which you let them know it's not their fault, that you both love them and are still a family, no matter what. Parents must manage the break-up in a sensitive and supportive manner, as this can significantly affect how the child copes with the situation.

Children thrive when they have set routines and predictability. Divorce affects children's stability and sense of security. Keep routines to minimize your child(ren)'s stress (and yours) as much as possible. Discuss how shared custody will affect established routines, and always listen to your children's concerns—even if you cannot change their reality. Open communication, reassurance, and maintaining a consistent routine can help provide stability and comfort during this challenging time.

Do not air your grievances with your partner to your child. They do not have the same perspective of their parents as you do and may not be mature enough to understand the complexities of adult matters. If you experience an acrimonious break-up, do your utmost to avoid your negative feelings about their other parent leaking into your discussions with your child. Instead, share your emotions with a close family member, friend, or therapist. If the break-up involves your child's safety, then you will have no option but to explain things at a level your child can grasp, especially regarding situations requiring supervised visits with their non-custodial parent.

Not all children of divorced parents experience these negative effects. Factors like parental cooperation and emotional support influence children's well-being. The positive outcomes include:

- ✓ **Improved Environment:** Divorce can remove children from a toxic or abusive environment and lead to a better quality of life and improved relationships.
- ✓ **Resilience:** Children may learn resilience and coping skills through their experience, which can serve them well when facing future challenges.
- ✓ **Quality Time:** When one parent becomes the primary

caregiver, the child might get more quality time and attention from that parent.
- ✓ **Better Relationships:** If the divorce reduces conflict between parents, it can create a more stable and positive environment for children, improving their relationships with both parents.

Divorce can profoundly affect parent-child relationships, and the effects can be negative and positive. The post-divorce environment and parental support influence children's outcomes. It is the responsibility of couples to look for ways to improve communication and foster more understanding. (We hope using this book will help!)

Relatives

Divorce often affects both the couple and their relatives. Here are the fundamental issues involving extended family members when a couple divorces:

- ❖ **Child Custody and Visitation:** Grandparents, aunts, uncles, and other extended family members might find their relationships with the children strained—especially if one parent gains full custody and limits the contact the children have with the extended family of the other parent.
- ❖ **Family Events and Gatherings:** Special occasions like weddings, birthdays, and holidays can become awkward as divorced parents and their families try to include everyone without causing discomfort.
- ❖ **Cultural or Religious Issues:** In certain cultures, divorce carries stigma and is forbidden, and your community shuns you. Family members may face societal judgements and pressure to maintain appearances in their community.
- ❖ **Estate Planning and Inheritance:** Divorce might cause

changes in estate planning, especially if you have shared assets. This can lead to disputes over inheritance and property division among extended family members.

Open and honest communication is key to mitigating these issues. Encouraging family members to express their feelings and concerns can help address misunderstandings and promote healing. Seeking the help of therapists or support groups can guide navigating these challenges and maintaining healthy family relationships during and after a divorce.

Friends

We may perceive a newly divorced person as a potential threat to our individual and couple friendships for assorted reasons:

- ❖ **Change in Dynamics:** A divorce often leads to significant changes in a person's lifestyle, routines, and social circles. Friends might worry that their group dynamics will shift because a newly single friend causes discomfort or awkwardness. The fear may stem from a lack of trust in their relationship or that it may happen to them. (Divorce might be contagious!)
- ❖ **Emotional Vulnerability:** Newly divorced individuals might be emotionally vulnerable and need support, which could lead to their relying heavily on friends. This heightened dependence might strain relationships if friends feel ill-equipped to manage the emotional burden.
- ❖ **Misunderstandings:** There may be assumptions or misunderstandings about the intentions of the recently divorced person. Friends may worry the divorcee is trying to break up other relationships or inappropriately seek emotional support.
- ❖ **Social Stigma:** In some cultures or social circles, there is a

stigma associated with divorce. Friends might fear judgement from others or worry about how others may perceive their association with a divorcee.

Friends should try to understand each other's perspective and openly discuss their concerns, fostering a supportive environment for everyone involved. Understanding and respect make maintaining positive relationships with other couples possible after divorce.

> **REFLECTION**
>
> 1. How would divorce affect your couple's friendships?
> 2. What kind of support would you seek from mutual friends if you were to divorce?

Getting Back on the Horsey

In every enchanting fairy tale that captures our hearts and imaginations, the prince and princess mount a majestic horse and ride into the vibrant sunset to their long-awaited Happily Ever After.

Despite the gruelling experience of divorce, a considerable number of individuals remarry. Statistics show that over eighty percent of divorcees take another chance at love and tie the knot again (Lindner, 2023, online). And of these, 60% of second marriages and 73% of third marriages end in divorce (Merchant Law Group, 2022, online). The sad reality is countless marriages end because individuals may overlook or dismiss the complexities and challenges that come with commitment—or they have not learned the lessons of their divorce. If you haven't done your inner work and are properly healed (addressed your blind spots) from your previous union, the risks are higher for a second (or third) divorce. And subsequent marriages are more likely to fail because there is much to balance around family and finances.

Remember: As humans, we have an unwavering need to connect. Despite the challenges and hardships we experienced in our previous marriages, many of us remain hopeful about finding happiness and companionship in new relationships. While the negatives of divorce are difficult, most divorcees are resilient and optimistic—ready to embark on another journey of love and commitment. Give yourself the time and space to heal so your next relationship can be even better!

Unfinished Business

You meet the person of your dreams, connect beautifully, and become serious—only to discover they have not yet divorced! They (or you) have put the inevitable off (procrastinated) for assorted reasons:

- ☐ You never felt the need to divorce or never got around to it.
- ☐ You don't want to pay for a lawyer.
- ☐ You are not making it official for the sake of kids/family.
- ☐ Your ex-partner lives in another province/state or country.
- ☐ You have too many shared assets or fear of losing assets/pension.
- ☐ You fear what others would think, being an outcast in the community or a disgrace to your family.
- ☐ You never thought you would want to marry again.

Consider your partnership status by reviewing the list of items above and checking all that apply.

Engaging in another intimate relationship while you are still in your current relationship (or have not had mental or legal closure on it) often applies to second and third marriages when people are in their middle to later years and have a lifetime of experiences, choices, and baggage. You must do the work to resolve your relationship status. Otherwise, you are not ready for a serious commitment to someone else. It's not fair to your new partner to start a new relationship without resolving things from your previous one (whether married, cohabiting, or long-term dating).

Kelly recently heard about a woman in a twenty-eight-year common-law relationship with a man who never divorced his wife. The couple went to see a notary seven years earlier to create wills together so she would be the beneficiary of his estate. When he died just last year, the surviving common-law partner was shocked to learn the notarised will meant nothing because since her partner never legalised his separation, all his assets (300K in savings and government pension) would go directly to his wife.

Two mistakes occurred here: 1) The common-law partner never insisted on her de facto spouse divorcing to protect their (allegedly) shared interests, and 2) The notary took the couple's money without regard for the finer points of their provincial laws governing cohabitation. Also, the man filed his taxes each year, claiming her as his common-law spouse. And adding insult to injury, the woman is now spending two-thousand dollars to go to court to prove the intent of her partner's will!

Remaining married to your ex-partner means you are legally bound to them. And this is a huge red flag of unfinished business! If you have not yet gotten a divorce, prioritising this step is crucial when trying to move forward, for yourself and especially with someone else. You must conclude and achieve closure on an intimate relationship where you are no longer interested or invested.

> **REFLECTION**
>
> 1. List the proof that you have legal, financial, emotional, and physical closure on your previous relationship?
> 2. How do you know your grieving process is complete?
> 3. What might hold you back?
> 4. What are specifically do you need to achieve closure?

Rebound Relationships

BOING! Speaking of unfinished business, you recently ended things with your partner, and you find yourself on the hunt for your next hookup, hoping for a relationship. Don't do it! When you seek a romantic involvement shortly after a previous committed relationship, this is rebounding. You may enter rebound relationships to cope with the emotional pain and loneliness of a breakup. The problem with these relationships is they may not entail as much emotional investment or seriousness. A rebound relationship can distract you from dealing with the loss and sadness of ending your previous relationship. And often, rebound relationships don't work out.

Rebound relationships have a greater risk of failing because:

- ❖ You may not have had enough time to fully process and heal from your previous relationship.
- ❖ Your focus may be more on filling a void rather than building a solid foundation, resulting in a lack of emotional depth and connection found in more established, long-term relationships.
- ❖ You may compare your new partner with your ex to validate

your decision to move on. And your new partner senses they are being (unfairly) measured against someone else.
- ❖ They are often short-lived. Once you heal and reflect, you may realize that the new relationship was about avoiding loneliness instead of forming a genuine connection.
- ❖ When you rebound into another relationship, you may not be fully emotionally available because you are still dealing with unresolved feelings, preventing deep investment.

Some rebound relationships can thrive and endure. Sometimes you can find a meaningful and lasting connection right after a breakup. Still, it is best to do your heart work and heal from your previous relationship. One rule of thumb is to take a year for every five years you spent with your previous spouse. Although that may feel long, take the time and space to learn about what you did or didn't do and how you might approach love differently for a more successful outcome.

Reality Check

How things are:

How I would like things to be:

Red Flag(s):

Deal Breaker(s):

One action I can take:

Chapter 17

Love and Legal Matters

Why does it matter?

Love and legal matters often intersect, particularly in relationships, marriage, and family. You must consider "What if?" ahead of the unthinkable. This means taking the initiative in legal planning by creating documents that reflect your desires and requirements. The descriptions below are brief and highlight the differences between the legal documents. You should research the laws of your province/state and meet with a notary or lawyer who qualifies to discuss the various protections and how they can be tailored to your needs. The following explores the main legal matters related to love:

Marriage

Getting married involves legal steps like getting a marriage license and having a ceremony officiated by a person legally allowed to perform a marriage. Marriage grants spouses certain legal rights and responsibilities, such as inheritance rights, tax benefits, and decision-making authority in medical emergencies.

Prenuptial Agreements

Some couples choose to enter a prenuptial agreement (See First the Prenup in Chapter 8) before marriage, a legal document that outlines the division of assets, spousal support, and other financial matters in the event of divorce or death. It helps protect both partner's assets and clarifies financial expectations.

Domestic Partnerships and Civil Unions

In certain districts, couples who choose not to marry may opt for domestic partnerships or civil unions. These legal relationships offer partners rights like healthcare decision-making, inheritance, and tax benefits.

Cohabitation Agreement

This document outlines the terms of your common-law relationship, specifically addressing how to divide any assets if you split up and especially if one partner is financially dependent, staying home to care for children.

Adoption and Surrogacy

When you want to grow your family through adoption or surrogacy, you must consider the legal aspects, such as complying with laws which vary by district. You may opt for local or international adoption, which entails each of its own set of criteria. Surrogacy laws are specific, often not allowing surrogates to profit, and instead, specifying paid expenses for medical care of the surrogate mother. Issues of legitimacy and legality can arise, so you must enlist the services of a legal professional should you embark on this option.

Separation and Divorce

When a married couple ends their marriage, they may begin with a legal separation: the legal process through which a married couple formalizes their separation without getting a divorce. Some couples choose legal separation over divorce for religious or financial reasons or to maintain certain benefits of marriage, such as social security or health insurance benefits. The specifics of legal separation can vary by area. A court order outlines the rights and responsibilities of both spouses while they are living apart, but still legally married.

If a married couple divorces, they must file for legal separation and follow the steps required by law. The court addresses issues such as:

- ❖ Who gets custody of the child(ren) and how much child support to pay.
- ❖ What alimony or spousal maintenance payments one spouse must pay the other to subsidize them during the separation.
- ❖ How to divide the couple's property, assets, and debts.
- ❖ What living arrangements each spouse will have during separation.
- ❖ Which health insurance coverage and other benefits one spouse might receive through the other spouse's employer and pension payouts.

❖ Visitation rights for the non-custodial parent if children are involved.

A legal separation can be a trial period to help you decide whether to end the marriage for good if you're not sure about getting a divorce. The process and requirements for legal separation vary significantly by province/state. If you are considering legal separation, you must consult with a family law attorney in your region to understand your rights and obligations.

Child Custody and Support

Whether parents separate or divorce, legal matters related to child custody and support arise. These matters determine where the child will live, visitation schedules, and both parent's financial obligations to support the child's upbringing, including education, healthcare, and other expenses.

Protection Orders and Restraining Orders

In cases of domestic violence or harassment within a relationship, you can seek legal measures such as protection orders or restraining orders. These legal tools protect people from further harm by restricting contact with or proximity to the offending party.

Laws and legal processes may vary by location, so consulting a family law attorney can offer accurate advice for specific situations.

Putting Your Affairs in Order

Many of us wait until a grim health practitioner tells us to go home and get our affairs in order—and they don't mean "Go out and have a fling!" Let's face it: death or disability is not something anyone wants to contemplate. A common myth or unconscious blockage is: "If I plan for my death, I will die." Newsflash: We are dying every day from the moment we are born! It's not the dying that may scare us, but the pain involved or the lack of control over our lives as we die. You must do your homework about the legalities, if not for yourself and your peace of mind, at least for those you will leave behind or who will need to advocate for you if you cannot speak for yourself.

Legal Will

Also called a last will, this notarised legal document states your wishes for bequeathing your money and goods when you die. If you do not have a will, the laws governing succession in your province or state will prevail when you die.

When Kelly broached his wishes with her aging hospitalised uncle, he avoided the subject, yet was open to giving her his house key. He was diagnosed with stage four cancer but was not forthcoming nor honest as to the severity of his diagnosis. The doctor sent him home with instructions for return hospital appointments for palliative chemotherapy. Two months later, he died without a legal will, which caused major headaches! His wife had died two months earlier of a heart attack—also with no will, and no children between them. The author and her brother collaborated with a notary to find the legal heirs of their aunt's and uncle's joint estate.

In the end, Kelly's uncle's estate was divided between a sole cousin on his mother's side, and on his father's side, an aunt with Alzheimer's disease with whom he had no relationship or contact. The aunt inherited half the estate, then died two months later, and it went to her two children, cousins with whom the author's aunt and uncle had no emotional connection or relationship. These people had never hosted Kelly's aunt and uncle for holidays, nor visited them. They didn't even know how their cousin died! But the provincial government succession laws prevailed.

As unpleasant a prospect as possible, you must make a will! Otherwise, you risk leaving your family members scrambling to settle your affairs. And your estate may go to people you had never intended as beneficiaries!

Power of Attorney

This legal document grants another person whom you trust the right to act on your behalf (with AND for you) regarding financial decisions. Your notary or attorney can help you outline the specific terms in a power of attorney document, which will determine whether this authority is broad or limited.

Protection Mandate

No one ever thinks they will lose their autonomy and require someone to advocate. But "Life happens to you when you're busy making other plans" (Saunders, 1957). If you become unable to make critical decisions, you can choose someone to take care of you and your property by signing a Mandate in Case of Incapacity in advance. Do your due diligence. You can download a sample protection mandate online, which you can sign before two witnesses. Work with your notary public or lawyer according to the laws of your province/state to draft this document, so it is authentic.

Living Will

This written document expresses your medical preferences for times when you cannot give consent. An example is a DNR (or Do Not Resuscitate order), which stipulates that cardio-pulmonary resuscitation will not be administered if you are dying. DNR does not mean do not treat, which is why you must spell out your wishes in a Living Will. Again, a legal representative or notary, depending on the laws of your province/state, can walk you through these documents.

Personal Property Memorandum

This is a list of personal items (furniture, art, jewellery) you bequeath to specific people. Your legal will must refer to this itemised, signed list.

Kelly's son recently shared his concerns about being an only child of divorced parents who may need care as they age, primarily since he lives out of the country. She had an open conversation about how he would navigate the situation based on her desires. It raised critical questions:

- ❖ Would his parents move closer to him if they needed care?
- ❖ What would happen if he needed to take time off work to settle his parents or their affairs?
- ❖ Who would be designated to help him from a distance?
- ❖ What are his parents' specific wishes regarding their care?
- ❖ How would he find information, such as computer passwords and critical documents?

Fortunately, both his parents are amenable to this conversation and transparent in their wishes to make things easier. This fruitful exchange yielded a brilliant solution: Kelly agreed to complete and update a document (Life Wishes and Personal Property Memorandum) containing detailed information regarding liquidating her individual property. She then uploaded the document to a shared computer drive. Of course, this does not replace a legal will. The shared document merely specifies the details not elaborated in the will. Kelly created the document, which she would revise regularly, and sent her son the link to the drive. It was an empowering exercise!

Here are common myths around legal planning:

Myth: It's only for those with a high net worth or estates that are complex.

Reality: Legal planning is necessary for people of all ages and estates of all sizes and should include healthcare directives, estate planning, and asset protection. Whether your assets are dollars or millions, having a will, power of attorney, and health care directive can provide peace of mind and ensure that your loved ones respect and follow your wishes.

Myth: It's a one-time event.

Reality: Legal planning is an ongoing process that develops with changes in your life, such as circumstances, family, and financial situations. Regularly reviewing and updating your legal documents ensures they reflect your current intentions and comply with any changes to the law.

Myth: There is only one aspect of legal planning: making a will.

Reality: Making a will is the starting point, and legal planning involves other crucial documents such as powers of attorney, healthcare directives, trust agreements, and beneficiary designations. These documents cover various aspects of your life.

Myth: Legal planning is only about death and taxes.

Reality: Legal planning encompasses more than estate planning and tax considerations. It also includes planning for incapacity, guardianship for minor children, difficult healthcare decisions, business succession, and asset protection. This not only protects your interests during your lifetime but can continue your legacy after your death.

Myth: It's cheaper to do legal planning yourself rather than have it done by a lawyer.

Reality: Despite the availability of cheaper online resources and templates, legal planning must be done with a qualified attorney. Laws can vary by province/state, and an attorney can advise based on your specific circumstances, ensuring your plan is legally valid.

Legal planning is crucial for following your wishes, protecting your assets, and providing for your loved ones. Consulting an attorney will help you navigate the legal planning process. It's the responsible thing to do!

REFLECTION

1. Do any of the above myths resonate with you?
2. Do you have a legal will?
3. Do you have a mandate granting all your medical and legal paperwork access? To whom?
4. Do you have a legal power of attorney granting your partner the power to act on your behalf?
5. Are there any other legal documents you need? What steps will you take to have them drawn up?

Reality Check

How things are:

How I would like things to be:

Red Flag(s):

Deal Breaker(s):

One action I can take:

Chapter 18

Your Happily Ever After

Happiness is a choice.

Whether contemplating life with your partner or solo, you have values, needs, wants, goals, and motivations. You desire a life with your partner, but not at the expense of your identity and well-being. You get to decide on your happiness and what that looks like. Consider *your* happily ever after.

REFLECTION

1. Do you unconditionally love your partner (warts and all) and feel fulfilled in your relationship?
2. Are you aware of your partner's visions and goals?
3. How does knowing these make your motivations clear?
4. What does moving forward look like?

> **EXERCISE A: Words of Love**
>
> Write a love letter to your partner for them to read when times are tough. Focus on what you love and appreciate about your Chosen One. Put the letter away somewhere secure and let someone close to you know where it is. Your partner must only open this letter when the time is right.
>
> If you're in a long-term relationship, take initiative in your communication by using a whiteboard. Once a week, list the things you love about your partner or the things they do you appreciate. And have your partner do the same for you. It's nice to be told, but having something in writing reminds us of the beautiful qualities both bring to the relationship.

An Alternative to Kissing Frogs

You may decide to step back from kissing frogs and celebrate yourself in all your glory. Some people opt to marry themselves. *Yes, marry themselves.* It's a practice called sologamy, a ritual where individuals vow to love, respect, and take care of themselves. The ceremony may include traditional wedding elements like putting on a ring, making vows, taking photos, and celebrating.

Many women are choosing sologamy as self-care and self-love. It allows them to prioritise their needs without relying on a partner. Self-marriage empowers women and boosts their self-worth, confidence, and independence, particularly after heartbreak or societal pressures. It sends a powerful message that people can be complete and fulfilled without depending on another person.

Sologamy can raise the question: "Why would one marry themselves?" Some people say doing so creates a mockery of marriage. Here is something to consider: people hold a variety of ceremonies. There are ceremonies where people dip into the water before their loved ones, celebrating a rebirth of themselves. So, how can it be inappropriate to throw a party to celebrate what you mean to yourself? Some women host divorce parties. Show your friends and family how you prioritise self-respect and deserve the best in relationships.

> **EXERCISE B: Celebrate Yourself**
>
> If the idea of marrying yourself doesn't appeal to you, there are other ways to celebrate and honour yourself while being single:
>
> 1. Write a love letter to yourself, then put it away for a while. Read it occasionally, especially if you feel lonely, unlovable, or plain sad.
> 2. Hold a dinner party with friends:
>   a) Provide squares of paper and one jar (with someone else's name on it) to every attendee.
>   b) Ask everyone to write five positive things they love and respect about their friend (whose name is on the jar) and place the papers in the jars.
>   c) Pass each jar around to your left until everyone has written something about each person.
>   d) When everyone has deposited their beautiful sentiments, pass the jars to the people whose names appear on them.
>   e) Every friend can read aloud the papers and bring their jar home as a souvenir. During challenging times, they can re-read the notes to reaffirm their value.
> 3. Make a mantra/vision for yourself by cutting words and images from magazines and pasting them on a poster board. Place it in your home where you will always see it. We can shape our reality by first setting an intention and

then envisioning what we want. Visualising positive outcomes triggers a thought, which creates positive results!

EXERCISE C: A Pledge to Myself

Vowing how you will care for and honour yourself is an exercise each must complete, no matter your relationship status. Write the following pledge and place it where you can see it as a reminder of your worth:

I, [insert name], take myself, [insert name], to be my life partner. I vow to love, honour, and cherish myself for all eternity.

I promise to always care for myself physically and mentally and never neglect my needs and desires.

I commit to being my best friend, confidant, and supporter. I will celebrate my victories and lift myself when I am feeling down.

I acknowledge I am my own person and that my happiness does not depend on anyone else. I am complete as I am, and I will never settle for anything less than the best for myself.

I promise to continue learning and growing and to always find joy and fulfillment in my own company.

This is my solemn vow and commitment to myself for the rest of my life.

Loving and respecting yourself is foremost. You can only build a home on a solid foundation. And once you have built your home, you have created the space to attract the love of your life—the *other* love of your life!

Parting Words

I was so preoccupied with trying to be enough for a partner that I never considered how I was enough for myself. The result was a relationship where I settled for less and tolerated more. After years in a dysfunctional cohabiting relationship, I wanted to be married and work toward common goals with a partner who cared enough to commit. I did the deep inner dive and found my Person Charming! All I had to do was show up exactly as I was. Being in my marriage has taught me about unconditional love. I've learned that sometimes I'm a sock, and other times, I'm a shoe! As a Coach, I often tell clients to cut through the chatter and listen to their intelligent inner voice because it usually knows the answer. (We hear it, but we may not like it!) So, my parting wish for you is to follow your intuition—there is no greater wisdom than your own!
Cheers,

Kelly
www.infiniteUcoaching.com

I have kissed many frogs and accepted a shitload of unhealthy relationships. Every time they ended, I felt devastated. I didn't know if I would ever find love and resolved to be a spinster with twenty cats. I hired a Life Coach, worked hard on myself, and I manifested an amazing man! As a coach, the advice I offer when you're feeling heartbroken is to never give up on what you want. With every relationship that ends, see the lesson, and use it to find the person who can be your best friend and partner. Constantly work to be healthy and happy and expect the same from your potential partner. Lastly, do not negotiate your values or worth for someone else's love.

xo *Laurie*

www.thefineartofyou.com

Bibliography

Advance Care Planning Canada. (n.d.). Retrieved April 22, 2024, from www.advancecareplanning.ca/individuals-families/

American Psychiatric Association. (2022). *Diagnostic and Statistical Manual of Mental Disorders (DSM-5-TR) Fifth Edition.* CBS Publishing: New York, USA.

American Society for the Prevention of Cruelty to Animals. (n.d.). *Home.* Retrieved April 22, 2024, from www.aspca.org

AMI Quebec. (n.d.). "Young Carers." Retrieved April 21, 2024, from https://amiquebec.org/youngcarers/#:~:text=A%20young%20carer%20is%20someone,problems%20related%20to%20old%20age

Angelou, M. (2015, June 12). "When someone shows you who they are, believe them the first time." X (formerly Twitter). Retrieved April 20, 2024, from http://t.co/7rks11m11C

APA Dictionary of Psychology. (2023, November 15). "Sexual Deviance." Retrieved April 22, 2024, from https://dictionary.apa.org/sexual-deviance

Arnold, C., & Hurst, C. (2022). "How Much Does It Really Cost to Own a Car?" *Finder.* Retrieved April 20, 2024, from www.finder.com/ca/cost-of-car-ownership

Aron, A. (1987). *36 Questions to Fall in Love* [PDF document]. Greater Good Science Center, University of California, Berkeley. Retrieved

April 22, 2024, from https://ggia.berkeley.edu/practice/practice_as_pdf/36_questions_for_increasing_closeness?printPractice=Y

Attachment Parenting International (API). (n.d.). "Eight Principles of Attachment Parenting." Retrieved April 21, 2024, from www.attachmentparenting.org/

Baumrind, D. (1966). Prototypical Descriptions of 3 Parenting Styles. Retrieved April 20, 2024, from www.devpsy.org/teaching/parent/baumrind_parenting_styles.pdf

Brenner, H., Ph.D. (2004, May 3). *I Know I'm In There Somewhere: A Woman's Guide to Finding Her Inner Voice and Live a Life of Authenticity.* Avery Publishing: New York City, USA.

Breus, M. J. (2018, June 7). "What Causes Sleep Violence?" *Psychology Today.* Retrieved March 15, 2024, from www.psychologytoday.com/us/blog/sleep-newzzz/201806/what-causes-sleep-violence

Brody, B. (2021). "What Are the Different Parenting Styles?" *WebMD.* Retrieved April 20, 2024, from www.webmd.com/parenting/features/parenting-styles

Canadian Centre for Addictions. (n.d.). *Life at CCFA.* Retrieved April 21, 2024, from https://canadiancentreforaddictions.org/life-at-ccfa/

Castleman, M. (2017, September 15). "The New Erotic Frontier: Sex in Nursing Homes." *Psychology Today.* Retrieved from tinyurl.com/456js8bm

Chapman, G. (2015). *The 5 Love Languages: The Secret to Love That Lasts.* Northfield Publishing, LLC: New York, USA.

Conversation Starters World. (n.d.) Two-Hundred Questions to Get to Know Someone. Retrieved April 23, 2024, from https://conversationstartersworld.com/questions-to-get-to-know-someone/

Crowe, C. (Director). (1996). *Jerry Maguire* [Film]. TriStar Pictures: USA.

Cunningham, A. Kiley, M., and Reiner, J., et al. (Directors). (2018).

Dirty John [Series]. Netflix. Retrieved from www.netflix.com/ca/title/80241855

Detweiler, G. (2021). "Love and Money: What Statistics Say." *Business Insider*. Retrieved April 22, 2024, from www.businessinsider.com/love-and-money-what-statistics-say-2012-2

Dey, T. (Director), Bevan, T. (Producer), Yorn, J. (Producer), Reitman, I. (Producer), Shapiro, S. (Producer), & Silver, J. (Producer). (2006). *Failure to Launch* [Film]. Paramount Pictures: USA.

Doran, G., Miller, A., & Cunningham, J. (1981). There's a SMART way to write management goals and objectives. Retrieved April 20, 2024, from https://cce.bard.edu/files/Setting-Goals.pdf

Emms., M., Fraser, R., and Smith, C. (Executive Producers). (2022). *Bad Vegan: Fame. Fraud. Fugitives* [Film]. Netflix.

Firestone, L., Ph.D. (n.d.). "In a Relationship with a Narcissist? What you need to know about Narcissistic Relationships." *PsychAlive*. Retrieved April 22, 2024, from www.psychalive.org/narcissistic-relationships/

Gallo, S. (2023). *Princess Love* [Vector art]. Silhouette Design Store. Retrieved April 21, 2024, from www.silhouettedesignstore.com/view-shape/177763#

Garcia, P. (2017, October 6). "Why Women are Choosing to Marry Themselves." *Vogue Magazine*. Retrieved April 20, 2024, from www.vogue.com/article/women-marrying-themselves-sologamy

Gardiner, D. (2004, November 28). "That marriage-wrecking MBA." *Financial Times*. Retrieved April 21, 2024, from www.ft.com/content/7fe60086-4165-11d9-9dd8-00000e2511c8

Grande, D. (2020, March 13). "Unrequited Love." *Psychology Today*. Retrieved April 21, 2024, from www.psychologytoday.com/us/blog/in-it-together/202003/unrequited-love

Government of Canada. (n.d.). Family Violence Resources Canada. Retrieved April 20, 2024, from www.canada.ca/en/public-health/services/health-promotion/stop-family-violence/services.html

Harvey, S., & Millner, D. (2014). *Act Like a Lady, Think Like a Man, Expanded Edition: What Men Really Think About Love, Relationships, Intimacy, and Commitment.* Amistad: New York City, USA.

Healthline.com. (n.d.). "Love Bombing: 10 Signs of Over-the-Top-Love." Retrieved April 21, 2024, from www.healthline.com/health/love-bombing#constant-attention

Herlihy, T. (Director). (1998). *The Wedding Singer* [Film]. Netflix.

Higgins, B. (Director). (2022). *The Tinder Swindler* [Film]. Netflix.

Holden, Karina and O'Clery, Cian. (Directors). (2022). *Love on the Spectrum U.S.* [Series]. Netflix.

Howarth, K. L. (2020, April 7). *Cycle of Abuse.* Graphic from *I Am Enough—Recovering from Intimate Betrayal.* p. 54. InfiniteU Press: Montreal, Canada.

Howarth, K. L. (2020, April 7). *I Am Enough—Recovering from Intimate Betrayal.* p. 127. Montreal, Canada: InfiniteU Press.

Indigenous Corporate Training (ICT) Inc. (2015, January 20). "First Nation Talking Stick Protocol." Retrieved April 21, 2024, from www.ictinc.ca/blog/first-nation-talking-stick-protocol

Indelicato, M. (2021, April 29). "In What Year of Marriage is Divorce Most Common?" Marriage.com. Retrieved April 22, 2024, from www.marriage.com/advice/divorce/what-year-of-marriage-is-divorce-most-common/

Investopedia. (2023). "Top 6 Marriage-Killing Money Issues." Retrieved April 20, 2024, from www.investopedia.com/articles/pf/09/marriage-killing-money-issues.asp

Geronimi, C., Jackson, W., and Luske, H. (Directors). (1950). *Cinderella* [Film]. Walt Disney Productions: USA.

Jenkins Reid, T. (2018, May 29). *The Seven Husbands of Evelyn Hugo.* Washington Square Press: Washington, USA.

Johnson, L. (2012, April 29). *Be The Ringmaster of Your Circus: Daredevil Tricks for Organizing your Life!* p. 4. Amazon Kindle. Retrieved

May 1, 2024, from www.amazon.com/RINGMASTER-YOUR-CIRCUS-Laurie-Johnson-ebook/dp/B007Z1IKZO/ref=sr_1_1?dib=eyJ2IjoiMSJ9.zRroq3SgWernr3SBDFZy-CA.6NID6yJbhOHy7xoMQm7i5hcwGlcPWJ3gjLILj_6iiG-k&dib_tag=se&qid=1714570607&refinements=p_27%3ALaurie+Laurie+Johnson&s=books&sr=1-1

Kessler, D. (2019, November 5). *Finding Meaning: The Sixth Stage of Grief.* Scribner: New York City, USA.

King, I. M. (Executive Producer). (2010-2017). *Pretty Little Liars* [TV series]. Alloy Entertainment, Long Lake Productions, and Warner Horizon Television.

Konish, L. (2022, March 29). "Couples Who Pool Their Money are More Likely to Stay Together." *CNBC.* Retrieved April 22, 2024, from www.cnbc.com/2022/03/29/couples-who-pool-their-money-are-more-likely-to-stay-together.html

Kreatics Web Development SL. (n.d.). "Maslow's Hierarchy." *Liveworksheets.* Retrieved April 21, 2024, from www.liveworksheets.com/bk1210800fn

Kübler-Ross, E. (2014, August 12). *On Death and Dying: What the Dying Have to Teach Doctors, Nurses, Clergy, and Their own Families.* Simon & Shuster: New York City, USA.

Labbé, S. (2022, October 28). "Canadian women do 50% more unpaid housework than men, finds StatsCan." *Times Colonist.* Retrieved April 20, 2024, from www.timescolonist.com/life/canadian-women-do-50-more-unpaid-housework-than-men-finds-statscan-5172421

LaGravenese, R., & Rogers, S. (Directors). (2007). *P.S. I Love You.* Alcon Entertainment, LLC: Los Angeles, USA.

Le Cunff, A.-L. (n.d.). "Are you a taker, a giver, or a matcher?" *Ness Labs.* Retrieved April 20, 2024, from https://nesslabs.com/taker-giver-matcher

Lee, S. (2019, October 10). "For Better Sex, 8 Tips No Couple Should

Go Without." *Healthline*. Retrieved April 20, 2024, from www.healthline.com/health/healthy-sex/improve-sex-life-couples

Lindner, J. (2023, December 20). "Remarried After Divorce Statistics: Market Report and Data." *Gitnux*. Retrieved April 21, 2024, from https://gitnux.org/remarried-after-divorce-statistics/#:~:text=About%2080%25%20of%20people

Lindner, J. (2024, December 20). "The most surprising affair statistics in 2024." *Gitnux*. Retrieved April 21, 2024, from https://gitnux.org/affair-statistics/%20who,to%2060%25%20of%20divorced%20women

Lisitsa, E. (n.d.). "The Four Horsemen: Contempt." *The Gottman Institute: A Research-Based Approach to Relationships*. Retrieved April 21, 2024, from www.gottman.com/blog/the-four-horsemen-contempt/

Lloyd, C., Levitan, S., Chandrasekaran, V., et al. (2009-2020). *Modern Family* [Series]. Netflix.

Loisier, M. J. (2009). "Law of Connection." *Wellness Central*, Hachette Book Group: New York.

Maslow, A. H. (1943). "A Theory of Human Motivation." *Psychological Review*, 50 (4), pp. 430-437.

McLaughlin, A. (2022, October 12). "Is it Love or is it Love Bombing? 5 Red Flags to Help You Spot the Difference." *Daily OM*. Retrieved April 21, 2024, from www.dailyom.com/journal/is-it-love-or-is-it-love-bombing-5-red-flags-to-help-you-spot-the-difference/

Merchant Law Group. (2022, April 14). "Canadian Divorce Statistics." Retrieved April 21, 2024, from www.merchantlaw.com/canadian-divorce-statistics/

Meyer, P. J. (2003). "Attitude Is Everything: If You Want to Succeed Above and Beyond. SMART Goals." MindTools.com. Retrieved from www.mindtools.com/pages/article/smart-goals.htm

National Association of Senior Move Managers (NASSM). (n.d.). "Level of Care Chart." *Assisted Living Today.* Retrieved April 21, 2024 from https://softlandingsforseniors.com/content/Understanding_Levels_of_Care.pdf

National Domestic Violence Hotline. (n.d.). The USA. Retrieved April 21, 2024, from www.thehotline.org/?gclid=Cj0KCQiAsoycBh-C6ARIsAPPbeLusNg3Ixh4zzDA-vCYX5BcaCp-d11frSy0Fx-ryDrCRegS0X2PERNQgaAi42EALw_wcB or call 1-800-799-SAFE (7233) / text START to 88788.

National Institute of Health (NIH) *National Library of Medicine.* (2020, January 24). "Social and cultural factors perpetuating early marriage in rural Gambia: an exploratory mixed methods study." Retrieved April 22, 2024, from www.ncbi.nlm.nih.gov/pmc/articles/PMC6974925/

Olson, C. (2013, December 6). "16 Organisations Working to Stop Child Marriage." *The Pixel Project's "16 for 16" Campaign.* Retrieved April 21, 2024, from https://16days.thepixelproject.net/16-organisations-working-to-stop-child-marriage/

Ontario Veterinary Medical Association. (n.d.). *Home.* Retrieved April 22, 2024, from www.ovma.org/

OurRelationship.com (2019, April 8). "Emotional Cheating—What is it and Where Should You Draw the Line?" Retrieved April 20, 2024, from www.ourrelationship.com.

Pannell, N. (2019, November 4). "Eleven of the Biggest Deal Breakers in a Relationship According to Experts." *Business Insider.* Retrieved from www.businessinsider.com/deal-breakers-relationships-dating-experts-2019-11

Pietrangelo, A. (2017, December 5). "What is Sexual Dysfunction?" Healthline.com. Retrieved April 22, 2024, from www.healthline.com/health/what-sexual-dysfunction

Psychology Today. (n.d.). "The Fundamentals of Sex." Retrieved April 22, 2024, from www.psychologytoday.com/ca/basics/sex

RAINN.org (n.d.). "Perpetrators of Sexual Violence: Statistics." *Sexual Violence Statistics*. Retrieved April 22, 2024, from www.rainn.org/statistics/perpetrators-sexual-violence

Rajendrakumar, J. (n.d.). "What Causes Contempt in Relationships?" *The Gottman Institute: A Research-Based Approach to Relationships*. Retrieved April 21, 2024, from www.gottman.com/blog/what-causes-contempt-in-relationships/

Rodgers, L. (2023, November 3). "Is Sex Important in a Relationship? Here's what Experts Say." *The* Healthy.com - *A Reader's Digest Brand*. Retrieved May 2, 2024, from www.thehealthy.com/family/relationships/is-sex-important-in-a-relationship/

Rogers, K. (2023, May 15). "What the five stages of grief are and how to get through them." *CNN*. Retrieved May 2, 2024, from www.cnn.com/2021/09/12/health/five-stages-of-grief-kubler-ross-meaning-wellness

Rose, M. (2022, June 8). *How to Build a Sex Room* [Film]. Netflix.

Rumour Juice. (2022, January 21). "How Marlon Brando Love-Tortured Rita Moreno." YouTube [Video]. Retrieved May 20, 2024, from www.YouTube.com/watch?v=JREuUENO82s

Sadeugra. (n.d.). "Hope you are a Real Prince!" *Getty Images Signature* and *Canva* Pro.com. Retrieved April 21, 2024, from www.canva.com

Saunders, A. (1957, January). *Quote Investigator*. Retrieved April 30, 2024, from https://quoteinvestigator.com/2012/05/06/other-plans/

Schwartz, J., & Savage, S. (Executive Producers). (2007-2012). *Gossip Girl* [TV series]. Warner Bros. Television.

Serrata, J. (2017). "The Cycle of Violence: Why it is no Longer Widely Used to Understand DV." *Promising Futures*. Retrieved April 29, 2024, from https://promising.futureswithoutviolence.org/the-cycle-of-violence-why-it-is-no-longer-widely-used-to-understand-dv/

Sethi, R. (2023, April). *How to Get Rich* [Series]. Netflix.

Shelter Safe. (n.d.). "Support for Victims of Domestic Violence." Canada. Retrieved April 21, 2024, from https://sheltersafe.ca/

Stress.org (2019). "The Holmes and Rahe Life Stress Inventory." Retrieved April 20, 2024, from www.stress.org/wp-content/uploads/2019/04/stress-inventory-1.pdf

Squirmy and Grubs. (n.d.). *Playlists* [YouTube channel]. YouTube. Retrieved April 21, 2024, from www.youtube.com/c/squirmyandgrubs

Suknanan, J. (2022, November 8). "National Debt Relief: 54% believe debt is a reason for divorce." *CNBC*. Retrieved April 21, 2024, from www.cnbc.com/select/national-debt-relief-survey-debt-reason-for-divorce/

The Canadian Andropause Society (affiliated to the International Society for the Study of the Aging Male). (1999). *The Aging Male*, 2:2, pp. 125-126. Retrieved April 21, 2024, from https://doi.org/10.3109/13685539909003175

The North American Menopause Society (NAMS). (n.d.). Retrieved April 22, 2024, from www.menopause.org/

The Oxford Learner's Dictionaries. (n.d.). Retrieved April 20, 2024, from www.oxfordlearnersdictionaries.com/definition/english/reality-check

TherapistAid.com (2016). "What Are Personal Boundaries?" *Therapist Aid LLC*. Retrieved April 20, 2024, from www.therapistaid.com/worksheets/boundaries-psychoeducation-printout

Therapy Jeff. (n.d.). *Ten Questions to ask Your Partner if you Want to go Deep Deep*. [Video]. Facebook. [Video]. Retrieved April 21, 2024, from www.facebook.com/reel/803669678166249

Tiny House Expedition. (2022). "His & Hers: 2 tiny homes parked side by side" [Video]. YouTube. Retrieved April 20, 2024, from www.youtube.com/watch?v=5AdynBTK-fI

Tracy, B. (2017). *Eat That Frog! 21 great ways to stop procrastinating and get more done in less time.* Berrett-Koehler Publishers, Inc.: Oakland, USA.

Travis, H. A. (2017, January 5). "Pets and Your Love Life: What the Experts Say." *PetMD*. Retrieved April 21, 2024, from www.petmd.com/dog/wellness/pets-and-your-love-life-what-experts-say

Walker, L. E. (1979). *The Battered Woman* (1st ed). Harper & Row: New York City, USA.

Wilson and Finkbeiner, Family Law Attorneys. (2022). "Divorce Statistics: Over 115 studies, Facts and Rates for 2022." *WF Lawyers Divorce Statistics and Facts.* Retrieved May 2, 2024, from www.wf-lawyers.com/divorce-statistics-and-facts/#

Wisner, W. (2023, June 5). "9 Types of Grief People May Experience, According to Experts." *Verywell Mind*. Retrieved April 21, 2024, from www.verywellmind.com/types-of-grief-people-may-experience-7504728

World Health Organisation. (2021, March 9) "Violence against women." *WHO Newsroom.* Retrieved April 21, 2024, from: www.who.int/news-room/fact-sheets/detail/violence-against-women

Young Caregivers Association. (n.d.). Retrieved April 22, 2024, from https://youngcaregivers.ca/

Zeltser, F. (2021, June 29). "A Psychologist Shares the 4 styles of parenting—and the type that researchers say is the most successful." *CNBC.* Retrieved April 20, 2024, from www.cnbc.com/2021/06/29/child-psychologist-explains-4-types-of-parenting-and-how-to-tell-which-is-right-for-you.html

www.ingramcontent.com/pod-product-compliance
Lightning Source LLC
Chambersburg PA
CBHW072145070526
44585CB00015B/1002